The Psychic Side of Sports

Michael Murphy • Rhea A. White

The Psychic Side of Sports

**ADDISON-WESLEY
PUBLISHING COMPANY**
Reading, Massachusetts
Menlo Park, California • London
Amsterdam • Don Mills, Ontario • Sydney

Other books by Michael Murphy

Golf in the Kingdom
Jacob Atabet

Other books by Rhea A. White

Surveys in Parapsychology (ed.)
Parapsychology: Sources of Information
(with Laura A. Dale)

Library of Congress Cataloging in Publication Data

Murphy, Michael, 1930 (Sept. 3)-
    The psychic side of sports.

    Bibliography: p.
    Includes index.
    1. Sports--Psychological aspects. 2. Mind and body.
I. White, Rhea A., joint author. II. Title.
GV706.4.M87   796'.01   78-14565
ISBN 0-201-04728-4
ISBN 0-201-04729-2 pbk.

Acknowledgments

The authors wish to thank the copyright owners for permission to
reprint the quotations appearing on the following pages of this text:

12: Reprinted with permission from *Runner's World,* P.O. Box 366,
Mountain View, CA 94043.

(continued on page 220)

ISBN 0-201-04728-4 H
ISBN 0-201-04729-2 P
ABCDEFGHIJ-DO-798

Second printing, October 1978

For my brother, Dennis Murphy,
who showed me these mysteries before I was
old enough to defend myself against them.
M.M.

For Harriet Edwards,
who read the true book, and understood.
R.A.W.

Acknowledgments

Our first thanks to Ann Dilworth of Addison-Wesley for encouragement and moral support and to George Harris, who helped bolster our courage.

Michael Murphy
Jim Hickman assembled some of the material in Chapters 5 through 7 and gave me the kind of helpful advice and criticism I have come to depend upon from him. Mike Spino, both my teacher and student in these matters, has done as much as anyone to kindle my love of sport. Richard Baker-Roshi, Abraham Maslow, David Meggyesey, Jerry Smith, and Sam Keen provided material for our thesis by the examples of their own lives and works. And George Leonard, as usual, gave inspiration and perspective to the enterprise from beginning to end.

And my special thanks to John Brodie, who is probably the chief catalyst for my attempting a sustained study of the spiritual dimensions in athletics. If he hadn't invited me to that 49'er training camp in 1972, I never would have appreciated how fully these phenomena pervade our sporting endeavors.

And, as usual, my wife, Dulce, helped out in a hundred ways. The work she puts into all my projects defies description.

Rhea White
I would like to express sincere thanks to Irving Adelman, for his informed and sensible advice and for his continual moral support. To Stephanie Becker, who not only typed beautiful copy but was able to read my handwriting. To Martin Bowe, for sharing the bulk of the literature search by tracking down some 1,500 books and scanning nearly 3,000; for making thousands of photocopies; for cogent edi-

torial suggestions; for his willing ear; and especially for his readiness to go anywhere and do anything, which provided me with literally hundreds of extra hours to devote to the book.

To Harriet Edwards, whose editing of the manuscript was a superb combination of sensitivity and sensibility, whose moral support was always both timely and just what was needed, and whose assistance in any task was a model of speed, efficiency, and effectiveness. To Caroline Rocek, head of the interlibrary loan department at the East Meadow Public Library, and to the other members of that staff: Mark Dubno, Inga Goldhammer, Doris Goodman, and Fran Saslowsky, for obtaining nearly 2,000 books and articles from libraries all over the country. To Susan Schnapf, for assisting with permissions and for her pertinent suggestions and useful feedback.

To Kristin Smith-Gary, who provided invaluable assistance in organizing and indexing vast amounts of material, devoting to the task nearly all her days off over a two-year period. In addition, she was always there with cheer and encouragement. To Jean Spagnolo, for devoting time she could not well spare to help with permissions, check quotations, and provide a willing ear from beginning to end, always ready with suggestions and support. Finally, I would like to thank the entire Reference staff of the East Meadow Public Library, each of whom was always ready to help, to suggest, to encourage, to overlook, and to understand.

Contents

INTRODUCTION

Where East Meets West: In the Body

T. George Harris

In his *New Yorker* profile on Michael Murphy, Calvin Tomkins did
better than anyone yet in reaching through the aura to the man.
That isn't easy. As founder and nonmanaging spirit at the Esalen
Institute, Mike has for years been hidden by the intellectual pyro-
technics flashing around him and billows of sensual smoke. The
New Yorker gave snapshots of the real Murphy at his everyday
chores: the scholar secluded in his well-thumbed library of classics in
mysticism, Western as well as Eastern, the rabid sport fan at pro
football games and golf tournaments, the gracious host to the widest
range of intrepid thinkers to be found in this golden age of new
paradigms.

"In addition to his other gifts," Tomkins wrote, "Murphy is
endowed with a warm, responsive nature, extravagant good looks,
and a wild Irish charm."

All true, but still way short of the mark. For one thing, Mike
has a rare capacity for friendship and a savage desire to hurt nobody's feelings. In the two decades I've known him, he has often
kept silent rather than cause discomfort to anyone.

That habit used to enrage me. Sam Keen, Princeton Ph.D. in
philosophy and theologian of love, once joined me in a plan to do a
Psychology Today conversation with our old friend. The three of us
spent two happy days and nights around a tape recorder, no holds
barred and no cautions. But when Sam started editing hundreds of
pages of transcript down to an article, Mike began to squirm. Ideas
to him have legs; they are inside the people he knows, his network
of seminal minds around the globe. He did not want to judge them
in print. Even if he said something good about one body of thought,
he hated to be critical, by indirection, of the opposing view. He was
then too much the gentle man to be the scholar.

Sam and I finally trashed the transcript and settled for something better: the private pleasure of Mike's witty, skeptical mind—he's especially skeptical of skeptics—and the excitement of watching him cut a path through the thicket of wild notions now sprouting in the rich, dark ground between the mind and the body.

This book is a sort of coming-out party. Murphy lays himself open, vulnerable to cheap slashes, without the protection of fiction. His two previous books were novels: *Golf in the Kingdom* and, in 1977, *Jacob Atabet, A Speculative Fiction. Golf* confirmed many a square-minded player's sense that something more perverse than mechanics controls the flow of energy in a small white ball. It became a door through the looking-glass in the locker room, a forerunner to Tim Gallwey's *Inner Game of Tennis.* Mike's current novel, *Atabet,* got its first orders mainly in the West, where people are less sure that they know everything, and in the psychic bookstores, where the customers tend to cherish the spooky whether they believe it or not. But rumors about the book soon built demand for it in hundreds of stores that normally weigh a writer's worth on the rusty scales of *The New York Times Book Review.*

Murphy is now doing this nonfiction book because of one fact: Rhea White. She's more than a coauthor who wrote Chapters 2, 3, and 4. She is the one person in the world with the particular combination of knowledge, skills, and interests to build the definitive bibliography on extraordinary experiences in sport—those that arouse suspicion of paranormal powers.

Rhea remembers the first time she was stunned by the extraordinary aspects of sports. She was watching a group of gymnasts working out in elementary school. "My conception of the limits of human achievement had been extended," she recalls, "I felt the same catch in the breath and quickening of the heart that I was beginning to experience when hearing music."

Rhea soon discovered this ecstasy in her own muscles when she took up golf. One summer's day on vacation with the family, while hacking around a mountain course, she suddenly hit one of those magic strokes, with a five iron, that the body never forgets. "Henceforth I played golf daily for the remainder of that vacation and several of those to follow," she admits. She entered every tournament in reach, chased stars like Byron Nelson and Patty Berg and

Cary Middlecoff around the exhibition courses. Though she found she lacked the talent to become a champion, "the motions of a correct golf swing never failed to thrill me."

These pleasures did not then connect with her intellectual interest in parapsychology. She had taken her A.B. at Pennsylvania State, but parapsychology lured her to Duke University for research in Dr. J. B. Rhine's lab. Working on experiments in extrasensory perception (ESP) and psychokinesis (PK), she was struck by a fact that seldom got mentioned in the parapsychology journals: the rigorous training and concentration that seemed necessary for any psychic to make progress, to improve PK or ESP skills. "I was awed by their dedication and discipline," she says. The training was much like that of serious athletes, she noted, as well as that of another gifted group she had begun to study: religious mystics.

With such parallels teasing in the back of her mind, and having attained a master's degree in library science at Pratt Institute, Rhea settled down in 1965 to bread-earning work as a reference librarian on Long Island. She became a mainstay at New York's American Society for Psychical Research in Manhattan and is one of the few people anywhere who has read deeply into the literature, old and new, on mysticism, parapsychology, and altered states of consciousness. Rhea has the archivist's impulse for building a cross-reference index on every aspect of paranormal experience—including those found in sports. Her home is so jammed with research boxes that even the bathroom doubles as handy storage space for a psychic index.

White discovered Murphy through his *Golf in the Kingdom*. "I couldn't figure out if it was a novel or for real, but either way I was mightily impressed by it." It reminded her of the late Gerald Heard's 1937 description of "the mind-body athlete" who will, he said, emerge in evolution's next step: "This athletic type will resolve the conflict of matter and mind, body and spirit. . . . It will create that state of being in which 'flesh helps soul no less than soul helps flesh.' "

Rhea didn't need to trade many letters with Murphy before he caught on. When he and wife Dulce flew East to see her, he could barely contain his enthusiasm about Rhea's file of 30,000 articles on parapsychology, the largest of its kind in the United States. Since their meeting, and with a book on the subject in mind, Rhea has expanded her index of extraordinary sports experiences to 4,500 references. She was aided in the job by Martin Bowe, a graduate school assistant. Rhea regrets that this present book cannot be encyclopedic, but she is considering remedying that with an exhaustive reference volume on the subject.

Some of the tall tales about athletes in this book seem innocent enough, even trivial. The one on Satchel Paige is a standard joke played out on the baseball diamond. Paige was a natural mystic who devised his own Zen-like Rules for Right Living. When his mind and body were in groove and he'd had no fried foods to "angry up the blood," he could throw so hard that the ball seemed to shift into a time warp. He once reared back and unlimbered a pitch so fast the batter never saw it, not even a blur—or so he claimed to his dying day. But then the story (pages 101–102) goes on beyond the stock joke. The catcher held the mitt where the ball was due to hit, of course, but when he fingered around in the mitt's pocket he did not find anything solid. So he and the umpire and the ball boy searched along the backstop—still no ball. Gone forever. Satch's biographer dutifully reported their account as if it were just one more footnote about the earthy mystic with the superhuman arm.

Today we'd have TV replays and stop-action cameras to make sure that Paige did not fling that yin-yang horsehide right into the next dimension. After I read the Paige yarn, I called Mike in California. Paige was a sly old pro, I said, and somebody should have checked his hip pocket. Mike's merry laugh rolled across the country, and I could all but see his eyes popping with their eerie energy. He instantly came up with another story about another immortal pitcher, Walter Johnson. "You know, Johnson did admit to pulling a stunt like that." In a pre-pitch huddle, he'd palmed the ball to the catcher, then delivered the pitch in pantomime. The catcher popped the ball loudly into the mitt pocket while a gullible ump called a strike. No self-respecting umpire would dare admit he hadn't seen a pitch, though he looked silly some years later when Walter, from the safety of retirement, took the mystery out of that invisible strike.

Mike told me the Walter Johnson story because he knew that the notion of trickery would comfort me. It puts the world back in order. It lets things work with the tinker-toy logic of classical physics—the way they did in the good old days before subatomic particles had a peculiar quality called "charm," before space started sprouting zits known as black holes, before astrophysicists started hunting a snipe called the quark. Deep down, and maybe not very deep, I'm homesick for the nostalgic world we had before some of our toughest scientists went around the bend.

But that simple reality has come unglued. And now Murphy and White are trying to push loose another piece of it. They are invading the core, the symbolic Rome, of Western orthodoxy: sports. I don't want to think of Billie Jean King as a witch, no matter what she says, or of pro football linemen as warlocks capable of auras and altered body shapes.

But nobody ever promised to keep reality tidy for my comfort. And if we have paranormal powers, the right place to look for them has to be among superbly trained jocks when they push themselves against their psychobiological limits. Here, if anywhere in the West, an accommodating body/mind would call out its secret reserves. In the public image, athletes were once viewed as muscular beasts, perhaps too dumb to experience anything requiring unusual powers of mind. But that myth has died with the data: pro football players, for instance, score in the top quarter on IQ tests. Also buried now is the psychoanalytic theory that many athletes are mainly masochists who seek pain, or sick people driven by a death wish, or latent homosexuals hunting macho security. For instance, psychologist Bruce C. Ogilvie of San Jose State has given batteries of standard psychological tests to champions in every major sport, both team and individual. They turn out to be uncommonly healthy in the head, with a vivid love of autonomy. "They are adaptable, resourceful and energetic," says Ogilvie, "and are willing to take the consequences of their own behavior."

The more risky the sport, he finds, the more stable the personality. Race drivers and parachutists are remarkably solid characters. Such daring athletes "have a periodic need for extending themselves to the absolute physical, emotional and intellectual limits . . . and there is a special form of psychic ecstasy found by living on the brink of danger." Other research suggests to me that there's an obvious reason for the bliss experienced in risk sports:

when one false move can wipe you out forever, your mind and body
move in focused harmony that must compare with the states
achieved through years of meditative rigor.

As you'll see in Chapter 4, trancelike techniques have begun to
help athletes meld the mind and body for superb physical efforts.
But going the other way, it's also clear that the body can alter the
psyche in predictable and regualr directions. At Purdue University,
A. H. Ishmail and L. E. Trachtman tested dozens of middle-aged
faculty men before they went on a jogging routine, then tested them
again months later. Their personalities had gone through measurable
patterns of change. Their characters had become more resolute,
stable, self-sufficient—and imaginative.

There's rising evidence that our logic-laden culture trains away,
or partly distorts, many of our natural gifts. Cutting the head off
from the breathing corpus, as our Western thought has done for at
least two centuries, we have also cut ourselves off from a great deal
of practical reality. That wound is now being healed as if by a
superdrug. We are rushing back into our bodies in droves. Jogging
and other participant sports have risen so fast, especially among the
cultural leaders, that we are in danger of becoming a nation of
Physical Puritans.

Our bodies have become the last frontier, the center of mystery.
Some 58 percent of all Americans now say that they have experienced ESP. Millions believe in spiritual or psychic healing. Some 27
percent of men and women say, when asked, that they have somehow communicated with a dead friend. And about 6 percent,
according to the National Opinion Research Council, have under-
gone deeply mystical experiences such as being bathed in light, like
St. Paul on the road to Damascus. My neighbor George Gallup says
he's never seen a change as dramatic as the shift toward physical
perfection, and on the religious side he reports that about a third of
all Americans are into some kind of mysticism, Western or Eastern.
Most of the vivid new religious thrusts have to do with body
mysticism, not with the more abstract forms of belief that were once
the grist of revivalism. God is not dead, He's in the gut.

Murphy and White in this book are raising the ante on body
mysticism. Murphy, having lived in an ashram in India and become
a student of Sri Aurobindo, is convinced, as was Aurobindo, that

Zen and other schools of Eastern psychology live up to their claims
of tapping into realistic knowledge about the body. In this tradition,
the disciplined meditator discovers certain internal vibhuti (perfec-
tions) or siddhis (powers) that go beyond the mechanical capacities
we normally expect. They include inner seeing and inner feeling,
almost literal perception of the kinetic activities of the muscles and
blood vessels. They also include a wide range of peculiar gifts such
as being able to slow down the flow of time, change body shape, or
even induce moments of invisibility. Perhaps they include the
Satchel Paige trick of making a ball defy gravity and laws of normal
physics.

In the pivotal Chapter 5, Murphy calls upon ancient literature
to support the tall tales told by modern athletes. When a football
player claims to see an aura over an opposing lineman, he argues,
the seer may not be just punch-drunk or lying. In effect, Murphy
and White use Eastern philosophers to defind the sanity and honor
of Western athletes.

Such suggestions still leave me shaking my head in caution, I
admit, but the evidence in the book builds, story by story, to an
acute sense that we cannot brush aside the whole idea. We have only
begun to explore, in psychosomatic medicine and in physiological
psychology, the remarkable ways in which the mind and body invade
each other's dominion. Many of the Eastern insights have already
paid off in research; we would never have believed, before Joe
Kamiya's biofeedback research, that a yogi could actually alter his
brain waves as well as body temperature and heart beat. The infu-
sion of Oriental ideas is now opening up other areas of research in
the West's labs. That combination can produce startling results. Yet
to me the scene is quite ironic. In *The Meeting of East and West,*
my college master at Yale, F. S. C. Northrup, laid down a turgid
argument that East and West would encounter each other on a high
philosophical plane, a sort of blue continuum. He was wrong. The
East now meets the West on very ordinary ground: right here in the
human body.

The Psychic Side of Sports

1
The Spiritual
Underground
in Sports

For the last six years, we have been investigating extraordinary psychic events in sport—moments of illumination, out-of-body experiences, altered perceptions of time and space, exceptional feats of strength and endurance, states of ecstasy. From personal interviews, books, magazines, letters and dissertations, we have gathered more than 4,500 of these incidents from famous and not-so-famous athletes. These tales are part of a sports underground—stories that athletes sometimes tell each other but that rarely appear in the sports pages. It's no wonder. Many of the experiences they reveal are surpassingly strange, and the athletes themselves often have trouble accepting them.

I (Murphy) encountered this underground of spiritual experience after writing a semi-fictional tale about a golf pro named Shivas Irons who taught the game with maxims from the Greek philosopher Pythagoras. The book, *Golf in the Kingdom,* triggered responses I had not expected. In the year following its publication, I heard dozens of bizarre and dramatic accounts about the spiritual mysteries of sport. Two such incidents illustrate the dilemma that many athletes face in trying to understand these strange events in their lives.

The first took place at the San Francisco 49'er training camp in the summer of 1972. John Brodie, the 49'er quarterback, liked *Golf in the Kingdom* and invited me to Santa Barbara, where the team was training, to see if we might write a book together on the psychic factors of athletics. Being a season ticket holder and long-time fan of Brodie's, I found his offer hard to resist. But on the second or third day there, a drama began that I hadn't expected. After an afternoon workout we drank beer with some of the team, and I was talking to some of them about our project. Before long I was telling stories about unusual psychic events that occur in the game of golf. During my dissertation one of the players said that the same kind of thing happened in football every now and then. Players sometimes changed their shape and size for a split second, and it wasn't just in the eye of the beholder. They *actually* changed, he had seen it, and he could get other players to say so too.

I asked him if he could say some more about it.

"Some days there are miracles out there," he whispered. "Yeah, miracles."

It was a hot day, around 80 degrees in this shady bar. Some of the players were getting up to go back to the training camp dinner. I asked him if he'd actually seen it happen—actually seen players change their shape and size.

"Five or six times," he whispered. "Yeah, I think so. I *know* so. The really great running backs. I saw MacArthur Lane do it." He laughed softly. "Ye-ees. Yes indeed. Got bigger once, then smaller. Couldn't have been my imagination."

Was he putting me on? As we went to dinner I wondered how my stories had set with him.

The next day I saw him again in the college dormitory the team was using for their training quarters. Did he want to talk some more about the things he had told me?

He towered above me in the corridor, masking a sense of surprise. Tell me about what? he smiled, about that *ghost story!* No—it had been the beer, and the heat. He hoped I didn't take it seriously.

"But you seemed so convinced," I said. "You weren't putting me on."

He seemed embarrassed. No, he hadn't been putting me on. He was just half-drunk. "Yes, I was *drunk,*" he said "and you got me going with those stories of yours. Got me goin'! But forget it." He turned and went up to his room.

I felt two kinds of emotion—embarrassment and a first sense of discovery. I had just seen a beautiful example of repression at work, and there was the thrill of unraveling a mystery about it! The thought occurred to me that I could track this story down like a detective.

Two days after our second meeting, he approached me during another beer-drinking session. Now he said he was confused about these "spooky things." But by God, the more he thought about them the more real they seemed. He had a hard time accepting them, but in the end he couldn't *reject* them. What was even worse, he remembered other experiences he had forgotten, like the time he heard a voice, a small disembodied voice, talking to him about a game that was under way. He hadn't talked to anyone else about it. The whole thing was a little upsetting, he said.

During the ten days I spent at that 49'er training camp I watched his struggle with these potentially disturbing memories. He was stepping into an aspect of himself he hadn't explored and probably hadn't recognized before—a territory that his coaches and teammates rarely talked about.

A similar incident took place later that summer when a woman phoned to say that my book reminded her of an experience she had while skydiving. Some of the events I had described sounded like a time she had been caught in a thermal upwind and had ridden her parachute, several thousand feet above the ground, for over an hour. During that ride in the sky, a ring of light had formed around her. And for a moment it had turned into a circle of dazzling figures—figures with human shapes made of nothing more substantial than light. She was a mother and sensible woman, a practical earthbound type, she said, but her experience had made her believe in something like angels. Could I tell her what they might have been?

I was cautious when I answered. Had she ever had visions before?

She said that she hadn't. Her husband thought it was some kind of hallucination, but the experience had been too sudden and too vivid for that. No, those figures had been utterly real.

I asked a few more questions, but could feel her backing away, responding to my caution with growing shyness about confiding in me. Finally she hung up without leaving her name or address.

That conversation was a good lesson in talking to people about these things. Skepticism can distance you from someone who has accepted the truth and power of an experience as strange as hers. That's why most sports reporters miss this element in their stories. Athletes will seldom make fools of themselves for the press. To understand these uncanny moments you must approach them sympathetically.

As other stories of this kind came my way in the months that followed, I began to realize that there was a side to athletic experience more complex than the conventional sports wisdom accounted for. There was something uncanny about hearing these things, a sense almost of déjà vu that I had felt before while watching or participating in certain athletic events. It was as if something secretly familiar was pressing to be recognized, something I had always sensed but could render only fictionally when I came to write about it. Then, as people began to tell me that *Golf in the Kingdom* encouraged them to accept these uncanny aspects of their experience, I decided to explore this domain more systematically. For several correspondents claimed that by acknowledging these sometimes strange experiences they found more excitement and significance in sport. Games, they said, were more interesting than ever if you did not suppress these mysterious openings.

In the summer of 1972 I began collecting stories like the 49'er player's and the woman skydiver's. A year later my efforts converged with Rhea White's. Like me, she had been a golfer and sports fan, and with 25 years of experience in parapsychological research she brought to our project a detailed understanding of phenomena like clairvoyance and psychokinesis. Also, on her own, she had systemically gathered a wealth of material on the mystical aspects of sports. She is also a professional reference librarian, and her experience in literature research has enabled her to locate and sift through a huge amount of material. As of this writing, she has read through some 4,500 books, articles, letters, and dissertations recounting incidents like the ones in this book.

In collecting these stories we have decided to define sports in a broad sense. Thus we are including feats of adventure like Lindbergh's flight across the Atlantic and Joshua Slocum's single-handed voyage around the world in the 1890s. Epic undertakings like these provide us with some of our richest material, for spiritual experience seems to depend to some extent on the distance a person has come from his or her ordinary habits and on a willingness to give up set responses. Stepping into *terra incognita* by deed seems to trigger openings into the *terra incognita* of experience. Mountain climbing, distance running, long sea voyages in small boats, and other sports that require a prolonged sacrifice of safety or comfort provide us with more startling spiritual encounters than low-risk games like racquetball or tennis. But low-risk games can become theaters of the occult too. Arthur Ashe [16]* and other tennis players talk about "the zone," a psychological space in which one's performance seems supernormal. There are times when the tamest games are as fierce and as trying as the ascent of a dangerous mountain.

The many reports we have collected show us that sport has enormous power to sweep us beyond the ordinary sense of self, to evoke capacities that have generally been regarded as mystical, occult, or reli-

---

* References will be found at the end of the book.

gious. This is not to say that athletes are yogis or mystics. Very few of us approach games with the lifelong dedication and conscious aspiration for enlightenment that the mystical path requires. It is simply to recognize the similarities that exist between the two fields of activity, both in their methods and in the states of mind they both evoke. The great seers of the contemplative traditions have explored the inner life more deeply than most of us, have opened up spiritual territories that we may or may not enter. But many athletes and adventurers have followed part way, however inadvertently, through the doorways of sport.

Yet we have found that athletes can be as shy or frightened about these things as our Victorian relatives supposedly were about sex. Some athletes have even denied stories that they had told us on previous occasions. Experiences of dramatically altered perception can be traumatic—and understandably so. Anyone would have trouble accepting these startling powers and strange states of mind if he or she had no context for them, no language or philosophy to support them. We hope to resolve that dilemma somewhat in this book. Chapters 2, 3, and 4 describe various psychic events, including mystical feelings and sensations, altered perceptions, and athletic feats that seem to defy normal explanations. In the last three chapters we examine some of the ways in which the timeless truths of our religious heritage, East and West, provide a framework for understanding such experiences as they appear in sports.

But when claims are made for the mystic or psychic aspects of athletics, there is inevitably a response from the skeptics. Many athletes and coaches are wearied by the recent notion that sport may be some kind of yoga. Marathon runner Frank Shorter, for example, said in a recent interview: "People are talking now about how running is supposed to produce some psychoelevating morphine derivative in the blood, or it's supposed to be some sort of religious experience. Maybe it is—but that shouldn't be the main reason you do it. It isn't a major reason for me, or even a minor one. I just like to go out and do it." (231: p. 37)

That attitude, that you should "just go out and do it," is a common one among athletes. There are several good reasons for it, among them a wisdom about talking the spiritual side of athletics to death and a refusal to build up false expectations about it. The athlete's silence about these matters is not unlike the old Zen Buddhist attitude: if you experience illumination while chopping wood, keep chopping wood. If there is something in the act that invites the ecstasy, it doesn't need an extra hype or solemn benediction. And there is wisdom in letting people discover these experiences their own way, for too many expectations can dampen the spontaneity and sense of release that are part of sports' glory. They can take the fun out of sports in the name of religion.

For *the mystical moment occurs as often as it does in sport in part because you don't have to have one.* You are simply there to have a good time or pursue a particularly delicious passion, when suddenly . . . it happens. Many coaches and athletes know this and therefore will not burden us with exhortations about the spiritual things they are doing.

Appreciating this, we come to our subject with some trepidation. By exploring these events in detail, will we raise false hopes that athletics is a special path to mystic insight? We will respond to part of that question at once by saying no, sport *does not* provide a guaranteed way to the Mysteries. It is not the same thing as religious discipline. Part of its glory is that it is not. Because both of us are avid fans—both as participants and as spectators—we don't want to ruin the fun we are having by loading sport with unnecessary baggage. Our aim instead is to enhance the understanding and enjoyment of sports by examining these phenomena. For there is some degree of blindness and fear about these things, an avoidance of the spirit in athletics. And this is as destructive to enjoyment and adventure as inflated claims or solemn incantations can be. Much that appears to be tough-minded wisdom turns out to be nothing but timidity and ignorance about the awesome richness of the human psyche that sport reveals.

2
Mystical
Sensations

Still high after a game—though his team had lost—Andy Russell of the Pittsburgh Steelers once told writer Roy Blount: "Some games you're distracted, by an injury or something, and you get down on yourself, question your character. This game I was away; into the *game*. We lost. But all I could think afterwards was, 'God damn, I had fun.' " (47: p. 310) Many people experience the same kind of intensity and release in sport. When anyone pushes against the psychobiological limits, the brain tissues record a remarkable range of pleasures.

In hundreds of reports from athletes, we have found that the sport experience produces many unusual feelings and ideas. We have noted sixty or more different kinds of sensation in their reports, from a simple sense of well-being to exotic moments when the body seems to stop time, or change shape, or free the self to travel out of the body.

A few sensations are so commonplace they have become newspaper clichés. The winner's confidence that marks many stars can radiate like an aura and be a palpable threat to every competitor. Pitcher Gene Conley says, "I'll never forget Ted [Williams] coming to the plate. You talk about a guy putting you back on your heels on the mound. He dug in, and he looked so *big* up there and the bat looked so light in his hands, and he didn't swish it around, he *snapped* it back and forth, and he looked so darned anxious, as if he was saying, 'Okay, kid, let's see what you've got.' Confidence just oozed out of him. He took something away from you even before you threw a pitch." (213: p. 203)

An entire team can catch the fever of invincibility. In *Life on the Run*, Bill Bradley describes a game the Knicks played against Milwaukee in which the New Yorkers trailed by 19 points with only five minutes remaining in the fourth quarter. With fans already heading home, Bradley reports, "Suddenly, we 'caught fire.' Everything we shot went in and our defense held Milwaukee scoreless for five minutes. We won by three points, accomplishing what came to be known as 'a believer feat.' Those who saw it believed in our invincibility. I even think we did." (56: p. 92)

When contagious confidence spreads through a team, conventional wisdom credits a nebulous group psych-up. But theologian Michael Novak argues in his *Joy of Sports* that something more concrete is going on:

When a collection of individuals first jells as a team, truly begins to react as a five-headed or eleven-headed unit rather than as an aggregate of five or eleven individuals, you can almost hear the *click:* a new kind of reality comes into existence at a new level of human development. A basketball team, for example, can click into and out of this reality many times during the same game; and each player, as well as the coach and the fans, can detect the difference. . . . For those who have participated on a team that has known the click of communiality, the experience is unforgettable, like that of having attained, for a while at least, a higher level of existence: existence as it ought to be. (362: pp. 135-136)

Beyond the aura of confidence and the click of teamwork that nearly everyone credits and purports to understand, athletes report other sensations that, true or not, happen fairly often. Their accounts support each other; men and women in very different sports tell stories that are quite similar. Their experiences range from surges of speed and power to moments of mystery and awe, from ecstasy to peace and calm, from instinctive right action to intimations of immortality, from detachment and perfect freedom to a sense of unity with all things, from a comfortable feeling of being "at home" to uncanny incidents when the body, as if weightless, tells the brain that it has taken up floating or flying.

The experiences reported in this chapter all involve transcendent feelings commonly described by artists, mystics, and lovers—and also by athletes. We give examples of eleven different categories of these feelings, but the number could be tripled. After we examine these, we will move on to extraordinary perceptions in Chapter 3 and to extraordinary athletic feats in Chapter 4.

Acute Well-Being

Anyone who exercises regularly will tell you that a sense of well-being is a natural attribute of physical fitness. Joe Namath touches on this feeling of happiness when he tells about throwing a touchdown pass: "It's pretty hard to describe how that feels, throwing a pass and seeing a man catch it and seeing him in the end zone and seeing the referee throw his arms up in the air, signaling a touchdown, signaling that you've done just what you set out to do. It's an incredible feeling. It's like your whole body's bursting with happiness." (347: p. 84)

Racing car driver Dick Simon says that "there is just something about the sensation you feel in a racing car at speed that is unlike anything else. It brings out all the good feelings in you."

Skiers, skydivers, and others have talked about these good feelings. But these days it seems we hear more about them from runners than from anyone else. A case in point is psychiatrist Thaddeus Kostrubala, who began running to improve his physical fitness and keep his weight down. After about two months, he reported:

> I became aware of two things. The first was the feeling that I was not at all fatigued after an hour of this type of running-walking. Strangely, at the end of the session I had a sense of energy and a kind of pleasure. It wasn't connected to any achievement factor that I could see, for I would feel that way even if I had not fulfilled my own present expectations—such as running a mile. I did not understand this odd shift in feeling. It was a sense of well-being, a sense of energy. . . . I seemed to be more cheerful. (259: p. 66)

Another runner, Dr. George Sheehan, says that he uses half an hour as the point beyond which he experiences distinct mental benefits:

> That first 30 minutes is for my body. During that half-hour, I take joy in my physical ability, the endurance and power of my running. I find it a time when I feel myself competent and in control of my body, when I can think about my problems and plan my day-to-day world. In many ways, that 30 minutes is all ego, all the self. It has to do with me, the individual.
>
> What lies beyond this fitness of muscle? I can only answer for myself. The next 30 minutes is for my soul. In it, I come upon the third wind (unlike the second wind, which is physiological). And then I see myself not as an individual but as part of the universe. In it, I can happen upon anything I ever read or saw or experienced. Every fact and instinct and emotion is unlocked and made available to me through some mysterious operation in my brain.
> (448: p. 36)

William Glasser, in *Positive Addiction,* collected a number of firsthand personal accounts from meditators, runners, and craftsmen. He concluded that they had formed "positive addictions" to these pursuits, "a trancelike, transcendental mental state that accompanies the addictive exercise. *I believe now that it is this same state, the positive addiction (PA) state of mind, that the exercisers reach indirectly and that the meditators are trying to reach directly."* (173: pp. 46-47)

Kostrubala, Sheehan, and Glasser all suggest that running is a physical means of obtaining the ecstatic state of consciousness that meditators seek by purely mental means. Another similarity is that athletes, like meditators, need to engage in a sport activity on a regular basis and for at least a half-hour period in order to achieve a state of heightened well-being.

Peace, Calm, Stillness

Almost all of us are caught up in lifestyles that offer little opportunity for true peace, or for the sense of renewal provided by stillness. But in areas where few people would expect to find it—in risk sports, in running, in the bruising melee of football—athletes do find stillness and peace.

This sense of peace can be found in any stage of a sport. Sometimes it precedes—although it is integrally related to—the actual act of participation. In Zen archery achieving and maintaining a state of calm is the primary goal before, during, and after the act of releasing the arrow. Sollier and Gyorbiró say, "The purpose of Zen archery is not to hit the target, but rather the concentration achieved by the archer in order to create a style that expresses his perfect mental serenity. When the archer does hit the center of the target in such a state of mental calm, it is proof that his spiritual discipline is successful." (465: p. 23) Sometimes this sense of peace or calm is the end result of a sports activity. Eric Ryback, who at the age of 18 hiked the entire length of the Pacific Crest Trail from Canada to Mexico, says that at the very end, when he saw his father running to meet him, "if I ever had a moment of complete peace on the trek, it was then." (419: p. 196)

This sense of stillness, however, is most often reported as occurring while the athlete is fully engaged. Steve McKinney recalled how he felt when he broke the world downhill ski record: "I discovered the middle path of stillness within speed, calmness within fear, and I held it longer and quieter than ever before." (304: p. 77) Malcolm Smith, describing what it is like to ride motorcycles at speed, says "you feel a calmness through your body, even though you know intellectually that you're right on the brink of disaster." (304: p. 179)

The experience is just as likely to occur in competition or in a team sport. Billie Jean King, writing of the perfect shot, says, "I can almost feel it coming. It usually happens on one of those days when everything is just right, when the crowd is large and enthusiastic and my concentration is so perfect it almost seems as though I'm able to transport myself beyond the turmoil on the court to some place of total peace and calm." (251: p. 199)

We have assumed that the words *peace* and *calm* in these descriptions refer solely to the athlete's subjective awareness, not to measurable objective factors. But there is evidence that certain athletes are able to maintain a state of physiological calm even in the most trying circumstances. For example, the breathing and pulse rates of deaf stuntwoman Kitty O'Neil were monitored continuously while she was achieving a speed of 612 miles per hour, strapped onto a liquid fuel rocket, in an attempt to break the men's land speed record. It seems hard to believe, but the instruments revealed that her pulse and breathing rates did not change. In fact, "Kitty O'Neil's pulse rate is the same when she's driving her body 600 miles per hour as it is when she's at rest." (247: p. 28)

Certain sports are more conducive than others to feelings of peace and calm. Stillness is almost inevitable in sports such as deep-sea diving, soaring, gliding, and mountain climbing, where silence is part of the environment. In a certain sense, going to the mountain heights or the ocean depths or flying alone high in the sky, in situations that stretch the athlete to the limit and strip away the comforts of everyday life, may create a silence like that which mystics reach through self-denial, withdrawal, and contemplation. These athletes too have withdrawn from the world for a time; temporarily, at least, they too have become ascetics; and the single-minded pursuit of their sport is in itself a form of concentrated meditation. Mountain climber Richard M. Emerson describes this mystical silence:

After so much effort, to *sit* there—totally alone at 25,000 feet, surrounded by a still and motionless world of rock and ice and blue-‵ black sky—was satisfying in a very special way. It was not the euphoria of altitude. It was the exhilaration of wilderness. Every feature of my surroundings gave evidence of violent force, yet all was calm and fixed—like a terrible battle scene suddenly frozen in a timeless tableau; the rock and ice polished by snow-blasting winds, the graceful sweep of flutings carved on the walls by avalance, the grind and furor of the icefalls far below. But everything was silent and motionless. (215: p. 154)

Colette Richard, a blind woman, learned to climb mountains and descend into deep grottoes. She once described what it was like to be resting high on a mountain: "I sat there listening with my whole being, and with my whole strength contemplating that mountain that I so dearly love. . . . Was there anyone in the world, at that moment, as happy as I?

"For the silence was not emptiness. The silence was Life, making one with the Word. That region was filled with silence—that is to say, filled with life." (403: p. 158)

She also took up caving, accompanying renowned speleologist Norbert Casteret. At her wish she spent a night alone deep in the earth, where she found "total silence." Later she observed, "Up in the heights the silence is white and luminous, a poetry of sunshine, glaciers, keen air and the scent of snow. . . . Underground it is a mineral stillness, immovable, a mysteriously living silence of dropping water and the smell of clay." (403: p. 158)

Howard Slusher, in *Man, Sport and Existence,* eloquently described the significance of these moments in the life of an athlete. He refers to the "*spirit* of the sport," and adds that it is associated with *quiet:*

In searching for the "sounds" of sport one quickly hears the roar of the crowd, the crack of the bat and the thundering of racing feet. But if one listens a little harder and a little longer, one comes to hear silence. There is silence within the performer, in the tenseness of the crowd, in the fear of the hunter and in the beauty of the ski slopes.

Man soon learns that silence is an integral part of life and that certainly it is prominent in sport. Silence is not simply the absence of sounds. Rather it is presence. It is the presence of the dimension of time. A realization of the instant and the situation. Furthermore, it is an expression of the completeness of the situation. In a very real way, silence is heard as an integral part of existence and, as such, provides for many combinations of feelings in the man of sport. (458: p. 168)

Detachment

It is easy to assume that during outstanding performances the athlete is supremely self-involved in what he or she is doing. In fact, this seems to be far from the case. The athlete's self-awareness in peak moments often differs radically from his or her everyday sense of self. There is a feeling of detachment—not only from self and from the surroundings, but also from the results of his or her performance. When he broke the four-minute mile, Roger Bannister says that halfway through the race, "I felt complete *detachment.*" (30: p. 238) Dancer Jacques d'Amboise also describes a sense of detachment in the supreme moments when he feels in command, that he can do anything with his body. "When you're dancing like that, you seem to be removed. You can enjoy yourself doing it and watch yourself doing it at the same time." (535: p. 9)

Before a race, driver Jackie Stewart insisted on isolating himself from everyone, including his wife, bending all energies to induce a state of detachment. In his book *Faster* he describes how he prepares for a race:

The process is akin to a deflating ball. The point of it is to shape my mood, really to expel mood, all mood. Beginning the night before, I start to pace myself into an emotional neutrality, a flatness or isolation that is imperative for a good start. By the time I go to bed, I will have obliterated all contact with people around me, Helen included. Usually I'll be reading, lying there beyond anybody's reach, trying to cleanse my mind, empty it of all extraneous thoughts, all impingements, anything that might encroach. Around eleven or twelve, perhaps, I'll go off to sleep. I'll awaken at half past six or seven, stay in bed, pick up my reading, then probably doze off to reawaken around nine. Breakfast in my room, always in my room, and usually alone, and perhaps, too, I'll have a massage, if one's available. Then back to sleep, up at noon, dress, and leave for the track.

By now I'm fairly bouncy. After the calm of being alone, the ball has started to inflate again. I'll have thoughts of what I'm going to do on the first lap, where I'm going to pass if someone gets off ahead of me, but immediately I'll then become aware of having to change my mood, of the need to put aside all these thoughts lest I lock myself into a plan that might interfere with my driving. More than anything, I know I need to stay loose, so I force myself to deflate, consciously, concentrating on it. I don't want Helen around me, I don't want to be bugged by reporters or film people or magazine photographers, by people wanting my autograph or by anyone. I'm into it, I need to be alone.

By race time I should have no emotions inside me at all—no excitement or fear or nervousness, not even an awareness of the fatigue that's been brought on by pacing myself. I'm absolutely cold, ice-cold, totally within my shell. I'm drained of feeling, utterly calm even though I'm aware of the many things going on around me, the mechanics, people running about, the journalists and officials and everything else.

Stress, I think, enters into it but mainly in a positive way. It's what really lies behind the routine of deflation, the knowledge or discipline, call it what you will, of anticipating what my emotions can become and anticipating too the need to rechannel them, negotiate them, as it were, into a more favorable currency. (474: pp. 30–32)

In an introduction to soaring, Richard Wolters asks why the new pilot tends to look down: "Is it because he is seeing old familiar things from a new perspective and they are strange and exciting? . . . Things seem unreal . . . you're detached. People and their emotions are down there only because you know it. When you break with below, there is a whole new vista. . . ." (533: p. 18)

In a study of parachute jumpers, Benjamin DeMott says, "Pressed for an account of his motives, the articulate jumper is likely to characterize the sport in terms suggesting that for him it amounts to a ritual of divestiture—a means of stripping off layers of institutional lies and myths that encrust the Individual. . . . Man diving is man alive; the ecstasy is that of non-connection—the exhilaration of sinking the world to nothingness, or at least to stillness, and thereby creating the self as All." (111: p. 110)

Charles Lindbergh noted during his famous cross-Atlantic flight: "How detached the intimate things around me seem from the great world down below. How strange is this combination of proximity and separation." It made him acutely aware of "the grandeur of the world outside. The nearness of death. The longness of life." (293: p. 228)

Freedom

A number of statements already quoted concerning the mental state at the apex of the sport experience mention a feeling of freedom and liberation. This feeling of release is a central facet of the experience. For some athletes the experience is not common. It is known only in those rare moments when everything is going right.

David Hemery, who set a world record at the 1968 Olympics in the 400 meters hurdle, winning by a wider margin than anyone had in 44 years, wrote of the event: "Only a couple of times in my life have I felt in such condition that my mind and body worked almost as one. This was one of those times. My limbs reacted as my mind was thinking: *total control, which resulted in absolute freedom.* Instead of forcing and working my legs, they responded with the speed and in the motions that were being asked of them." (200: p. 57)

But other athletes say the feeling of freedom is a constant factor in their sport. Scuba diver Jim Gott says: "Beneath the seas, the diver enters a totally new world. He flies, unburdened even by the law of gravity. His every movement has a feeling of freedom to it." (76: p. 199)

The same sensation is frequently described by airplane pilots:

To fly over open country, to fly just for the sake of flying, is to know freedom. Not just to *feel* free, which can be mere delusion, but to *know* it, to be aware that you are totally free. In flight, the world is open to you. Light is a message, a dialogue, in which the sun and clouds and the radiance of the land are all participants; at night, it is radiated in pinpoints of brilliance that mark autos, towns, isolated houses, and huge cities. Even in cloud, flight means the freedom from or the mastery of that which we normally fear, for flight in cloud can mean the mastery of intelligence over mystery. . . .

The best joy is flight itself: to know you are *up there,* seeing from where you see, feeling the coolness of new breezes, making for yourself the choices of involvement or detachment, and knowing, above all, that for the moment you are a completely separate entity. (150: p. 229)

Mountaineers, while exerting every muscle and all their energy to remain attached to a vertical piece of earth, nonetheless value climbing in part because of the moments of freedom from gravity which it provides. Lionel Terray says that what he and his climbing companion, Pierre Lachenal, "loved about climbing was the sensation of escaping from the laws of gravity, of dancing on space, which comes with technical virtuosity. Like the pilot or the skier, a man then feels freed from the condition of a crawling bug and becomes a chamois, a squirrel, almost a bird." (487: p. 192)

Floating, Flying, Weightlessness

One of the most pleasurable experiences sport can provide is the feeling of floating or weightlessness. It is built into the very structure of some sports, such as skiing, parachuting, and flying. Steve McKinney says that when he broke the world record in speed skiing, it was like "riding the substance of dreams, a magic carpet of air, into which our will power was sensuously intertwined. It was this air carpet, about four to six inches in depth, that we found at speeds over 100 mph. We left the snow and actually flew through the speed trap." (304: p. 74) The feeling is also captured in scuba diving. As Jacques Cousteau puts it: "To halt and hang attached to nothing, no lines or air pipe to the surface, was a dream. At night I had often had visions of flying by extending my arms as wings. Now I flew without wings." (94: p. 6)

In the sports just mentioned one has the feeling of floating because one actually *is* floating, but often, even when an athlete is on the ground, there is a feeling of lightness, a floating sensation, even a sense of weightlessness. Sometimes the athlete even feels as if he or she were suspended above the ground.

Long-distance runner Bill Emmerton, completely exhausted after 600 miles of running, suddenly "had this *light* feeling, I felt as though I was going through space, treading on clouds." (279: p. 40) Marathon runner Ian Thompson observes: "I have only to think of putting on my running shoes and the kinesthetic pleasure of floating starts to come over me" (10: p. 61) Another runner, John Roemer, says "I want to stick my arms out and float." (173: p. 110) William Glasser administered a questionnaire to runners and found repeated mentions of wanting to float or fly. In *Art of the Dance,* Isadora Duncan conceives a type of dancer who can

> . . . convert the body into a luminous fluidity, surrendering it to the inspiration of the soul. This . . . sort of dancer understands that the body, by force of the soul, can in fact be converted to a luminous fluid. The flesh becomes light and transparent, as shown through the X-ray—but with the difference that the human soul is lighter than these rays. When, in its divine power, it completely possesses the body, it converts that into a luminous moving cloud and thus can manifest itself in the whole of its divinity. This is the explanation of the miracle of St. Francis walking on the sea. His body no longer weighed like ours, so light had it become through the soul. (124: p. 51)

The experience of becoming lighter, of being weightless, or of rising in the air—bears a strong resemblance to the experience of mystical ecstasy, in which the feeling of being outside oneself is a primary feature. It is also experienced in some of the newer approaches to the study of consciousness. The editor of *Brain-Mind Bulletin,* Marilyn Ferguson, reports that floating is a common experience of "participants in muscle-relaxation and alpha biofeedback training. It is a typical meditation phenomenon. Mystics frequently speak of enlarging, of loss of body sensations, bubbling up, or becoming airborne. Sensory-deprivation subjects may lie quietly in their isolation chambers, then suddenly feel as if they have risen several inches and are buoyant." (142: p. 68)

Ecstasy

Describing a Yale-Princeton football game, Richard Harding Davis wrote: "People forgot for a few precious minutes to think about themselves, they enjoyed the rare sensation of being carried completely away by something outside of themselves, and the love of a fight, or a struggle, or combat, or whatever else you choose to call it, rose in everyone's breast and choked him until he had either to yell and get rid of it or suffocate." (107: p. 13) What these spectators were experiencing was a form of ecstasy. The contemporary writers on mysticism in daily life observe that a primary element of the ecstatic experience is an "intense, overpowering joy" which seems literally to life those who have the experience out of themselves. They point out that sometimes ecstatics think they can "actually see themselves from the outside." (179: p. 12)

In Pele's first World Cup appearance in 1958, which his team won largely due to his efforts, he believed that "he played that whole game in a kind of trance, as if the future was unfolding before his own disinterested eyes. His feeling is confirmed by newsreel footage of the Brazilian squad moments after the final whistle. As he twists and turns in his teammate's arms, Pele's youthful face is gripped by an almost pained wonder. He looks like a child, caught in the tortuous grip of some unnamed, private ecstasy. Each time he looks at the camera, he turns away quickly." (48: p. 27)

Some may think that the experience of ecstasy attributed to athletes by writers and spectators is just a projection. But to the athletes themselves, these moments are utterly real. Quarterback Francis Tarkenton says that he plays football for one reason: "I love it. Nothing in my life compares to the ecstasies I get from this game." (428: p. 94) Leuchs and Skalka say that while skiing, the athlete can experience "the magic moment when you are right on the mark, when everything falls into place and the only sensation you feel is the ecstasy of what you are doing. Skiier, skiing, skied are one." (281: p. 5) Mountain climber Lionel Terray says he climbed mountains because "the simplest climbs made me crazy with joy. The mountains were a sort of magic kingdom where by some spell I felt happiest." (487: p. 23)

Jesse Francis Lewis questioned 53 students regarding their ecstatic experiences and the contexts in which they occurred. He found that a common facet of the ecstatic experience was a surge of energy. In fact, he notes, "with great regularity, ecstasy involved either activity or the impulse to activity. . . . This may appear as a sort of release of energy, in screaming, jumping, walking or running, or may be more quiet as in smiling or standing." (284: p. 43) The students mentioned that winning sports events was one of the most common triggering events. Similar findings were reported in a classic study of ecstasy made by Marghanita Laski, who studied the "triggers," or circumstances, leading up to the experience of ecstasy. She found that one of the major triggers was movement. In particular, she says, "the kinds of *exercise* or *movement* that seem to be relevant to ecstasy are two: regular rhythmical movement such as walking, jogging along on a horse, riding in a carriage, etc.; and swift movement, such as running, flying, galloping." (273: p. 198)

Almost all of the risk sports involve regularity or swiftness of motion, and these are sports in which euphoria and ecstasy are frequently experienced. Ian Jackson tells about his first experience of surfing: "I began an accelerating paddle rhythm. . . . If you've ever had a close brush with death . . . you know the feeling that shot through my body. It was a pure adrenalin flash. . . . As I pulled out over the shoulder of the wave, I balanced for a moment in ecstasy. Then my knees buckled and I toppled into the warm water, laughing uproariously. It was an instant addiction." (224: p. 17) A woman participant in Outward Bound said of her first rappel while rock climbing: "It must be like flying, it's so exhilarating, so euphoric. It's a giddying rush that's free of any effort on my part." (86: p. 33)

Rhythmic dancing has long been known to trigger ecstasy. Heinrich Zimmer, a scholar and student of Indian culture, points out that "dancing is an ancient form of magic. The dancer becomes amplified into a being endowed with supra-normal powers. His personality is transformed. Like yoga, the dance induces trance, ecstasy, the experience of the divine, the realization of one's own secret nature, and, finally, merging into the divine essence." (537: p. 151) This ecstasy can be experienced by the audience as well as the dancers. Writing of her sister-in-law, Isadora Duncan, Margherita Duncan says, "When she danced the *Blue Danube,* her simple waltzing forward and back, like the oncoming and receding waves on the shore, had such an ecstasy of rhythm that audiences became frenzied with the contagion of it, and could not contain themselves, but rose from their seats, cheering, applauding, laughing and crying. . . . We felt as if we had received the blessing of God." (124: p. 23)

At least one religious group, the Dervishes, uses dance as a means of inducing ecstasy. Their dance progresses through successive stages of intensity, the last of which is "a species of ecstasy which they call *halat*. It is in the midst of this abandonment of self, or rather of religious delirium, that they make use of red-hot irons. . . . These fanatics, transported by frenzy, seize upon these irons, gloat upon them, bite them, hold them between their teeth, and end by cooling them in their mouths." (67: p. 281)

Power, Control

Self-mastery and a sense of power are among the supreme rewards of sport. In some cases the power does not seem to originate in oneself but from outside, as if from the air or the sea or the rock beneath one's feet; at other times, it wells up from within. This feeling can occur in almost any sport, although in our collection of cases it appears to happen most when high risk is involved. University of Illinois psychotherapist Saul Rosenthal (160) has, through surveys of many athletes, identified a powerful form of well-being that comes from risk in sports like skiing and auto racing. An account of bullfighter El Cordobes has described many performances in which he was " 'crazy happy.' He was hypnotized by his own success with this animal, unable to think of anything else but that splendid, drunken feeling of power each movement, each pass of the bull, gave him." (88: p. 305)

This intoxicating power is often felt above the earth. It is one aspect of the "break-off" phenomenon experienced by pilots at high altitudes. Richard Wolters says of being caught up by a thermal, which is the peak moment in soaring: "You'll stumble into it, but you'll know what it is . . . instantly. Then you'll become a believer! It'll push up right from the seat of your pants. Its strength will astonish you, and you will truly climb on wings. . . . This is the power; to use it is the skill. This is what the whole thing is about." (533: p. 62)

When this sense of power happens frequently enough so that it can be expected to recur and its coming can be counted on, it is transformed into a feeling of invincibility. Decathlon champion Bruce Jenner says that part way through the 1976 Olympics

> . . . a strange feeling began to come over me. In four events so far, I'd set three personal bests and come within a couple hundredths of my electronic p.r. [personal record] in the hundred. I started to feel that there was nothing I couldn't do if I had to. It was a feeling of awesome power, except that I was in awe of myself, knocking off these p.r.'s just like that. I was rising above myself, doing things I had no right to be doing. (228: p. 77)

Often the sense of control in sport extends to one's equipment or surroundings. In auto racing on good days drivers feel they can do anything with their cars. "They say they can attach a lawn mower to the car and mow the lawn." (254: p. 94) An experience of oneness and of being in effortless control is described by surfer Midget Farrelly:

> Sometimes you reach a point of being so coordinated, so completely balanced, that you feel you can do anything—anything at all. At times like this I find I can run up to the front of the board and stand on the nose when pushing out through a broken wave; I can goof around, put myself in an impossible position and then pull out of it, simply because I feel happy. An extra bit of confidence like that can carry you through, and you can do things that are just about impossible. (141: p. 23)

Chris Bonington, a well-known mountain climber, says that control can even be extended to one's environment. "With experience, one gains greater control. This led to a real pleasure in a struggle with the elements at their worst—certainly my most memorable, and in a way most enjoyable, days climbing have been in violent storms in the Alps, when the wind and snow have torn at my anorak-covered body; when my wits and judgment have been extended to the full and yet, in spite of all, I have remained on top of the situation." (53: p. 22)

At its fullest, the feeling of being in control is a unifying experience involving the athlete's entire sense of self, the environment, and even his destiny. Champion race driver Mario Andretti insists: "Only a race driver can know—can feel—the joys of motor racing. When a man is competing in a race car, when he is pushing himself and the machine to the very limit, when the tires are breaking free from the ground and he is controlling his destiny with his own two hands, then, man, he is living—in a way no other human can understand." (8: p. 5)

Andretti's experience is corroborated by a study of racing car drivers which concludes that

> . . . the need to feel in control is satisfied by handling a machine delicately and skillfully at high speeds. Driving these speeds and performing a task which is quite obviously highly dangerous at the limits of one's ability and the limits of the car's capacity, gives rise to a particular exhilaration and feeling of successful control of objects and oneself. (264: pp. 193–194)

A sustained feeling of power develops into a sense of being in control, which contributes to the "high" often experienced in sport. Although it sometimes originates outside the individual, as when an athlete identifies with the power in a wave or the lift of a thermal, most often it wells up from within, resulting from the athlete's mastery of his body, his equipment, his sense of self, and even the environment.

Being in the Present

Regardless of the sport, successful athletes say that when they are performing at their best they are immersed in the present moment, totally involved in whatever confronts them. John Brodie, former San Francisco 49'er quarterback, has said that "a player's effectiveness is directly related to his ability to be right there, doing that thing, in the moment. All the preparation he may have put into the game—all the game plans, analysis of movies, etc.—is no good if he can't put it into action when game time comes. He can't be worrying about the past or the future or the crowd or some other extraneous event. He must be able to respond in the here and now." (343: p. 20)

When athletes are truly immersed in the present, they are totally unaware of distractions. Auto racer Jochen Rindt told Peter Manso that when driving "you completely ignore everything and just concentrate. You forget about the whole world and you just . . . are part of the car and the track. . . . It's a very special feeling. You're completely out of this world. There is nothing like it." (308: p. 168)

Apparently Ben Hogan, one of golf's legendary concentrators, was singularly unaware of his competition. On one occasion, Clayton Heafner finished second to Hogan in a big tournament, in which Hogan came from behind to defeat him, although Heafner was playing his best golf. All through the round Heafner had been aware of Hogan, and at the end consoled himself with the thought that it was not he who had lost the tournament but Hogan who had won it by "shooting the lights out." Later, in the locker room, Heafner bumped into Hogan, who looked up from a telegram he was reading and said, "Oh, hi, Clayt, how'd it go today?" (49: p. 53)

Football player Jack Snow says he concentrates "to the point of self-hypnosis. I pick out a spot in the end zone or behind the end zone and I tell myself I won't let anyone stop me from reaching it, and I don't. If a plane crashed in the stadium, I don't think I'd notice it until the play was over." (287: p. 49)

The single-minded concentration of the athlete creates in him or her both a sense of detachment from the surroundings and an awareness of being in "another world." Golfer Arnold Palmer writes that this experience in tournament play:

> . . . involves a tautness of mind but not a tension of the body. It has various manifestations. One is the concentration on the shot at hand. The other is the heightened sense of presence and renewal that endures through an entire round or an entire tournament. There is something spiritual, almost spectral about the latter experience. You're involved in the action and vaguely aware of it, but your focus is not on the commotion but on the opportunity ahead. I'd liken it to a sense of reverie—not a dreamlike state but the somehow insulated state that a great musician achieves in a great performance. He's aware of where he is and what he's doing, but his mind is on the playing of his instrument with an internal sense of *rightness*—it is not merely mechanical, it is not only spiritual; it is something of both, on a different plane and a more remote one. (371: p. 141)

Instinctive Action and Surrender

Despite the many long years of instruction, study, practice, and training that most athletes put in, they generally do not act consciously when they make outstanding plays. The conscious knowledge of correct and incorrect moves serves as kindling and logs to a fire, but in the white heat of the event they are burnt into nonexistence, as the reality of the flames takes over—flames originating in a source beyond conscious know-how, melding athlete, experience, and play into a single event. This is not to belittle deliberate training and practice, for without wood there can be no flame. Perhaps we can speak of two stages, conscious and unconscious, neither of which could operate without the other. Because we can talk about it, think about it, read about it, the conscious aspect is familiar to all of us; to some, it is the only reality. We must, however, give equal recognition to the lesser known, unknown, unconscious aspect—the state that can be recalled only after the play has been made, when the athlete talks about being "unconscious," "out of my mind," "in the twilight zone," "out of my gourd," playing "over my head." He doesn't know how he made the play—he just did. "It was instinct."

Masters of the martial arts are generally more conscious of the second, unconscious stage than their Western counterparts. In a sense the latter are in a paradoxical situation: that of being unconscious of being unconscious, as it were.

E. J. Harrison, a Westerner who made firsthand observations of martial artists and other renowned fighters around the world, tells of a demonstration given by Matsuura, a high-ranking instructor at the Kodokan School of Judo:

Sitting on his knees with his back to me and his hands together, he made his mind blank of any conscious thought. The idea was that I was to remain behind him for as long a time as I desired. Then with all the speed and power I could muster I was to grab him by the throat and pull him over backwards. I sweated it out for maybe two or three minutes without making a move. Then I put all the power and speed I could into the effort. My next step was to get up from my back where I landed in front of him. His explanation was that the action was not conscious, but rather sprang from the seat of reflex control, the *tanden,* or second brain. These things are not taught in the Judo College. (394: p. 409)

One does not consciously have to plan how to act; instead, one lets the appropriate responses happen of themselves. This open secret at the heart of the sports experience has been well described by writer and philosopher Michael Novak:

> This is one of the great inner secrets of sports. There is a certain point of unity within the self, and between the self and its world, a certain complicity and magnetic mating, a certain harmony, that conscious mind and will cannot direct. Perhaps analysis and the separate mastery of each element are required before the instincts are ready to assume command, but only at first. Command by instinct is swifter, subtler, deeper, more accurate, more in touch with reality than command by conscious mind. The discovery takes one's breath away. (362: p. 164)

A famous explication of the importance of unconsciousness in sport is German philosopher Eugen Herrigel's description of his efforts to learn Zen archery. The Zen master who taught him insisted that "the shot will only go smoothly when it takes the archer himself by surprise. . . . You mustn't open the right hand on purpose." (203: p. 48) Former heavyweight champion Ingemar Johansson found something similar in boxing. He insisted there was something about his right hand—the hand that delivered the knockout punch—that was strange. He told a *Life* reporter that it worked independently of his conscious mind and was so fast he couldn't even see it. "Without my telling it to, the right goes, and when it hits, there is this good feeling. . . . Something just right has been done." (232: p. 43)

Many athletes recognize the importance of not acting deliberately during peak moments. They seem to know that conscious thought must be held in abeyance. Catfish Hunter, in describing the perfect game he pitched against the Minnesota Twins in 1968, says, "I wasn't worried about a perfect game going into the ninth. It was like a dream. I was going on like I was in a daze. I never thought about it the whole time. If I'd thought about it I wouldn't have thrown a perfect game—I know I wouldn't." (220: p. 37)

O. J. Simpson insists "Thinking . . . is what gets you caught from behind." (288: p. 180) So instead, on game day, he says, "My biggest thing is to clear my mind. . . . I just try to clear myself and relax my body and get into my breathing pace, my own pace. I can't be thinking about one element of it. I'm not thinking about anything, so hopefully I'm thinking about everything. Pulling in what I need to pull in. You just react instead of consciously thinking about it." (73: p. 28)

Sometimes the unconscious, instinctive action in sport is perceived as coming from a greater power beyond oneself. Utah State University basketball star Wayne Estes, who in his senior year ranked just above Princeton's Bill Bradley and just below leading scorer Rick Barry of the University of Miami, scored 48 points in his final game. In a radio interview following the game he said "I was just putting the ball up. . . . Somebody else was putting it in for me." (252: pp. 25–26)

In the 1953 World Series, George Shuba pinch-hit a home run. Blinded by the sun, he could barely see the ball, but he hit it out—the second player ever to pinch-hit a homer in a series. However, says Shuba, ". . . it wasn't me. There was something else guiding the bat. I couldn't see the ball, and you can think what you want, but another hand was guiding my bat." (241: p. 238)

The necessity for remaining open and empty, and the need for surrender, also figure prominently in the religions of the world. The purpose of surrender, of letting go, in both religion and sport, is not to diminish one's self but to achieve a level of functioning otherwise impossible. The feeling of a greater self taking over, so graphically described by the athletes in this section, has its counterpart in St. Paul's ". . . not I live, but Christ liveth in me." From the Eastern point of view, there is Lao Tse's "when once you are free from all seeming, from all craving and lusting, then will you move of your own impulse, without so much as knowing that you move." (311: p. 182)

Mystery and Awe

Although most of us view the world of the West in the twentieth century as almost totally secularized, a sense of the numinous, of mystical awe, is surfacing in unlikely places. For many persons this sense of the numinous is experienced on athletic fields and playgrounds. In interviews with 20 athletes, physical education professor Kenneth Ravizza (396) found that 18 had experienced what they called awe and wonder during their peak moments in sport. Maurice Herzog, in describing the successful ascent of Annapurna, says that as he and Pierre Lachenal approached the summit:

> I felt as though I were plunging into something new and quite abnormal. I had the strangest and most vivid impressions, such as I had never before known in the mountains. There was something unnatural in the way I saw Lachenal and everything around us. . . . all sense of exertion was gone, as though there were no longer any gravity. This diaphanous landscape, this quintessence of purity—these were not the mountains I knew: they were the mountains of my dreams. (205: p. 132)

This sense of awe, which may linger on after the experience, was felt by a surfer who, after riding his biggest wave, said: "Afterward I just sat there. I didn't want to talk about it. It happened so quickly. I didn't realize the magnitude of it until I was sitting on the beach." (396: p. 118)

At these times athletes feel they are treading on sacred ground—or even that the divine has invaded their lives. Basketball player Patsy Neal writes:

> There are moments of glory that go beyond the human expectation, beyond the physical and emotional ability of the individual. Something *unexplainable* takes over and breathes life into the known life. One stands on the threshold of miracles that one cannot create voluntarily. The power of the moment adds up to a certain amount of religion in the performance. Call it a state of grace, or an act of faith . . . or an act of God. It is there, and the impossible becomes possible. . . . The athlete goes beyond herself; she transcends the natural. She touches a piece of heaven and becomes the recipient of power from an unknown source.
>
> The power goes beyond that which can be defined as physical or mental. The performance almost becomes a holy place—where a spiritual awakening seems to take place. The individual becomes swept up in the action around her—she almost *floats* through the

performance, drawing on forces she has never previously been aware of. (350: pp. 166–167)

This can be a frightening experience; it can literally raise the hairs on the head. George Plimpton relates a conversation he had with tennis player Sidney Wood on what it is like to be charged up during a match. "He described the effect as 'total vision,' . . . in which the feeling of omnipotence is overwhelming. 'You simply become more than yourself,' Wood said. 'When it happens, there are physical manifestations as well. The hair stands on end and starts to get all prickly.' " (385: pp. 59–60)

Dick Schaap has written a whole book centered on the moment at the Mexico Olympics when Bob Beamon broke the world record in the long jump by nearly two feet, a record no one has approached since. After the footage had been determined, and Beamon had donned his warm-up pants, Schaap, who relived the event with Beamon, says:

Suddenly, the enormity of what he had done sank in, and Beamon fell to his knees, leaned his head against the Tartan running track, almost as if he were kissing the ground, then clasped his head in his hands. Waves of nausea rolled over him, and his heart pounded as it had never pounded before, and he could see stars in front of his eyes. "Tell me I am not dreaming," he mumbled. It's not possible. I can't believe it. Tell me I am not dreaming." Beamon thought he was going to vomit, and an American physician offered him some bicarbonate. Beamon turned it down and asked instead for a cup of coffee. "If I had had high blood pressure," said Beamon later, "I would have had a stroke." (427: p. 97)

This fear, which sometimes may even border on terror, may be due in part to the fact that "the athlete many times finds that things go beyond what he understands, and what he knows should happen logically." (350: p. 166) The German theologian Rudolf Otto describes the human encounter with the awesome aspect of sacred—with "that which is alien to us, uncomprehended and unexplained . . . that which is quite beyond the sphere of the usual, the intelligible, and the familiar, which therefore falls quite outside the limits of the 'canny' and is contrasted with it, filling the mind with blank wonder and astonishment'' (366: p. 26) and a ''consciousness of the absolute superiority or supremacy of a power other than myself.'' (366: p. 21) Thus the athlete knows that being in perfect control of the football, or the puck, or the bat may be a matter more of grace than of will, and that one can only ''do it'' by letting it happen, by letting something else take over, as it were. And it is the awareness of and closeness to that ''something else'' that can lead to terror. Otto calls it ''the emotion of a creature, submerged and overwhelmed by its own nothingness in contrast to that which is supreme above all creatures.'' (366: p. 10) George Leonard describes something very similar that occurs in sport:

> Pressing us up against the limits of physical exertion and mental acuity, leading us up to the edge of the precipice separating life from death, sports may open the door to infinite realms of perception and being. Having no tradition of mystical experience, no adequate mode of discourse on the subject, no preparatory rites, the athlete might refuse to enter. But the athletic experience is a powerful one, and it may thrust the athlete, in spite of fear and resistance, past the point of no return, into a place of awe and terror. (279: pp. 39–40)

Feelings of Immortality

It is not uncommon for athletes to experience a sense of immortality in one form or another. Charles Tekeyan, for example, feels that the sense of immortality some athletes speak of is solely a matter of continued excellence in the flesh. He says, ''An athlete at his peak feels invincible and immortal and intends to remain that way as long as possible.'' (485: p. 2) This idea of *physical* immortality, however, is only one form of immortality found in sports. Another is the sense of continuity with ages past. Long-distance runner Bill Emmerton once saw himself in the chain of life stretching over many generations. According to George Leonard:

> Once, while making the run from John 'o Groat's to Lands End in Britain, he ran steadily for thirty-five hours with only the briefest of necessary stops. After some thirty-two hours of that run, be-

tween two and three a.m., he found himself in a fog on the Cornwall moors, totally alone, miles from anyone. Emmerton, Australian-born-and-bred, knew that he had ancestors in that region of England.

"I was completely, utterly exhausted," he told me. "I'd just put six hundred miles behind me, fifty miles, day in and day out, through all kinds of weather conditions—six inches of snow, the fierce winds from the North Sea, the pelting rain, the hailstorms. Then, all of a sudden, I had this *light* feeling, I felt as though I was going through space, treading on clouds. I didn't know what it was, but I heard a voice saying, 'We're here to help you.' I reached out my arm and someone was there to help me. I could feel spirits, the spirits of my ancestors they said they were, and they gathered around me, coming so close I felt I could *touch* them. I've never revealed this to anyone before—*never*. But they were *right there*. And I was talking to them. I just started *talking*. It was this *warm* feeling, almost like an orgasm. And I was saying, 'Thank you. Thank you for taking care of me.' " (279: pp. 40-44)

Some sports, more than others, seem to draw back a curtain that ordinarily screens out all intimations of immortality, thus revealing a reality that has been there, unguessed, all the time. This occurs with some frequency in mountaineering and is exemplified by Frank Smythe's experiences in the Himalayas:

There is something about the Himalayas not possessed by the Alps, something unseen and unknown, a charm that pervades every hour spent among them, a mystery intriguing and disturbing. Confronted by them, a man loses his grasp of ordinary things, perceiving himself as immortal, an entity capable of outdistancing all change, all decay, all life, all death. (464: pp. 136-137)

Thus in sport as elsewhere there are various ways in which a sense of immortality arises—through a sense of one's endless bodily strength, or in the awareness of being a link in a never-ending chain of being, or as part of a spiritual essence that cannot die. In such moments the athlete experiences an incontrovertible reality that makes *this* world seem like a dream.

Unity

There are many levels of unity experienced in sports: a union of mind and body; a sense of oneness with one's teammates; and in the highest reaches of experience, a feeling of unity with the cosmos.

An experience of inner unity is the apex of the sports experience for many athletes. Boxer Randy Neumann says of running to exhaustion: "It's an amazing sensation to feel your mind and body become a single force against . . . gravity. This is also the sensation experienced in a rare fight when you pull your whole being together and pit it against an opponent." (353: p. 91)

Patsy Neal descibes the oneness that can be experienced in a moment of competition:

> There seems to be a power present that allows the individual to "walk on water," or to create miracles in those precious moments of pure ecstasy. He runs and jumps and *lives* through the pure play process, which is composed of joy and pleasure and exuberance and laughter; even the pain seems completely tolerable in these few precious and rare moments of *being*, and of knowing that one is just that . . . a oneness and a wholeness. (350: p. 90)

Sometimes the sense of identity extends to teammates and even to opponents. The latter is especially noticeable in the martial arts. A teaching manual states that when judo is practiced properly, "There will be no curtain to separate you from your opponent. You will become one with him. You and your opponent will no longer be two bodies separated physically from each other but a single entity, physically, mentally, and spiritually inseparable. Therefore the motion of your opponent may be considered your motion. And you can lure him to any posture you like and effectively apply a large force on him. You can throw him as easily as you can yourself." (508: p. 33)

Athletes also feel a sense of unity with their equipment. Jimmy Clark, one of the greatest auto racers of all time, once observed: "I don't drive a car, really. The car happens to be under me and I'm controlling it, but it's as much a part of me as I am of it." (289: p. 171) Similarly, Donald Bond, who made a study of flyers, found that they "commonly speak of the plane as if it were an extension of their own bodies." (51: p. 26)

Sometimes the athlete feels at one with his or her immediate natural surroundings. Writer Matthew Fox says, "In the ecstasies of sport, we experience again our communion with nature: our bodies and whole selves are once again immersed in our origins—water, sky, earth and, because excellence is demanded of us, fire. Consider the surfer's union with the waves, the sea, the sky and wind." (153: p. 7)

In the ultimate experience of oneness, there is no longer any separation between the athlete and the universe itself. In fact, the founder of aikido, Morehei Uyeshiba, taught:

> The secret of Aikido is to harmonize ourselves with the movement of the universe and bring ourselves into accord with the universe itself. He who has gained the secret of Aikido has the universe in himself and can say, "I am the universe." I am never defeated, however fast the enemy may attack. . . . When an enemy tries to fight with him, the universe itself, he has to break the harmony of the universe. Hence at the moment he has the mind to fight with me, he is already defeated. (501: p. 177)

This sense of unity can also be experienced in the form of perceiving the world as if through the eyes of God. This is illustrated by the following experience, which Yukio Mishima had when flying an F104 at speeds of over 1,000 miles per hour:

> . . . if this stillness was the ultimate end of action—of movement—then the sky about me, the clouds far below, the sea gleaming between the clouds, even the setting sun, might well be events, things, within myself. At this distance from the earth, intellectual adventure and physical adventure could join hands without the slightest difficulty. This was the point that I had always been striving towards. (327: pp. 1–2)

Explorer Richard Byrd, alone for months in the Arctic, living in primitive conditions at subzero temperatures, one evening knew the unity of the universe. He writes:

> The day was dying, the night being born—but with great peace. Here were the imponderable processes and forces of the cosmos, harmonious and soundless. Harmony, that was it! That was what

came out of the silence—a gentle rhythm, the strain of a perfect chord, the music of the spheres, perhaps.

It was enough to catch that rhythm, momentarily to be myself a part of it. In that instant I could feel no doubt of man's oneness with the universe. The conviction came that that rhythm was too orderly, too harmonious, too perfect to be a product of blind chance—that, therefore, there must be purpose in the whole and not an accidental offshoot. It was a feeling that transcended reason; that went to the heart of man's despair and found it groundless. The universe was a cosmos, not a chaos; man was as rightfully a part of that cosmos as were the day and night. (72: p. 85)

3
Altered
Perceptions

Former quarterback John Brodie once said, "Often in the heat and excitement of a game, a player's perception and coordination will improve dramatically. At times, and with increasing frequency now, I experience a kind of clarity that I've never seen adequately described in a football story." (343: p. 19)

In this chapter, we report on several altered perceptions that occur in sport. They range from subtle heightenings of alertness to alterations of time and space, to extrasensory perceptions and the apprehension of disembodied entities. Like the feelings and sensations we examined in the preceding chapter, some of these altered perceptions occur quite commonly, while others are strange and infrequent. Taken together, they resemble the range of altered perceptions reported in the literature of yoga and mysticism.

Shifts in alertness are experienced by many athletes. These may involve a sharpening of vision or hearing, or a keener sense of interior (kinesthetic) sensations, or indeed of the whole person. Such fresh awareness can occur in the thick of vigorous action.

Pro football's Mike Reid wrote music and played the concert piano professionally at the same time he was playing defense for the Cincinnati Bengals. He reported, "Mentally I'm more alert. I do my best work at the piano after a game." (399: p. 51) Aerobics research suggests that Reid's charged-up body could not return to his normal nonathletic state until about five hours after he played a game. So his alert state at the piano comes as no surprise. Senator William Proxmire finds that merely walking can bring the senses out of their "normal" daze:

> The most surprising physical aspect of walking is the energizing effect. . . . This contradicts everything I expected of walking, and it's a mystery to me why it takes place. I can start off tired and weary at the end of a long day in the Senate, with all kinds of frustrations, feeling too tired to sleep and far too tired to walk, and after that first difficult quarter-or-half-mile, not only does the frustration ease but, after my vigorous striding begins, I begin to feel more rested and then fully alert. (392: p. 53)

Kathy Switzer, one of the first women to run in the Boston Marathon, says that after she took up running she discovered that "while I was running I found myself being able to think clearly. . . . I thought

about my writing, my schoolwork—everything came so clear to me."
(140: p. 100) She also discovered that it made her more sensuous. "When
I'm training, I'm more physically sensitive to food, to weather, to
touch . . . everything. . . . I also become more mentally sensitive to social problems, the ills of the world and so on. When I'm not in training,
I'm more lethargic and apathetic.

"Everything I see and feel is more extreme when I'm in training. If
I'm happy, I'm happier. If I'm sad, I'm sadder. If I'm emotional, I'm
more emotional. I once ran thirty-one miles and after that there was
nothing in the world I thought I couldn't do." (140: p. 97) Descriptions like
this have been given by many joggers and runners. In fact, the clarity
that Kathy Switzer describes is one of the reasons for the great popularity of the sport.

This phenomenon has been confirmed by systematic research.
Dorothy V. Harris, Director of the Center for Women and Sport at
Pennsylvania State University, finds mental alertness and clarity associated with all sports. In a systematic study she found that after vigorous exertion most people are "more alert, they can think more clearly,
and are more effective mentally. . . ." (191: p. 53)

As a result of this heightened sensitivity, sport participants often
report more sharply etched and vivid perceptions. Not only do their
minds *feel* clear, but they actually do *perceive* things more fully and
vividly. Everything looks and feels fresh and new, as if encountered for
the first time. The senses, opened as if to a new world, often register
things that one never catches in normal consciousness. Valentine
Menkin, twice an Olympic yacht-racing champion, when asked what he
focused on during a race, replied:

I try to feel the yacht with my body and watch the sea and the air
with my eyes. To me every air current has a color of its own. I try
to feel every wave with my feet. Like on horseback, I hold on with
the tips of my toes. At the Mexico City Olympics, where I made
my best showing, I saw all the air currents and made almost no
mistakes. On the other hand, when I am in poor shape, the air becomes invisible. When the wind is weak, all the perceptions I've
tried to develop since childhood are weakened, and then my feet
take over. I feel the water with my feet, like a car feels the road
with its springs. (367: p. 63)

Adam Smith tells of a diver who was skeptical about peak experiences occurring while engaged in sport: ". . . then one day, in just 30 feet of water, something happened, and he said that suddenly he felt absolutely at one with the ocean, and he could *hear grains of sand on the bottom,* and he spent almost an hour listening to the grains of sand, and his life has been changed ever since." (460: p. 37)

Athletes have exceptionally vivid memories of these moments of heightened sensory involvement. As pitcher Whitey Ford writes, "You know the way Jack Nicklaus can remember every shot he took in a golf tournament? Well, I think I could tell you just about every pitch I threw in those 3,170 innings. And Mickey [Mantle] could tell you just about every pitch that was thrown to him. . . . Most guys have this total recall about the things they saw or did in ball games." (152: p. 174)

A horsewoman, Mary Lindsay Dickinson, wrote one of us (White) about two outstanding rides she had:

> Riding makes you god-like and takes you beyond the limitations of the human body—especially jumping fences so high and solid you can't see over or through them.
>
> So—one show in Houston, Texas—the other in Ruleville, Mississippi, both the same. The course calls for a preliminary circle before the first fence. As I made the circle, before we even took off, I knew and I'm sure the horse did too that this was special. Every step took a long time. The fences were just at the right place. . . . The horse jumped like a stag and I was in ecstasy. I believe the horse was too.
>
> You can't describe these sensations. All I know is this suprastate was clearly visible because both times total strangers sought me out to tell me they'd never seen anything like it. And ten years later my parents and I were talking about my show career and I said, "I've never talked about this before but 2 rounds were special." My Mom said—with no hesitation—"Yes—that time in Houston" and my Dad said, "And Ruleville, too." I know that for those few moments what we did was sublime and if Michelangelo had seen it he would have tipped his hat. (116)

The obvious explanation for the vividness of Mary Lindsay Dickinson's memory is that it involved two outstanding events in her ath-

letic career. It is to be expected that hitting a timely home run, or winning one's first major tournament, or running one's first marathon
would certainly be memorable events. But what about the claims of
Mickey Mantle and Jack Nicklaus? Presumably they remember the
major portion of *all* the events in which they participated. This
amounts to almost total recall for specific areas of their lives, whereas
presumably in other areas they remember only the high spots. It
appears that their experiences were memorable because of the unusual
state they were in, a state of mind that apparently contributed to their
outstanding performances. (Could it be that some superstars are in this
exceptional frame of mind much of the time?) Does their exceptional
state of mind determine both the quality of the performance and the
vividness of the recollection of it, not the other way around as is
usually assumed?

Altered Perception of Size and Field

A number of changes in spatial perception are experienced in sport.
These changes are not common but seem to occur at peak moments
when the athlete is in a state which differs from his or her more routine
state of consciousness. Some athletes report being able to perceive
many more details than is customary for them. And the details stand
out much more sharply than usual.

St. Louis slugger Stan Musial told Roger Kahn that he didn't guess
what a pitch would be, he *knew*. Musial added, "I can always
tell . . . as long as I'm concentrating." He went on to tell Kahn:

> "I pick the ball up right away," he said. "Know what I mean? I
> see it as soon as it leaves the pitcher's hand. That's when I got to
> concentrate real hard. If I do, I can tell what the pitch is going to
> be."
> "When can you tell?"
> "When it's about halfway to home plate. . . . I can tell by the
> speed. . . . Every pitcher has a set of speeds. I mean, the curve
> goes one speed and the slider goes at something else. Well, if I con-
> centrate real good, I can pick up the speed of the ball about the
> first 30 feet it travels. I know the pitcher and I know his speeds.

When I concentrate, halfway in I know what the pitch is gonna be, how the ball is gonna move when it gets up to home plate."

Musial mentally sorts the deliveries of some 80 or 90 pitchers. Allowing four pitches to each, this means that in any given season he has classified something over 320 distinct deliveries. Then, through his great coordination and eyesight, he applies the knowledge during the three-fifths of a second it takes a typical pitch to reach him from the mound. The frequent result, professor, is what we in the trade call a clean blow. (242: pp. 15–16)

Perhaps, as Musial feels, the concentration is the crucial thing. There is no doubt that it is important, but there may be other factors involved. For, as parapsychologists have noted, when conscious attention is centered on one thing, this act may allow other, more subtle perceptual abilities to come into play. Maybe the important thing in Musial's case was simply that he believed he could see the pitches if he concentrated, so that when he succeeded in concentrating, he actually did hit more pitches than he would have otherwise. We are suggesting that what occurred may not have been simply a matter of heightened visual acuity but rather some intuitive factor.

Under special conditions objects appear to be much larger than they are in reality. For instance, in the 1955 U.S. Open Golf Championship, dark horse Jack Fleck came from behind to defeat Ben Hogan. In looking back on the final round, he says the turning point was the fifth hole, "after I had made four pars. I can't exactly describe it, but as I looked at the putt, the hole looked as big as a wash tub. I suddenly became convinced I couldn't miss. All I tried to do was keep the sensation by not questioning it." (359: p. 23) Other players report similar experiences; baseball players talk about how large the ball is when they're at bat, and basketball players see the hoop getting bigger and bigger.

Some athletes can perceive an entire field including all the players. Newspaperman Chris Lydon wrote of Bobby Orr: "He sees all the action on the ice and knows where everyone is going to be moments before they get there. He thinks of passes that occur to nobody else. Like Bob Cousy in his early days with the [basketball] Celtics, he hits open men who didn't realize they were open and weren't ready to receive a pass." (114: p. 62)

Soccer's Pele had a similar gift: "Intuitively, at any instant, he seemed to know the position of all the other players on the field, and to sense just what each man was going to do next." (352: p. 205)

The startling difference between the widened perception developed by athletes and "normal" perception is described by Paul Martha of the Pittsburgh Steelers. "I always knew that a free safety man is supposed to watch the quarterback and the receiver, too, but it was always difficult for me. . . . Then all of a sudden, midway through the 1967 season, I realized I was following the quarterback all the way—and the receiver, too. It just happened. It was like I had stepped into an entirely new dimension." (538: p. 161)

Although the ability to be aware of the entire field and all the players on it is partly a matter of alertness and concentration, peripheral vision also plays a large role. Bob Cousy was noted for this ability. According to John Devaney, "as Cousy drove toward the foul line, his astonishing wide-angle vision would allow him to see Oftring and Kaftan on either side of him. If an opponent moved toward Cousy, *zip* went a pass to whoever was free, and *justlikethat* Holy Cross had scored again." (113: p. 91) Cousy himself admits that he has "unusual peripheral vision. I can see more than most people out of the corners of my eyes. I don't have to turn my head to find out what's going on at either side. It sometimes appears that I'm throwing the ball without looking. I'm looking all right but out of the corners of my eyes." Joe Marcus reports that Pele has "about twenty-five percent better peripheral vision than other athletes." (310: p. 31)

In studying brain surgery patients, California Institute of Technology scientist Dr. Colwyn Trevarthon discovered a second sight system that controls peripheral vision. Trevarthon hypothesizes that this system evolved from the primitive type of visual awareness belonging to birds, reptiles, and other lower forms of animal life, allowing an automatic response to action in the surrounding space. Thus, if there is unexpected movement in that space, Trevarthon explains, it "registers first through this second, more primitive system before the classical visual system becomes aware of it." (438: p. 14) Perhaps those athletes who have exceptional peripheral vision are not natively any better endowed than those who do not seem to have it. The difference may lie in the fact that somehow they have discovered a way to allow the more primitive system to function.

Alterations in Time Perception

In peak moments in sport, the athlete's sense of time is also altered. Often it is perceived as moving more swiftly, as in the case of a chess player who said, "Time passes a hundred times faster. In this sense it resembles the dream state." (161: p. 36) Or time can be compressed into a centered moment in which there is neither before nor after. In an article on outstanding experiences in sport, Jo Ann Houts observes, "The sense of time is disoriented. A single play may seem like forever or an inning may seem like only a second. There is no conscious sense of past time or future time. The moment-to-moment passage of time is all that is relevant; in-the-moment perception is all that the player possesses." (218: p. 71)

That the extraordinary moment in sport is fraught with immense possibility is illustrated in a graphic description by football player Gary Shaw. He calls it "the moment on a football field that for me soars above all others." (447: p. 233)

> My life-long friend, Dee Wilson, and I frequently spent our late summer afternoons running pass patterns and playing touch football. Some days I would be quarterback and Dee the receiver, and on others it was vice versa. One September day we were playing two other friends on the otherwise empty field of a high school stadium. We were in good shape and had been playing for almost two hours. But now all of us were tired and it was getting dark, so we agreed the next play would be our last. Dee and I had been working on one pass pattern for a couple of days, and though it had been unsuccessful that afternoon, we had decided to try it again on this final play. What followed was an experience I'd never had before.
>
> At the end of this pattern, Dee was to be about thirty yards downfield angling for the corner of the end zone. But as I dropped back and pointed my eyes toward his full strides into late afternoon, I began to feel some inexplicable postponement of time. My mind was quick and clear, yet all physical movement fell into a lingering genus of departure. With a sudden calmness, I could see the whole field and the three small figures elegantly brushing its top. As I watched their grace, I could feel the empty stands and their

suspension of a lost past. This changeless spell brought an acute sense of temporariness and the feeling of inevitability fading with the dusk. Yet just as acute was the sense that this present intimately belonged to both past and future. This time and our movements were one. As I released the ball with the giving length and completeness of my arm, I could see the beginning of its easy soft arc. And it somehow seemed perfectly coordinated with the stadium, the ground, early evening and the four of us. As the ball was coming down some thirty long yards into the distance, two figures in ballet stretched into the air to meet it. In one easy motion of symmetry, Dee took the pass and lissomely yielded to a surging turf. Then slowly and gently separating himself from the stadium ground, he turned to me and grinned. I knew we had connected. (447: p. 234)

Although some athletes talk about time speeding up, most experience it, as Gary Shaw did, as slowing down. This slow-motion experience can be important to the outcome of a performance, according to racing car driver Jackie Stewart:

Some days you go out in a race car and everything happens in a big rush. You don't seem to have time to change gears or brake and the corners are all coming up too quickly. You're not synchronized. And thus the most important thing is to synchronize yourself with the elements that you're competing against, the motor car and the track. Your mind must take these elements and completely digest them so as to bring the whole vision into slow motion. For instance, as you arrive at the Masta you're doing a hundred and ninety-five mph. The corner can be taken at a hundred and seventy-three mph. At a hundred and ninety-five mph you should still have a very clear vision, almost in slow motion, of going through that corner—so that you have time to brake, time to line the car up, time to recognize the amount of drift, and then you've hit the apex, given it a bit of a tweak, hit the exit and are out at a hundred and seventy-three mph. Now, the good driver will do this in a calculated way such that as he gets out the other side he'll say, "Whew, I did that well." It wasn't a case of coming out and trying to catch the car and regain control. The driver who's fighting it, who doesn't have a mental picture in advance, will arrive at the corner to find that it's all happening very quickly. He's too heavy on the brake, the car is sliding too much, it's a big, deep breath in and a hope that I get around. Now this man doesn't have it. (308: pp. 180–181)

Runner Steve Williams says "if you do a 100 right. . . that 10 seconds seems like 60. . . . Time switches to slow motion." (333: p. 34) Williams says he feels he can even control time to some extent. He recalls a race when he fell behind. Hating to lose, he says, "At my own decision, I froze those people where they were. My next recollection was being in front and through the tape." (333: p. 34)

In the most intense moments of a football game John Brodie claims that "time seems to slow way down, in an uncanny way, as if everyone were moving in slow motion. It seems as if I had all the time in the world to watch the receivers run their patterns, and yet I know the defensive line is coming at me just as fast as ever. I know perfectly well how hard and fast those guys are coming and yet the whole thing seems like a movie or a dance in slow motion." (343: pp. 19–20)

The experience of time slowing down has also been noticed by spectators, implying that there may be an objective aspect to this experience. Veteran ballet reporter Herbert Saal says of the skill of Mikhail Baryshnikov:

The most exquisitely chilling weapon in the arsenal of this complete dancer was his *ballon,* his ability to ascend in the air and stay there, defying gravity, especially in the double *tour en l'air,* in which the male dancer revolves two full terms before landing. The Stuttgart Ballet's Richard Cragun can turn three times in a blur of motion. But Baryshnikov did it in slow motion. And it was unbelievable. He blasted off with the hesitation and majesty of a space-ship. He turned—once, twice—and every thread on his costume was plainly visible as he soared high above the audience like an astronaut looking back at earth. (420: p. 84)

If slowed perception is a feature of exceptional performance in sport, then most athletes would naturally want to induce this altered perception of time. A number of athletes, especially golfers, have recognized the importance of slow motion and have deliberately tried to swing more slowly in the interest of achieving *more power*. Bobby Jones is said to have felt it was not possible to swing a golf club too slowly. (237) This advice is given by many golfers. Dick Aultman reports that during the start of his downswing, Jack Nicklaus' hands move more slowly during the last part of his backswing. This is even more significant when one considers that his is one of the slowest backswings on the golf tour. Aultman cites a British scientist, Dr. David Williams, who has concluded "that, all things being equal, the more leisurely the hands and arms start down, the greater the clubhead speed at impact." (19: p. 30)

Several golfers carry this advice a step further and advocate slowing down the pace throughout the entire round. Among them are Bruce Devlin, Henry Ransom, Sam Snead, and Jane Blalock. For example, Larry Dennis reports, "[Tom] Weiskopf credits last summer's [1973] startling streak of five victories and a bunch of near misses to a decelerated pace on the golf course." (112: p. 81) But some golfers carry it still one step further and suggest getting ready for a tournament by moving slowly even when they are off the course.

Cary Middlecoff tells a story about fellow golf pro George Knudsen who held the lead going into the final round of a tournament. Knudsen was driving Middlecoff and another pro, Fred Hawkins, to the golf course at the rate of about 16 miles per hour. When urged by his impatient passengers to hurry it up, Knudsen says Middlecoff: ". . . just looked . . . through those dark glasses and said, 'Man, this is my way to cool it. I started thinking this way last night.' " (175: p. 88) Knudsen shot a 65 that day and won the tournament.

It is exciting to consider that even though the passage of time has not actually slowed down, nevertheless the fact that it *feels* as if it has apparently enables the athlete to accomplish more, just as he would if in fact he did have more time, more amplitude.

A classic study of what is known as "time distortion" was made by Cooper and Erickson in 1954. (93) Working with 14 subjects, they used hypnosis to slow down the subjects' perception of the passage of time. Under these conditions the subjects could accomplish far more work than usual. For example, a college student who was gifted in designing clothes took 10 seconds to design a dress while in a state of hypnotic time distortion. Later she said that to her the session seemed to last an hour. (Ordinarily, designing a dress took her several hours.)

It has been suggested that altered time perceptions, as well as altered states of consciousness such as hypnogogic imagery and creative reverie, are associated with various brainwave patterns. [Pioneer studies have been reported in this area by Barbara Brown (65) and Elmer and Alyce Green (181)]. Keith Floyd speculates that time perception is related to brainwaves and that this may explain some superior athletic feats:

> Having seen that time (and/or motion) goes slower the slower the brainwave rhythm, it would not be at all surprising to discover that those with superior skills—great athletes, for example—may merely be blessed with basal brainwave firing significantly slower than that of the general population. This may prove to be the critical difference between the "star" and the "superstar." The baseball player firing alpha, for instance, might perceive the ball at no more than half the speed perceived by his teammate firing beta. One firing theta could carefully observe the approach and spin of the ball, examine the stitches, read the label, and have up to four times as much "time" to regulate the swing of the bat and make his moves. (148: p. 50)

The Backward Glance and Life Review

Among a number of other altered time perceptions which may be experienced in sport are brief and long-range glimpses of the past, déjà vu, and the life review. Transatlantic sailor Robert Manry was awed by "the ocean's . . . enormous breadth and depth, by the ghostly presence of all the famous and infamous ships and men and women it has carried through the centuries." (307: p. 67) Los Angeles doctor Steve Seymour says, "I can blink my eyes and look out at a javelin thrower and see tens of thousands of warriors marching across the field and I can hear the voices of antiquity." (253: p. 40)

At other times, athletes experience déjà vu—the feeling that "you've been here before"—probably the most common of all the altered states of consciousness. Especially striking is a series of experiences described by Bob Brier, who holds a Ph.D. in philosophy and is a well-known parapsychologist, a distance runner, and an Egyptologist to boot. Of his experiences playing basketball in college, he says:

We were playing at home and I was dribbling the ball in the left corner, near the out-of-bounds line. Suddenly I had the feeling I had been in this situation before. By *situation* I mean the crowd, my position with the ball, the man guarding me, etc. Now I had played on this court many times and realized that I had probably been in *similar* situations, but this had that special déjà vu feeling. . . . I had the feeling that I was going to take a turn-around jump shot and it was going to go in. Almost automatically and in a bit of a daze I took the shot and it went in. (This was not a shot that I normally took as I was the center and tended to stay close to the basket.) I didn't think much of the event till our next game, which was away. In the first half of the game I had the feeling again when I was in the left corner with the ball. Again I took the turn-around jumper and it went in. . . .

In all I had the feeling six times during my senior year. The third time I had it I knew I couldn't have been in that spot before because I had never played on that court. Still I had the feeling, took the turn-around jumper, and it went in. . . .

The last time I had the feeling it was at a crazy time to take the shot. I was guarded closely by a man at least four inches taller than I. Still I went up, arching the ball much higher than I normally would to clear his hands, and it went right in. My overall field goal percentage for that year was 43%, so the 100% on the six shots was considerably higher than my average. (61)

Brier's account is particularly interesting because it recurred several times, unlike many déjà vu experiences, and because successful shooting was associated with it.

During special moments in sports, some athletes have seen their entire lives flash before them. This life review is also quite common at moments near death, as Raymond Moody (331) has recently shown. Tom Simons, who trained and raced with Steve McKinney when the latter broke the world speed ski record, writes, "While going down [the slope], the flow of events through my brain was a viewing of my life, and possibly six previous ones as well." (304: p. 77)

In his book *The Perfect Game,* Tom Seaver writes that after his first victory in the 1969 World Series, when Rod Gaspar scored the winning run,

. . . as Rod Gaspar's front foot stretched out and touched home plate, in the fraction of a second before I leaped out of the dugout to welcome him, my whole baseball life flashed in front of me, the perfect game I'd pitched when I was twelve years old, the grand-slam home run I'd hit for the Alaska Goldpanners, the first game I'd won as a member of the New York Mets, the imperfect game I'd pitched against the Chicago Cubs, one after another, every minor miracle building toward that one magic day.

I never realized before that a man's whole life could be encompassed in a single play, in a single game, in a single day. (440: p. 71)

Time Stopping

There are moments in sport when time seems to be arrested, only to proceed on its way again as before, but not quite, leaving behind a wake of pleasurable exhilaration similar to the sense of shock experienced when that other metronome of our existence—the heart—stops beating for a second. Players and spectators both refer to moments when time stops or even, as some put it, the world stops.

Julius Erving, one of basketball's great slam dunk artists, has said that a great dunk shot is "a time suspension." (373: p. 52) That is what Jimmy Breslin felt when watching Erving: "There were these moments when Doctor J. exploded, going up so high and his body bending and swaying so spectacularly, that he made you forget the world for an instant." (59: p. 301)

It has been observed that "there is a common experience in Tai Chi of seemingly falling through a hole in time. Awareness of the passage of time completely stops, and only when you catch yourself, after five or ten minutes, or five or ten seconds is there the realization that for that period of time the world *stopped*." (216: pp. 180, 182)

The experience of Roger Bannister in the midst of his record-breaking race was similar: "I felt that the moment of a lifetime had come. There was no pain, only a great unity of movement and aim. The world seemed to stand still, or did not exist. The only reality was the next two hundred yards of track under my feet. The tape meant finality—extinction perhaps." (30: pp. 213-214)

Extrasensory Perception

A "sixth sense" is sometimes attributed to certain star athletes by their teammates, opponents, and others as well. What it seems to boil down to is the ability to be in the right place at the right time. It is dubbed *a* sixth sense, but it is probably more useful to think of it as a composite of several sensory modalities and abilities such as timing, knowledge of the opponents' style of play, muscle memory, and subliminal perception. Sometimes it may even include an X ingredient not yet differentiated that galvanizes the player into an action uniting the right movement at the right moment.

A number of athletes have gained reputations for this uncanny sixth sense. Middle linebacker Ray Nitschke nominates former Cleveland Brown fullback Jim Brown as the smartest runner he ever played against. He says Brown "had a sixth sense that told him how the defense would react. Then he'd react accordingly. He was an artist—a brilliant football player who could not only beat you physically but mentally." (361: pp. 125–126)

Some remarks that Lou Brock has made about how he steals bases suggest that it is more a matter of empathy and intuition than it is of speed and muscle. When asked if it is a matter of surprise, if not speed, Brock replied:

> Not likely. How much surprise do you think I can generate when I get on first base nowadays? Maybe about as much as the sun when it rises in the East. What's really surprising is if I don't make any move at all, right? Actually, the only thing the pitcher doesn't know about me is the precise moment I'm going to go, and he knows that too, damn near.
>
> You can surprise a rookie, maybe, but most of the time what you're doing is fishing in a very clear pool, where you can see the fish you're after and you lead him gently and patiently to the bait, and when he takes it, you yank.
>
> You just gotta know when that is, which is the part that gets to be intuitive after a while. There's no place for it in the textbook. It's a little like knowing what an intimate friend is going to say a split-second before he says it. So you try to make that pitcher your

very close buddy, by empathizing with all his moves and all his thoughts. You know at one point he has to commit himself, and then he can't go back on it. I have to too, but he has to first, and that makes a big difference. (62: p. 183)

Brock's emphasis on such mental factors as empathy and intuition and his de-emphasis of physical qualities such as speed and surprise raises the possibility that there may be something more involved—something not yet generally recognized—and not only in base stealing, but in many aspects of sports. It may be possible that in addition to "luck," or coincidence, and picking up on subliminal sensory cues, there is an element of extrasensory perception, or ESP, in sports. In fact, the "sixth sense" is an older term for what today is known as ESP, or psi ability. ESP includes the ability to obtain information about the contents of someone's mind (this form of ESP is known as telepathy), and the ability to obtain information directly from events themselves (clairvoyance). There is also ESP of the future, or precognition.

It is almost impossible to isolate ESP in the form of telepathy or clairvoyance in the sport situation, even if it is occurring, because almost all sports take place in settings where the players are within sensory range of one another; so sensory cues cannot be absolutely ruled out. In certain plays that are unusual, although some form of ESP may have occurred, it is more likely that the needed information was available through subtle sensory cues.

For instance, Walt Frazier, former basketball star of the New York Knicks, praises fellow Knick Bill Bradley's passing skills, which, combined with Frazier's own ability to get the ball in the basket, led to some great plays. Frazier (1970) says that "as a game goes on, some defensive men get tired and careless. If I notice my man is watching the ball and taking his attention away from me for an instant, he's a pigeon. All of a sudden I just streak to the basket, going backdoor, and Bill hits me almost every time. Sometimes he has passed the ball before I've taken the first step. It's like telepathy. We look each other in the eye and he knows the mischief I'm thinking about." (158: pp. 162-163) But as long as they can look each other in the eye, sensory cues cannot be ruled out, even if they were neither deliberately given nor consciously received. It *is* like telepathy, but we can't say that it actually is.

Although something extraordinary seems to be happening in all the incidents we have described in this section, some factor imperfectly understood—possibly if so, an extrasensory factor—it is involved in a matrix of sensory factors that prevents us from *definitely* saying ESP is occurring. There are other incidents, however, in which it seems more likely that ESP *is* involved. Flyer Jackie Cochran reports that on one occasion when her friend and fellow pilot Amelia Earhart was visiting her, they tried to see if Ms. Cochran could deliberately exercise her psychic ability.

> The first night there, we heard that a passenger plane had disappeared en route from Los Angeles to Salt Lake City and Amelia asked me to try to locate it. We sat together for about two hours during which I gave names of various mountain peaks and the locations of roads and transmission lines and even of a pile of telephone poles up in the mountains near Salt Lake City. I also gave the location of the plane. Neither of us knew that area so Amelia called Paul Mantz in Los Angeles and asked him to verify names and locations on an air map and call us back. He called back with complete verification. Amelia, thoroughly excited by that time, dashed back to Los Angeles by car through the night and took off for Salt Lake in her plane at daybreak. She searched the area for three days and verified all my descriptions but found no wreckage of the transport and gave up. Next spring, when the snow on the mountain had melted, the wreckage of that plane was found within two miles of where, on the night it went down, I said it was.
>
> A few weeks later, Amelia called me from Los Angeles with the news that a transport airliner en route to Los Angeles had gone down somewhere on the last leg of the flight. Would I try to give her the location? Within an hour, I called her back, told her exactly where the plane was, which way it was pointing down the mountainside and the condition of the occupants as between the dead, the injured and the safe. The plane was located promptly just where I said it would be; all my information proved correct.
>
> (82: pp. 88–89)

Before Amelia Earhart made her ill-fated flight, Ms. Cochran had several disturbing hunches about it. She mistrusted the navigator's ability, and supplied her friend with a bright-colored kite in case she was forced down, as well as fishhooks, lines, and a knife with blades for many uses. When Ms. Earhart made a preliminary solo flight, Ms. Cochran had told her husband that one of the plane's engines had caught fire, but that it was being put out with little damage. The fire was reported later by the news media. Then the report came that Ms. Earhart's plane was missing.

> With all this ability and preliminary work with Amelia, why didn't I locate her when she went down? The answer is that I did, or at least I think I did, but can never prove it one way or the other. . . . I told . . . where Amelia had gone down . . . but that Amelia was alive and the plane was floating in a certain area. I named a boat called the *Itasca* which I had never heard of at the time, as a boat that was nearby, and I also named another Japanese fishing vessel in that area, the name of which I now forget. . . . Navy planes and ships in abundance combed that area but found no trace. I followed the course of her drifting for two days. It was always in the area being well-combed. On the third day I went to the cathedral and lit candles for Amelia's soul, which I then knew had taken off on its own long flight. I was frustrated and emotionally overcome. If my strange ability was worth anything it should have saved Amelia. Only [my husband's] urging . . . ever prompted me to try my hand at this sort of thing again and he hasn't urged me for several years for he knows it upsets me. (82: p. 91)

John Fairfax, who rowed across the Atlantic, took his bearings from the planet Venus, and regarded her as his guiding "star." Near the end of the voyage he was approaching the Hogsty Reefs. Trusting to luck, he rowed on through the rain. The next day, he recorded this in his log:

> I hope I am on course. Haven't seen any land, but it must be near. Feeling a bit wary about the Hogsty Reefs. Got a sixth sense for this sort of thing, and now something tells me I'm heading straight for them. It would be very bad luck indeed to have come so far only to pile up onto a flipping reef. . . . Come, Venus; you ought

at least to come out—let me have a peep at your lovely body. No chance. I just can't get a sight, not even a single position line. Well, let's trust luck.

June 26   157th day

Near dawn and—ye gods! Saw her!—just as she was rising through a hole in the clouds. Horizon unbelievably black and low. How she managed to get through for me to see her I'll never know; but see her I did, for about two minutes, and all during that time she blinked and flashed at me like mad. Planets don't twinkle, so I knew right away there was something wrong somewhere and she was trying to warn me. Stopped rowing at once. Hit by a squall immediately after, and for two hours it was as if the sea and sky had gone mad. Lightning, thunder, rain, and the wind north-east, gusting up to Force 6 and 7. Magnificent spectacle of raw, naked fury! I felt, as never before, as if I were part of it and, deliriously happy, cursed and sang throughout it all, at the top of my voice, while *Brittania,* frightened out of her wits, screamed bloody rape. I felt full of energy suddenly, and the strength and power of the gods burned like lava in my veins. And I positively itched to grab the oars and row, row, row. But I didn't. My beloved had warned me not to and I heeded her, which probably saved my life. (139: pp. 191, 192)

This case is a good example of what Dr. Louisa E. Rhine, in her pioneer studies of psychic experiences reported by the general public, has called the "dramatic form." (401) In such cases the percipient, instead of seeing a photographic representation of what is happening at a distance or is about to happen, sees the event dramatized in a meaningful way. In this case Venus, unlike an actual planet, was seen to "twinkle," thus dramatizing to Fairfax the fact that something was amiss.

These examples show how ESP could occur in sport. But we can never rule out coincidence or luck, and faint sensory cues may be available, although in the Cochran and Fairfax cases it seems unlikely.

Another sport situation in which ESP *may* or *may not* be involved is the "called play," in which the athlete predicts what he or she is going to do and then successfully does it. One of the best-known called plays in history was the home run hit by Babe Ruth against Charley Root of the Chicago Cubs in the 1932 World Series. In his autobiography Babe Ruth says he and his wife were heckled and spat upon prior to the game. He writes:

I was so hopping mad by the time we got to our suite upstairs that I told Claire I'd fix them, somehow.

"I'll belt one where it hurts them the most," I said, without knowing just what I'd do—or how.

I guess it was while I was angry that the idea of "calling my shot" came to me. It wasn't exactly a new idea with me. I had hit a few home runs after promising to hit them, and in most of those cases I had been able to pick the very spot.

For instance, back in my early days with the Yanks, when we still played at the Polo Grounds, I teed off on one late in a tight ball game. The ball went up into the lower right field stands and hit a tall iron girder down the middle of which ran a white foul line.

I started to trot toward first base, but Billy Evans, umpiring behind the plate, called me back by yelling "Foul!"

I came back and walked up to him. "What was wrong with that?" I asked him, waving my arms and throwing my cap down to indicate to the fans that I was madder than I really was.

"It was an inch to the foul side of the line," Billy said.

"Okay," I said, stepping back into the batting box, "watch this one. It will be an inch fair."

I hit the next pitch almost exactly as I hit the first one. It went on a line into the stands and hit the same upright girder. I looked around at Billy.

"It was an inch fair," Billy said. "Go ahead.". . .

There was a funny one in 1928, too. The Yanks were playing an exhibition game in Fort Wayne, Ind., and one of the first fans to show up at the ball park was the father of Ford Frick. He thought Ford might be traveling with us, but Ford had made other arrangements. So I fixed old man Frick up with a seat in a box behind the Yankee dugout. Even got him a cushion, for he was in his 70's then and mighty brittle-looking.

Fort Wayne gave us a lot of trouble that day. At the end of eight innings we were still tied up, and as I walked toward the plate I took a look at Mr. Frick. He looked very tired.

"I'll end it for you, Pappy," I called to him, "so you can trot home and get your nap." In the distance a long train of open cars was passing.

"See those cars, Pappy?" I yelled above the noise. "Watch."

I hit one over the right-field fence and into one of the cars—which may still be traveling, for all I know. . . .

Some of these memories came back to me as I made up my mind to do something about the Cubs, and Cub fans in general, in that hotel suite in Chicago in 1932.

The Yanks and Cubs were two of the sorest ball clubs ever seen when they took the field for the third game, with George Pipgras pitching for us and Charley Root throwing for them. . . . While Root was getting ready to throw his first pitch, I pointed to the bleachers which rise out of deep center field.

Root threw one right across the gut of the plate and I let it go. But before the umpire could call it a strike—which it was—I raised my right hand, stuck out one finger and yelled, "Strike one!"

The razzing was stepped up a notch.

Root got set and threw again—another hard one through the middle. And once again I stepped back and held up my right hand and bawled, "Strike two!" It was.

You should have heard those fans then. As for the Cub players they came out on the steps of their dugout and really let me have it.

I guess the smart thing for Charley to have done on his third pitch would have been to waste one.

But he didn't, and for that I've sometimes thanked God.

While he was making up his mind to pitch to me I stepped back again and pointed my finger at those bleachers, which only caused the mob to howl that much more at me.

Root threw me a fast ball. If I had let it go, it would have been called a strike. But this was *it*. I swung from the ground with everything I had and as I hit the ball every muscle in my system, every sense I had, told me that I had never hit a better one, that as long as I lived nothing would ever feel as good as this.

I didn't have to look. But I did. That ball just went on and on and on and hit far up in the center-field bleachers in exactly the same spot I had pointed to.

To me, it was the funniest, proudest moment I had ever had in baseball. I jogged down toward first base, rounded it, looked back at the Cub bench and suddenly got convulsed with laughter. (418: pp. 191–194)

So goes Babe Ruth's version of the famous home run, many years after the event. Reviewing a number of Ruthian biographies, Roger Angell says, "The consensus of his biographers (. . . except for Mr. Sobol, who calls the whole thing an invention of Ted Husing's) is that Ruth did not point to the bleachers beforehand, but that he did hold up his fingers to count off the first two strikes and then held up one more, making his intentions unmistakable. Then he hit the homer, the longest, everyone agrees, ever struck at Wrigley Field." (12: p. 7) In other words, Ruth took two called strikes and then *did* predict he would hit a home run, even though the consensus of what occurred is not exactly as he recalled it in his memoirs.

A number of shots have been called in golf, including some amazing ones by Walter Hagen, who liked to bet on his ability to call them. In his autobiography, Hagen describes an occasion when Horton Smith, the leader in the clubhouse, came out to watch and good-naturedly taunt him. Hagen says:

I figured for a moment. "I have a good chance to tie you," I told him. "I merely have to make the last three holes in six shots." I raised my voice for the gallery to hear. "Horton," I said, "I can make a 3, a 2 and a 1 to tie you."

I hit a long tee shot—long for me at least—and away we went up the hill, followed by the whole gallery. I hit my second shot to a plateau and found my ball about six feet from the hole. I gave it a quick glance, knocked it in and turned to the gallery. "Well, there is my 3. Now for a 2."

I hit a five-iron on the seventeenth about twenty feet from the hole. I could scarcely see the hole, for it was getting quite dark. I looked over the green, gave the ball a rap and to my surprise it holed.

"There you are," I said casually. "Now for a hole in one!"

I ran to the eighteenth tee, pulled out my two-iron, then had to wait while gallery fans were chased off the fairway. The hole was approximately 190 yards. Now about all I could see in the distance was the club house. I aimed for that hoot in the grill. I hit the ball well and a very loud cheer went up. I thought I had made it. Instead I had hit the flag gently and stopped about six inches away. The 2 gave me a second place. (187: pp. 203-204)

The most remarkable called play, or set of called plays, that we have come across is an *entire round* that golfer Joe Ezar is said to have predicted. The president of Fiat Motor Company told Joe he would give him 5,000 lire if he shot a 66, or 10,000 lire for a round of 65. Instead, Joe asked how about a 64. For a 64 he was promised 40,000 lire. Ezar then wrote on a scorecard what he would shoot on each hole to get a 64, ending with a birdie on 18. His playing partner, British golfing great and three-time winner of the British Open Henry Cotton, told him he was crazy. Joe retired to the bar where he put in a good night, waking the next day protesting he was too hung over to play. His caddy, who had a bet on the day's round, put him in a cold shower and got him to the first tee. Cotton advised him to drop the whole thing. He considered it an impossible feat, tantamount to asking for 18 miracles in a row. But Joe then scored as predicted for the first eight holes. He then got a 4 instead of the predicted 3 on the ninth, countered by a 3 in place of a predicted 4 on the 10th. On each of the remaining eight holes he again scored as predicted, ending up with a 64. Cotton said "You could call that round the biggest fluke of all time. . . . He had all the luck in the world, chipping in and holing impossible putts, but the figures came out just as Joe had predicted." (119: p. 67)

Another famous called play was Joe Namath's prediction that the Jets would beat Baltimore in the 1968 Super Bowl. One of his teammates, Randy Rasmussen, said:

At the time I thought, jeez, Joe, just keep your mouth shut. But before I knew it I'd reexamined what was going on—everybody had—and we realized we all felt the same way. We'd seen the films, we *knew* we could win. Joe just said it, was all. And the thing is, the papers played it up like he was wisecracking. But he was serious as can be.'' (486: p. 82)

This is a good example of the self-fulfilling prophecy in sport. Namath's prediction, based on his own confidence, fired the confidence of his teammates, and together they got into that supercharged state in which it is almost impossible to lose. In fact, all these examples could be instances of fierce conviction and the self-fulfilling prophecy.

But what about true precognition? What happens when there are no sensory cues, when there is no self-fulfilling prophecy? Do some athletes have the ability to predict events before they happen? If so, then we have the best evidence for ESP in a sport situation.

Racing car driver A. J. Foyt has had more than one hunch that proved to be correct. Bill Libby writes that "going to Riverside to race stock cars the day after his thirtieth birthday in January, 1965, A. J. Foyt had a premonition of impending danger. He recalls, 'Usually I like to run there, but that one time I just didn't want to go. Before I left the airport, I called Lucy and told her where I'd parked the car and where to find the keys. That's something I'd never done before.' '' (286: p. 133) During the race he went over a 35-foot embankment in the worst accident of his long career.

He also had a premonition involving the 1967 Indianapolis 500 when he predicted that Andy Granatelli's jet car, driven by Parnelli Jones, would not complete the race. He said, "I knew dead certain inside me that the jet car was going to break." (286: p. 86) In practice the new turbocar had awed all the other racers. Bill Libby writes, "Few realized that the car had problems, but Foyt guessed it. He figured the gearbox would go. He said it before anyone else said it, before the car had qualified. . . . 'It won't last half the race,' he said. . . . 'It will take time to develop it. Its time may come, but it's my time now. I feel like I'm gonna win this race.' '' (286: p. 160) Foyt did win the race, and the turbocar failed to finish because of mechanical troubles.

One of the most dramatic examples of what may be precognition in sport happened in the case of Wayne Estes, who was the second leading college basketball scorer in 1965. Early in his last game, against Denver, Estes asked the coach to remove him from the game because he had lost his touch: In fact, he had no feeling in his hands. The coach refused, telling him the baskets would start to drop if he kept shooting. He was right. At halftime Estes had scored 24 points. But his hands still felt numb. He scored another 24 in the second half, and set a new single-game scoring record for Utah State's Nelson Fieldhouse. The trainer pricked Estes' finger with a pin after the game. Wayne did not react normally: the strange numbness was attributed to his being keyed up, but it was suggested he have a thorough examination if it didn't go away in a few days.

On the way home from the game, Estes and some friends passed a car accident and stopped to see if they could be of assistance. An ambulance had already arrived, however, and there was nothing they could do. Walking back to the car, "a sagging wire from a bent telephone pole was swaying overhead, its lowest point almost six and a half feet from the ground. His friends passed under it. Estes' forehead brushed the live wire. Several thousand watts of electricity shot through his body, killing him. 'Wayne's hands started to smoke, and he fell to the ground,' John Vasey, one of Estes' companions, said later." (252: p. 26) Could it be that the numbness and tingling in his hands that Estes experienced during the game was a symbolic precognition of the manner in which he was to meet his death a few hours later? In fact, two months before his death, Estes had bought a $10,000 life insurance policy—but only after asking "whether the triple-indemnity clause for accidental death applied to death by electrocution." (252: p. 26)

Perhaps the most common way an athlete foresees the future is in a dream. This is also true of precognitive experiences in the general population. (400) In his autobiography, Sugar Ray Robinson describes a nightmare he had the night before he fought Jimmy Doyle for the welterweight championship:

> In the dream, Jimmy Doyle was in the ring with me. I hit him a few good punches and he was on his back, his blank eyes staring up at me, and I was staring down at him, not knowing what to do, and the referee was moving in to count to ten and Doyle still wasn't moving a muscle and in the crowd I could hear people yelling, "He's dead, he's dead," and I didn't know what to do. Then I woke up. (410: p. 140)

In another account of the fight, he said:

> I got up the next day and I called the fight off. I called the commission and everybody and I said I'm not fighting. They said, Ray,

it's just a dream. I said, no, I've had premonitions before, and I'm just not going to do it. They called in all the priests, Catholic priests, and Protestant, got them to talk to me and everything, and I said all right. They talked me into going through with the fight. I went through with the fight, like I had said, knocked him out. He died right there in the ring. Boy, what a feeling I had. I felt like it was premeditated and I knew about it and still went ahead and did it. But it happened. That ain't the only time. I've had many. Several times I've had other experiences like that, to make me think. I don't do it no more, though. I get the premonitions. If I get one now, I won't do it. (148: pp. 278–279)

A. J. Foyt, who had the premonitory experiences involving the 1967 Indianapolis 500 already described, also had a precognitive dream about that race. The race had been called part way through because of rain. Parnelli Jones, driving the turbocar, was leading by 12 seconds. Bill Libby records that "that night Foyt slept fitfully. He was disturbed. He had a sort of vision in which he was leading on the last lap when a smashup took place in front of him and he had to brake to beat it." (286: p. 162)

When the race resumed, Jones in the turbocar led all the way until the one hundred ninety-seventh lap, when the jet car lost its power with only 10 miles to go. Foyt drove on, well out in front with two laps left. Nothing, save an accident or mechanical failure could keep him from winning. Libby says:

> He came through the next-to-last lap and into the last lap and around and into the last turn. All the while his mind was working hard and he thought about an accident and he slowed sharply.
>
> "It was as though I had a premonition," he said later. "I had dreamed about it, and then I came around the last corner and there it was! If I hadn't already slowed down, there is no way I could have gotten through it." (286: p. 163)

Thus, prepared by his vision or dream, Foyt edged through and won his third Indianapolis 500.

Sometimes relatives, coaches, or other persons close to athletes have precognitive experiences involving them. Miler John Walker says of his grandmother: "Sometimes it is almost as if we were one person. . . . She's so psychic you wouldn't believe it. She doesn't talk in terms of 'me' and 'you' when we're communicating—we are jointly 'us' to her." (509: p. 9) At the Montreal Olympics, after Walker had failed to win the 800 meters run, but a day before he was to win the 1500 meters, he received the following letter from his grandmother: "Don't worry about the 800 meters—I see us on the victory dais later in the Games. I hear the crowd cheering us. I see us running the lap of honor. We will triumph, we will win the 1500 meters gold medal." (509: p. 9)

Willie Shoemaker tells of a dream Ralph Lowe, owner of the horse the Shoe was to ride in the 1957 Kentucky Derby, had about "his rider standing up and misjudging the finish in the 1957 Kentucky Derby." (452: p. 58) Lowe told Shoemaker the dream the Friday night before the race. Shoemaker assured him it would not happen. But it did.

When runner Jim Ryun fell in the Munich Olympics where he eventually finished last, his wife reports she dreamed about the fiasco in advance. "I had a dream that night before the race, and in my dream, Jim fell down. I didn't warn him because I thought it would upset him. I've often wondered if I should have . . . if it would have made a difference." (376: p. 265)

In reviewing these cases it appears that athletes use every means available to accomplish their ends. When the usual sensory channels are blocked, they sometimes make use of a more subtle kinesthetic sense or even, at times, of ESP. It is even possible that blockage of sensory abilities triggers psi capacities. Bob Banner (29) describes a group that deliberately uses physical exercises, especially basketball skills, to develop psychic abilities. They have observed that in order to activate "extraphysical powers," they must first master physical skills. Then, at key moments, something else occasionally takes over.

This possibility has been proposed by a physicist interested in parapsychology, Joseph H. Rush. In a provocative monograph, Dr. Rush introduced the term *psi enhancement*, for a complementary relationship between normal sensori-motor functioning and the operation of some form of psi. He suggests that psi enhancement might be present in sport, providing that "extra edge of precise muscular control in a fast game." (415: p. 42) Furthermore, he hypothesized that psi enhancement tends to operate when the usual sensori-motor skills are frustrated or blocked, which seems to be the case in some of the preceding examples.

The fact that the athletes themselves use the term *sixth sense,* a synonym for ESP, lends credence to this possibility.

Out-of-Body Experiences

In Chapter 2 athletes described certain moments of feeling detached from the swirl of events; others reported moments in which they seemed to be "floating" or "flying." There are other, more extreme accounts in which athletes say they were literally out of their bodies. Parapsychologists have established that some people can both "see" events happening at a distance as if they were actually there and "see" their own bodies as if from a point outside themselves. Even if this feeling is illusory, it remains a vivid experience. Moreover, objective information about the world outside is sometimes obtained in this state. A rock climber doing a solo climb recalls that

> About 15 or 20 feet above the ground, I slipped and fell. . . . Objectively, the height wasn't great, but I think that I was very frightened of the coming pain or death, and for a moment abandoned the idea of living. As I fell, I seemed to be about 5 or 10 feet out from the rock face, looking at my body falling (in contact with the face). I vaguely recollect wondering if I could investigate this odd sensation by moving around to the other side of my body to look at it. Once I hit the ground, I was immediately preoccupied with my pain. (180: p. 25)

British chemist Robert Crookall made a lifelong study of out-of-body experiences. He has published hundreds of cases, among them the following experience of Robert Kyle Beggs:

> From my present perspective of more than twenty years I look back with awe upon the moment in July, 1929, when I drowned.
> It was one of those grey, windy, rainy days. . . . Mildred Johnson, an excellent swimmer, and I had gone out a little way to ride

the breakers, when I became aware of the murderous undertow. I was just about to call to Mildred that I was going back to shore when, over the sound of the waves, I heard a faint cry for help.

As I rode a high wave I saw a small boy desperately clinging to a piece of board. I shouted to Mildred to get help. . . . I managed to boost the frightened youngster up onto the small piece of board.

Suddenly a mountainous wave broke over me. I went down, down, down into the quiet depths. I was so tired that I did not care. I felt peace settle over me. Well, I thought, I had tried, and I was so very tired. It seemed then that a wonderful transition occurred. *I was no longer in the water but rather I has high above the water looking down upon it. The sky, that had been so grey and lowering, was iridescent with indescribable beauty. There was music that I seemed to feel rather than hear. Waves of ecstatic and delicate color vibrated around me and lulled me to a sense of peace beyond comprehension.*

In the water beneath me, a boat came into view, with two men and a girl in it. The girl was Mildred. Then I saw a blob of something floating in the water. A wave tossed it and rolled it over. *I found myself looking into my own distorted face. What a relief, I thought, that that ungainly thing was no longer needed by me.* Then men lifted the form into the boat, and my vision faded.

The next thing I knew, it was dark and I was lying in the beach cold and sick and sore. Men were working over me. I was told later that they worked over me for more than two hours. I was given credit for saving a youngster's life. (99: pp. 11-12)

In at least one instance, an athlete used this kind of unusual experience to his advantage: "a well-known long-distance swimmer . . . who prefers to be anonymous, [said] that whenever his physical body is exhausted during a marathon competition, he relaxes it by floating overhead in his double while continuing to swim. When he reenters his body, he feels refreshed and can go on for quite awhile without fatigue. The man added that athletes in other sports also go out-of-body during competition, but they don't talk about it." (182: p. 339)

Charles Lindbergh describes an experience he had which bears considerable resemblance to an out-of-body experience:

For unmeasurable periods, I seem divorced from my body, as though I were an awareness spreading out through space, over the earth and into the heavens, unhampered by time or substance, free from the gravitation that binds men to heavy human problems of the world. My body requires no attention. It's not hungry. It's neither warm nor cold. It's resigned to being left undisturbed. Why have I troubled to bring it here? I might better have left it back at Long Island or St. Louis, while this weightless element that has lived within it flashes through the skies and views the planet. This essential consciousness needs no body for its travels. It needs no plane, no engine, no instruments, only the release from flesh which the circumstances I've gone through make possible. (293: pp. 352–353)

There is a large literature on out-of-body experiences, and the phenomenon has been studied by parapsychologists since the 1880s. It is beyond the scope of this book to summarize all the evidence for this type of experience, but further sources of information are listed in the bibliography. (See especially 99, 100, 101, 180, and 330)

Awareness of the "Other"

Sometimes, especially in arduous and solitary sports that tax mind and body to the limits of endurance, the athlete becomes aware of some "other"—a sense of divine presence, a disembodied spirit, a source of strength outside the self, a nebulous figure, or a recognizable apparition. The athlete may even carry on a conversation with the figure or may be guided or aided by it in some way. Explorers, sailors, and mountaineers are particularly prone to these visitations.

Strange visions and presences are encountered with some frequency by sailors at sea, especially when they are alone. Joshua Slocum, during his single-handed voyage around the world in the 1890s, suffered from food poisoning, became delirious, and could no longer man his sloop. When he came to his senses, the boat was plunging through a heavy sea. To his amazement he saw a foreign sailor at the helm. The phantom doffed his cap and identified himself as a member of Columbus' crew. "Lie quiet, senor Captain, and I will guide your ship tonight," the vision said. Slocum slept through the entire night, and awakened to find that his boat had covered 90 miles and maintained a true course for the 24 hours he had been incapacitated. Feeling better, he spread his wet clothes in the sun and again fell asleep. "Then who should visit me again but my old friend of the night before, this time, in a dream. 'You did well last night to take my advice,' said he, 'and if you would, I should like to be with you often on the voyage, for the love of adventure alone.'. . . I awoke much refreshed, and with the feeling that I had been in the presence of a friend and a seaman of vast experience." (456: p. 42)

Charles Lindbergh, in his pioneer solo flight across the Atlantic in 1927, encountered some strange visitants:

These phantoms speak with human voices—friendly, vapor-like shapes, without substance, able to vanish or appear at will, to pass in and out through the walls of the fuselage as though no walls were there. Now, many are crowded behind me. Now, only a few remain. First one and then another presses forward to my shoulder to speak above the engine's noise, and then draws back among the group behind. At times, voices come out of the air itself, clear yet far away, traveling through distances that can't be measured by the scale of human miles; familiar voices, conversing and advising on my flight, discussing problems of my navigation, reassuring me, giving me messages of importance unattainable in ordinary life. (293: p. 389)

Sometimes the sense of presence is personified, yet remains vague and unidentifiable. One of the best-known of such encounters occurred during Sir Ernest Henry Shackleton's exploration of the South Pole in 1916. The following is taken from his memoirs of the trip:

When I look back at those days I have no doubt that Providence guided us, not only across those snowfields, but across the storm-white sea that separated Elephant Island from our landing-place on South Georgia. I know that during that long and racking march of thirty-six hours over the unnamed mountains and glaciers of South Georgia it seemed to me often that we were four, not three. I said nothing to my companions on the point, but afterwards

Worsley said to me, "Boss, I had a curious feeling on the march that there was another person with us." Crean confessed to the same idea. One feels "the dearth of human words, the roughness of mortal speech" in trying to describe things intangible, but a record of our journeys would be incomplete without a reference to a subject very near to our hearts. (445: p. 211)

Shackleton's impression was shared by F. A. Worsley, whose account of the expedition was as follows:

While writing this seven years after (almost), each step of that journey comes back clearly, and even now I again find myself counting our party—Shackleton, Crean, and I and—who was the other? Of course, there were only three, but it is strange that in mentally reviewing the crossing we should always think of a fourth, and then correct ourselves. (534: p. 197)

Frank Smythe, while climbing Everest in 1933, had a similar experience:

All the time that I was climbing alone, I had the feeling that there was someone with me. I felt also that were I to slip I should be held up and supported as though I had a companion above me with a rope. Sir Ernest Shackleton had the same experience when crossing the mountains of South Georgia after his hazardous open-boat journey from Elephant Island, and he narrates how he and his companion[s] felt that there was an extra "someone" in the party. When I reached the ledge I felt I ought to eat something in order to keep up my strength. All I had brought with me was a slab of Kendal mint cake. This I took out of my pocket and, carefully dividing it into two halves, turned round with one half in my hand to offer my "companion." (499: p. 234)

The 1975 British conquest of Everest is renowned for its dramatic examples of these helpful companions. Climbers Doug Scott and Nick Estcourt both said they saw or sensed phantom climbers:

Scott states that while tackling the very dangerous ridge of ice cornices he felt as if they were accompanied by another person who guided them by some sort of mental speech and warned them where the cornices, etc., were dangerous. He writes, "I had a mental chat with it . . . seemed like an extension of my mind outside my head. In the bivouac at 28,700 feet, on our way down from the summit, I also felt this presence, same sort of thing— replied to it—it to me. Seemed quite rational then . . . a bit queer now. (523: p. 320)

Nick Estcourt described a similar experience, though he was not climbing with Scott. It happened early in the morning as he delivered an oxygen bottle from Camp 4 to Camp 5:

I set off on my own at about 3:30 in the morning, pulling up the fixed ropes leading up to Camp 5. . . . I was about two hundred feet above the camp when I turned around. I can't remember why, but perhaps I had a feeling that someone was following me. Anyway, I turned round and saw this figure behind me. He looked like an ordinary climber, far enough behind so that I could not feel him moving up the fixed rope, but not all that far below. I could see his arms and legs and assumed that it was someone trying to catch me up.

I stopped and waited for him. He then seemed to stop or to be moving very, very slowly; he made no effort to signal or wave; I shouted down, but got no reply, and so in the end I thought, "Sod it, I might as well press on." I wondered if perhaps it was Ang Phurba coming through from Camp 2, hoping to surprise us all by being at Camp 5 when we arrived that morning.

I carried on and turned around three or four times between there and the old site of Camp 4. . . . and this figure was still behind me. It was definitely a human figure with arms and legs, and at one stage I can remember seeing him behind a slight undulation in the slope, from the waist upwards as you would expect, with the lower part of his body hidden in the slight dip. . . .

I turned round again as I reached the old site of Camp 4, and there was no one there at all. It seemed very eerie; I wasn't sure if anyone had fallen off or what; he couldn't possibly have had time to have turned back and drop back down the ropes out of sight, since I could see almost all the way back to Camp 4. The whole thing seemed very peculiar.

These two incidents, occurring as they did at different times and to different people during the 1975 Everest expedition, were given an even more bizarre twist. (54: pp. 176–177) C. J. Williamson, writing in the *Journal of the Society for Psychical Research*, related that after a friend of his died, he tried to contact him by means of automatic writing. He began to receive messages purporting to come from his deceased friend, who had been a radio operator. Many of the messages Williamson received could be verified, but he could also see that some of his own memories or thoughts could have been their source. He therefore devised a "test" for his friend, asking for information that presumably was not known to any living person. In 1974 he asked for the details of the Everest expedition of 1924, in which Mallory and Irvine disappeared. He got back several details about the expedition, including the information that the two climbers had reached the summit before they disappeared. Williamson's friend also mentioned the upcoming 1975 British expedition. Williamson says, "There were hints coming through . . . that something psychic was being planned to happen on the mountain during the British 1975 expedition." (523: p. 318) He immediately wrote to Chris Bonington, the leader of the expedition, asking him to make special note of anything strange that might happen to any member of the party. Then Williamson got another communication from his friend:

> Finally I got a "message" I thought of such importance that, on January 17th 1975, I lodged it in a sealed envelope with the Bank of Scotland Ltd., Lerwick, for safe keeping. This letter lay there untouched until, after the expedition had returned home again, I heard through the Press and TV that something really strange had indeed been experienced by some of the climbers. (523: p. 318)

Williamson contacted the president of the Society for Psychical Research, John Beloff of the Psychology Department, Edinburgh University, asking him to open the sealed message and compare its contents with what had been reported on the 1975 expedition. Beloff did so, in the presence of a witness, and read the following message that Williamson had received through automatic writing. It went as follows:

> . . . Everest again. I know that you want to reveal to the world the survival of Mallory and Irvine. I read your thoughts and letters

weeks ago. You don't have to speak or write you know. Andrew Irvine is always compliable. They will wait he says. He speaks of Smythe. Everything possible they will do to lead them or save them if need be. Bonington is co-operative—he will not be disappointed even should they not reach the summit. They will come back with better news than that. On the mountain they will see others, not of their own party, others who simply could not be there in the physical body. He will tell you all when they arrive back. Will they reach the summit you ask? Weather will be difficult and ice crevasses. Disaster to some but Bonington will come back safely. Hastie or is it Haston will be in very great danger and I doubt and trust for his safety. (523: p. 319)

The message was accurate in a number of details, but they *did* reach the summit in spite of bad weather conditions. Bonington came back safely, but one member of the expedition died. Another member, Dougal Haston, was one of the first to reach the summit, climbing with Doug Scott. On the way down they were overtaken by darkness and were forced to spend the night in the highest bivouac yet attempted, at 28,700 feet, without oxygen. Haston's life was in danger, but he survived.

In his book, Bonington (54) discusses but rejects the possibility that Estcourt hallucinated the figure because he wasn't acclimatized to the altitude. Bonington suggests that this lack of acclimatization probably was the cause of Frank Symthe's similar experience in 1933. But Estcourt was much lower than Smythe had been—between 23,900 and 24,500 feet, whereas Smythe had been at 27,000 feet. In addition, Estcourt was well used to that altitude. Bonington suggests that Estcourt had a psychic experience related either to the death of a member of the expedition that was to take place later that day, or to a past tragedy: Estcourt was near the spot where a Sherpa "who had worked very closely with Nick in the autumn of 1972, had perished in an avalanche in the autumn of 1973." (54: p. 177) Williamson also discounts lack of oxygen and the altitude, observing that Everest had often been climbed with and without oxygen but with no reports of strange encounters except for this 1975 expedition, as had been predicted in the communication he received from his friend. (He was evidently unaware of Frank Smythe's experience, although the communication he

received did refer to him.) But after all these qualifications and explanations have been considered, the startling fact remains that
Williamson's message, received through automatic writing, did successfully predict that "on the mountain they will see others, not of their
own party. . . ."

The same Dougal Haston (195) who took part in the 1975 Everest
expedition describes what may have been an apparition in his autobiography (published prior to the 1975 expedition). Climbing in the Alps,
he and his companion spent the night in an empty climbers' hut. About
2 a.m. he was jerked awake by noises. He heard footsteps walking
around in the room above and then descending the stairs. The
doorlatch was rattled but not opened. Next he heard footsteps going up
the stairs, followed by silence. In the morning he said nothing, but his
companion mentioned that he had heard the sounds, so Haston knew
he hadn't been dreaming. Together they combed the hut, but found
nothing. Because of bad weather they had to spend a second night in
the hut, and at 2 a.m., the same sounds were heard once more. They
got up and checked the corridor, finding nothing, but they didn't feel
up to tackling the floor above. The following day, Haston was flipping
through the climbs book and found a note in it concerning the death of
the hut's Guardian in an avalanche.

In the 1972 single-handed Transatlantic yacht race, a number of
hallucinations and illusions were experienced, some of them premonitions. Glin Bennet (43), who reported on the race, stresses the harmful
effects of fatigue and prolonged exposure to the elements. He points
out, and rightly so, that sensory deprivation often leads to disturbances
in perception and thinking.

Bennet's warnings are sound, but he tells only one side, the dis-
tressful side, of what happens in stress and overexposure. The visions
and figures perceived by explorers, mountaineers, and sailors are likely
to be hallucinatory projections. Nevertheless, they often play a helpful
role and guide the person who sees them even as dreams often guide the
dreamer. They may act as a source of strength and insight not otherwise available to the conscious mind. Often it is while the mariner or
mountaineer is unconscious, ill, or otherwise unable to cope, that these
compensatory figures appear and somehow personify inner resources
of strength and insight that the beleaguered person is not able to call on
in the ordinary way.

Extraordinary conditions call forth extraordinary capabilities. What does it matter if the aid seemingly comes from "outside"? The important point is that the aid *is* forthcoming. If it cannot be consciously summoned, then it often breaks through from our unconscious depths. It is almost as if, to use Shaw's phrase, "there is a friend behind the phenomena." A number of explorers testify to some such reality. Adventurer Wilfred Noyce (215), explaining what it is that draws some of us to the heights and depths and lonely places of the globe, says, "We go out because it is in our nature to go out, to climb the mountains and sail the seas, to fly to the planets and plunge into the depths of the oceans. By doing these things we make touch with something outside or behind, which strangely seems to approve our doing them." (215: p. 153)

The altered states of perception experienced by athletes indicate that there are ways of perceiving ourselves, each other, and our world, that can enable us to extend our boundaries. We can go beyond our limits, and experience a rewarding oneness both within and without. "Thou art That," the Indian sages have always taught. In sport, the Beyond that is Within begins to perceive its oneness with the Beyond that is Without.

Extraordinary
Feats

One night Bobby Orr of the Boston Bruins "took a pass from goalie Cheevers and detonated a ninety-foot shot that was so fast—despite its distance—that Detroit goalie Roger Crozier stood dumbfounded as it went by. Cheevers, who has never received a point in his career, was awarded an assist on the play. 'It's easy,' the goalie explained, 'to get an assist with Orr.' " (146: p. 7)

The literature of sport is filled with examples like this of outstanding performances turned in by a single player.

The New York Mets' diminutive shortstop Bud Harrelson says his own favorite play was made in a game in St. Louis: "Joe Torre hit it. It was a high bounder hit hard to my right. I had no time to backhand the ball or anything like that. I jumped up and took the ball up high bare-handed, and while I was still going up I threw to first. I came down and saw the ball beat Torre by a step. Joe just stopped and looked at me like he couldn't believe it. I couldn't believe it myself." (285: p. 156)

There are many stories of outstanding plays turned in by the legendary Julius Erving of the Philadelphia 76'ers. In one game he brought his team from a 24-point deficit at the beginning of the last quarter to a victory in the final second: "It was pure magic and Philadelphia fans went nuts. This was no longer basketball, but a kind of religious exercise with Erving as shaman." (507: p. 108) In an All-Star game Julius "stole the show with a single play, a play that had to be seen to be believed. It can best be described in words as a dunk that started near the foul line and somehow ended with Julius whipping the ball around his head and into the basket. The crowd came to its feet in disbelief, and the stomping and cheering and sounds of sheer amazement rocked the arena. The NBA Milwaukee Bucks' Oscar Robertson, who had been guarding Julius, took some time to recover from his utter bewilderment at the play. Fans who witnessed it still talk about it." (194: p. 84)

Sometimes an outstanding performance is turned in by an entire team—like the New York Giants of 1951 who came from behind in the closing weeks of the season to win the National League pennant from their arch rivals, the Brooklyn Dodgers. Over that period of time, many unexpected and outstanding plays were made by the entire team, climaxed by Bobby Thompson's famous home run, "the shot heard round the world." When it was over, sportswriter Red Smith wrote ". . . there is no way to tell it. The art of fiction is dead. Reality has strangled invention. Only the utterly impossible, the inexpressibly fantastic, can ever be plausible again." (249: p. 150) Thomas Kiernan wrote a book about the Giants' march to victory: *The Miracle at Coogan's Bluff*.

> At the time Red Smith was right. There was no way to tell the story of that season and its monumental climax. People were too close to it—the players, the writers, the fans, everyone. It unfolded too quickly, too abstractly for human perception. The emotions it generated were like a metaphysical siren that only higher beings—perhaps the gods—could hear. (249: p. 150)

Throughout his book, Kiernan questions the members of the miraculous team, trying to establish the possibility of what he comes to refer to simply as the "Question"—namely, whether or not "some kind of extraterrestrial energy . . . sort of took over the club and made it perform feats that were beyond its ordinary human capabilities." (249: p. 235) Although he doesn't actually say he believes that was the case with the Giants, the reader gets the impression that he felt so. We propose that there *are* moments in sport when players tap levels of ability that go far beyond what we have come to expect as the normal range of human accomplishment.

Deep in our Western tradition is the feeling that athletes can be superhuman. "To the Greeks, the gods were athletic; then athletes must try to be godlike." (188: p. 365) At its best sport hints that human capacities may be limitless. Some extraordinary sport feats seem to break through into another order of existence.

Exceptional Energy

One key to outstanding athletic performance is the ability to call on unusual reserves of energy. José Torres, in his book on Muhammad Ali, says of the turning point in the second Frazier fight: "He [Ali] is using those mysterious forces. I can't explain it any other way." (495: p. 212) Having himself been a professional boxing champion, Torres would not talk about mysterious forces if other explanations were handy.

This sense of exceptional energy is not confined to individuals. John Brodie, of the San Francisco 49'ers, refers in his autobiography to certain "times when an entire team will leap up a few notches. Then you feel that tremendous rush of energy across the field." Brodie does not feel there is anything unusual or mystical about this. He says, "When you have eleven men who know each other very well and have every ounce of their attention—and intention— focused on a common goal, and all their energy flowing in the same direction, this creates a very special concentration of power. Everyone feels it. The people in the stands always feel and respond to it, whether they have a name for it or not." (63: pp. 151–152)

Several researchers, including Hans Selye, have described a pleasant form of stress that seems to be invigorating. Some have termed it "eustress." Researcher Dorothy Harris notes that "eustress is associated with excitement, adventure, and thrilling experiences. This stress is fun, it enhances vital sensations, it 'turns on' individuals, and in the process of turning on, *it releases energy*." She also suggests that "eustress may be more than energy consuming, it may be energy mobilizing as well. . . . Most people have far more energy resources than they are aware of, and do not realize they have the capacity to *generate energy* for other activities." (190: p. 109) (Our italics.)

Western athletes frequently experience these energy bursts and are familiar with the fact that expending energy can generate higher levels of force. In the main, however, these surges of new energy seem to occur spontaneously. Athletes in the West are hampered by the fact that their training programs are not grounded in an underlying philosophy that would meaningfully account for and encourage the systematic development of these unusual forces. Instead they have to trust blindly that by steadfast practice and perseverance their hidden reserves will eventually be mobilized.

The Eastern martial arts, however, include specific methods for mobilizing energy and uniting mind and body. Their methods are embedded in a conception of human nature that sees the development of unusual capacities as accessible to everyone. The concept of unusual energy is basic to them. In Japan it is called *ki*, in China *ch'i*, in India *prana*. Like yoga, the martial arts teach methods for deliberately tapping exceptional energy. Some writers use the word *intrinsic* to differentiate this inner resource from energy that is produced by muscles. Ratti and Westbrook, a husband and wife team, both black belts, who are undertaking intensive studies of various martial arts, point out that by practicing Eastern methods of concentration and mind-body uni-fication, a type of energy is produced which, if not different from, is at least "far more encompassing and comprehensive in both substance and intensity than the common type of energy usually associated with the output of man's muscular system alone." (394: p. 381)

According to some teachings, the range of this unusual energy is infinite, and its development takes place in three stages, each encom-passing more of the universe than the preceding level: The first stage, which is the one most relevant to current athletics, involves individual coordination and centralization of *ki*. In the second stage, the influence of *ki* extends beyond the individual and touches others. The final stage—rarely tapped—puts the athlete in touch with the center of life itself with a resonance that knows no bounds.

All techniques for developing *ki* have the same goal: the unity of mind and body. Aikido expert Koichi Tohei writes:

The things that one can do when he is sincere and when his spirit and body are one are astonishing. The cornered rat has been known to turn on the cat and down him. People often display powers in time of fire that they would never dream of in ordinary life. Women have been known to lift automobiles to drag children out from under them. In desperate situations of life or death people come up with unheard-of wisdom. All of these cases involve manifestations of power made possible by the unification of the spirit and the body. (494: p. 23)

Although the many methods for developing *ki* differ in some respects, most include five major elements: (1) relaxation and letting go, (2) concentration, (3) breathing exercises, (4) emptying the mind of thought, and (5) rhythmic activity. (See References 33, 174, 370, 394, and 516)

Relaxation and concentration are emphasized in Western sports. However few athletes try to enhance these states by deliberate means such as meditation. Psychiatrist Thaddeus Kostrubala explains how athletic activity and meditation can both generate energy:

I liken . . . running itself to one of the major techniques of medi-tation, and sometimes prayer, employed by virtually all disciplines both East and West: the constant repetition of a particular word or series of words, whether it be, "Om, na pad na, om na," or the Hail Mary. It matters little what value that particular philosophy or religion attaches to the use of the word, phrase or prayer. It is clearly intended to be an opening into another aspect of awareness. In short, by means of the repetition, the phenomenon sought—namely, the touching of another state of consciousness— is achieved. I think the same process occurs in the repetitive rhythm of slow long-distance running. Eventually, at somewhere between thirty and forty minutes, the conscious mind gets exhausted and other areas of consciousness are activated. (259: p. 103)

If this is the case, then even though most Western athletes have made little use of meditation, nevertheless they may have been achieving comparable results through the use of rhythmic activity engaged in faithfully over a long period of time.

Breathing plays an essential role in many Eastern disciplines. Westbrook and Ratti say, "One frequently mentioned method of developing this Inner Energy is by the regular practice of deep or abdominal breathing, since *ki* is held to be closely connected with breathing and has indeed even been called the 'breath of life.' " (516: p. 23) W. Scott Russell notes that "when faced with stress, the karateist automatically begins his patterned breathing. And when he begins that breathing, he automatically feels calm and in control. But that's not all that happens. The karateist's controlled breathing not only keeps him calm and composed, but also gives him a tremendous surge of energy." (417: p. 55)

Although in the West it is rare to find breathing exercises systematically practiced, many athletes use something similar at moments of stress. Basketball's Bob Pettit wrote that he relaxed "before shooting a free throw by taking a deep breath, then slowly let the air out of my lungs." (380: p. 128) Racing car driver Mario Andretti says, "Jackie Stewart told me he used to practice deep breathing at certain spots around the circuit." (337: p. 23)

Another method used to develop *ki* is the achievement of a detached state of mind. Karate expert Masutatsu Oyama advises one to "forget yourself, forget your enemies, forget winning and losing, and when you have done so, you will be in the spiritually unified state that is called *mu*, or nothingness, in Zen. When you have spiritually reached the state of impassivity you will have entered a corner of the Zen world of *mu*." (370: p. 320) As we saw in Chapter 2, many athletes have discovered that they perform best in a state of detachment. Tom Nieporte and Don Sauers, in a survey of professional golfers' ideas concerning the mental side of golf, conclude, "It is generally accepted among the pros that there are times when exceptionally gifted players at the top of their games can play tournament golf with 'blank minds.' Their swings and tempos are so well grooved, and their concentration is so deep, that they do everything automatically." (359: p. 64)

Another aspect of creating *ki* is the development of an effective rhythm. Sugar Ray Robinson stresses the importance of rhythm as he prepares for his first professional bout:

> Now, in the minutes before I would box, I was searching for that rhythm. In some of the bootleg shows there had been a band playing between the bouts, and that music would be blaring as I came into the ring. I always wished they had continued to play while I was boxing. I think I would've boxed better.
>
> Rhythm is everything in boxing. Every move you make starts with your heart, and that's in rhythm or you're in trouble.
>
> Your rhythm should set the pace of the fight. If it does, then you penetrate your opponent's rhythm. You make him fight *your* fight, and that's what boxing is all about. In the dressing room that night I could feel my rhythm beginning to move through me, and it assured me that everything would be all right. (410: p. 75)

O. J. Simpson says the key to the success of great runners is that "they get into a certain rhythm and make instinctive moves without any reason for them." (25: p. 70)

Western athletes, then, like practitioners of the martial arts, often depend on relaxation, concentration, breathing exercises, mental emptying, and rhythm to achieve exceptional performances. Even though they don't have a training system as sophisticated in this regard as yoga or the martial arts, they manage nevertheless to incorporate these elements into their practice and performance. Through intrinsic energy or in concert with it athletes often discover extraordinary capacities for strength, speed, balance, and ease.

In addition, they sometimes demonstrate abilities that are generally assumed to be "impossible." There are accounts of abilities to leap over rocky terrain without looking; to climb smooth walls without artificial aids; to be unharmed by hard, well-aimed blows, delivered not only by hand but with swords or other hand weapons; to elude bullets and pass through walls; to rise and hang in the air; and even to disappear. We have no absolute proof that these possibilities are facts. At this stage all we can say is that sport gives rise to legends of this kind. Even if such capacities do not exist, it is certainly interesting and possibly significant that wonder tales of the sort commonly associated with saints and yogis are now being connected with sporting feats.

Extraordinary Strength

At peak moments athletes find themselves in possession of extraordinary strength. In a term paper, a high school wrestler describes one such experience:

> Late in that last period something strange happened. I stopped thinking about anything and just started to wrestle. Fatigue was no longer any problem. I needed a pin to win because I was too far behind in points to catch up. If I were being logical, I never could have done what I did, because I went for a reverse cradle, where the man on the bottom tries to cradle the top man—a difficult move to get. Even if one can get it, it is almost impossible to pin a man with it. Somehow I got this hold and reversed him. He was in a near-pin position but far from actually getting pinned. I should have known that I couldn't pin him. But it was as if my mind was turned off; just my body was working with strength I didn't know I had. Then it was over. I had pinned him! It was as if I had come back to reality. I couldn't believe what I had done; defeated a seemingly superior wrestler by a move that took the strength and skill that I know I didn't really possess.

Seasoned golf pros have learned to adjust for abnormal strength when they are charged up playing in a tournament. Under such conditions Tom Weiskopf says, "That adrenalin gets flowing and I'll hit the ball 15 to 25 yards further than under normal conditions." (441: p. 256)

Golfer Frank Beard tells how, toward the close of his first tour championship, he began to compensate deliberately according to his mental state:

> I was still about two hundred yards from the middle of the green, and something popped into my mind, that good rule I still follow: when you're pumped up, always take less iron than you think you need because you'll hit it farther than you normally would. For two hundred yards, I'd normally take a three-iron. I took a five-iron. On a normal lie, under normal conditions, I couldn't hit a five-iron two hundred yards if my life depended on it. But I busted the ball right in the middle of the green, maybe twenty feet past the pin. If I'd hit a three-iron, I probably would've gone over the club-house. (38: p. 85)

Pittsburgh Steeler Sam Davis, pondering aloud to Roy Blount about the extraordinary strength of teammate Joe Greene, said, "I'm beginning to believe it's a mental thing." Under ordinary circumstances Greene is not one of the team's strongest men, "but on the pass rush [he] can lift two guys. I've seen him hit guys with one hand, rushing in, and knock them flat on the behind. If that ain't strength, I don't know what it is." (47: p. 79)

There are many cases in the martial arts literature which suggest that Eastern athletes can deliberately tap extraordinary amounts of energy and strength. Morehei Uyeshiba, the founder of aikido, is said to have relocated a large stone that ten laborers had been unable to move. He often performed such feats, and once said, "I taught myself that an extraordinary spiritual power or soul power lies within a human body." (501: p. 153)

Among the most astounding feats of strength practiced in the martial arts are those performed by karateka, those who practice karate. Don Buck, karate sensei, is known for his eerie power in winning arm-wrestling contests. "On at least one occasion he won such a contest, using only his little finger," Glen Barclay writes. "His explanation is that using one finger put him at an advantage, because he was able to 'focus the same amount of strength into a smaller area.'" (33: pp. 47–48)

John Gilbey traveled all over the world in the 1960s observing extraordinary feats of strength and prowess. In Taiwan, he

. . . saw gifted boxers of every description. Men who could slice bricks like your wife would a cake; men who could lightly touch your body and bring a bright red blood line immediately to the surface; men who could support over a two hundred pound weight attached to their genitalia; men who could catch flies (alive!) with their chopsticks; men who could plunge their arms up to the elbow in unprepared, rather hard soil. (172: pp. 13, 14)

He also observed a man who struck a steel stanchion a glancing blow. Gilbey says:

I looked at the huge steel stanchion. And what I saw made my eyes pop. The impress of the blond chap's fist was clearly and unmistakeably engraved in the steel to a depth of a full quarter inch! The stanchion was not of deficient steel. Fool that I am, I tested it (my hand is still numb) and no posterity will see my work because it isn't there. (172: p. 147)

A recent book on kung fu by David Chow and Richard Spangler includes several photographs of outstanding feats which they observed. One shows an 82-year old Chinese Ch'i Kung master who drove an eight-inch nail through four inches of board with his bare forehead. (80: p. 179)

Most of us have a strong impulse to reject such tales as legends or mere fantasies, indulged in by peoples who are less gifted than Westerners at separating subjective from objective realities. However, there are so many stories like these that it is difficult to believe that none of them is true. Moreover, many of these unusual feats have been witnessed and attested to by knowledgeable observers. Since we are primarily interested in describing the extreme limits of performance in athletic endeavor, we must include some of these astounding stories. As more people become aware of these feats and the methods behind them, we will be able to prove, for ourselves and for each other, which are true and which false.

Extraordinary Speed and Endurance

Sometimes athletes are able to call on level upon level of speed or to achieve extraordinary endurance at exceptional speeds. Derek Sanderson insists that his (then) teammate Bobby Orr "has sixteen versions of fast.'' (423: p. 119) John Walker describes his win in the 1500 meters at the 1976 Olympics this way:

> . . . when I hit the front I got a flash of compelling certainty. I didn't look over my shoulder, but I sensed someone coming up on me fast. . . .
>
> I was already at full stretch. But I went into a sort of mental overdrive, and my subconscious mind took over completely—I've experienced it in races before, and I can't explain it. I burned Wohlhuter off and went to the tape with my hands over my head. (509: p. 9)

Ian Jackson describes a type of run with Rich Delgado, who was normally a faster runner than Jackson:

> I never knew how it happened. We would be easing along at 7:00 per mile and one of us (I never knew which one) would surge very slightly. Then we'd both be onto the pace of the surge. Later, there'd be another surge—just a little, almost unnoticeable increase in pace. But we kept pushing it up. Once we were moving, we didn't back off. Back and forth we'd play with the pace. He'd throw in a little more tempo. I'd match it and throw in a little of my own. Within a mile we'd go from 7:00 down to 6:30 pace. Two miles later, we'd be under 6:00. Another mile and we'd be down to about 5:30. It was so smooth you hardly knew it was happening. Finally, we'd be flying at 5:15 or 5:10, and the miles would reel by effortlessly. (224: p. 34)

It is evident from these examples that unusual energy reserves were being tapped. At first blush one is tempted to say that the athletes were simply stronger than their opponents, but apparently more is involved. Referring to fastball pitcher Nolan Ryan, Ron Fimrite says: "No one can say what causes him to throw so much harder than anyone else. . . . Sheer physical strength is not the source of his speed, although at 6'2" and 198 pounds, Ryan has a good pitcher's build. . . . But muscles do not give a man arm speed. 'If they did,' says Oriole Manager Weaver, 'I'd have everybody working out with weights. No, it's not that. No one knows what it is. It's like asking what makes a man run fast.' '' (144: pp. 37, 39)

A rare and dramatic example of extraordinary speed and endurance are the *lung-gom-pa* runners in Tibet. In her book *Magic and Mystery in Tibet*, Alexandra David-Neel says that they undergo a special kind of training that develops "uncommon nimbleness and especially enables its adepts to take exraordinarily long tramps with amazing rapidity." (105: p. 199) She adds that although many undertake the *lung-gom* training, few become really good at it. But one day she encountered such an adept. Her companion urged her not to interrupt him, as he was running in a trance and to awaken him suddenly might cause death. When the man drew close, "I could clearly see his perfectly calm impassive face and wide-open eyes with their gaze fixed on some invisible far-distant object situated somewhere high up in space. The man did not run. He seemed to lift himself from the ground, proceeding by leaps. It looked as if he had been endowed with the elasticity of a ball and rebounded each time his feet touched the ground. His steps had the regularity of a pendulum." (105: pp. 202-203).

The major emphasis of these *lung-gom-pa* runners is not on speed, but endurance. The same pace is maintained over all kinds of terrain for several consecutive days and nights. According to some reports, thousands of miles are covered in this manner by the *lung-gom* adepts. David-Neel takes pains to point out that the feats accomplished are more a matter of mind than of muscle. She says, "It must be understood that the *lung-gom* method does not aim at training the disciple by strengthening his muscles, but by developing in him psychic states that make these extraordinary marches possible." (105: p. 209)

> Some initiates in the secret lore also assert that, as a result of long years of practice, after he has travelled over a certain distance, the feet of the *lung-gom-pa* no longer touch the ground and that he glides on the air with an extreme celerity.
>
> Setting aside exaggeration, I am convinced from my limited experiences and what I have heard from trustworthy lamas, that one reaches a condition in which one does not feel the weight of one's body. A kind of anesthesia deadens the sensations that would be produced by knocking against the stones or other obstacles on the way, and one walks for hours at an unaccustomed speed, enjoying that kind of light agreeable dizziness well known to motorists at high speed. (105: p. 215)

Lama Anagarika Govinda, a European by birth, experienced something similar to the trance of the *lung-gom-pa* runners when he was traveling in Tibet. He had spent a day far from camp painting and exploring, and did not turn toward home until dark. He had to cover many miles of boulder-covered ground in the dark of night. In spite of these obstacles, he found that

> . . . to my amazement I jumped from boulder to boulder without ever slipping or missing a foothold, in spite of wearing only a pair of flimsy sandals on my bare feet.
> One false step or a single slip on these boulders would have sufficed to break or to sprain a foot, but I never missed a step. I moved on with the certainty of a sleepwalker—though far from being asleep. I do not know how many miles of this boulder-strewn territory I traversed; I only know that finally I found myself on the pass over the low hills with the plain and the magnesium swamp before me. . . . Still under the influence of the "spell" I went right across the swamp without ever breaking through. (177: p. 78)

Only later was Govinda able to find an explanation for his experience, after reading the account we quoted from David-Neel. Govinda says that unwittingly he had followed the *lung-gom* rules, adding, "I clearly reached a condition in which the weight of the body is no more felt and in which the feet seem to be endowed with an instinct of their own, avoiding invisible obstacles and finding footholds, which only a clairvoyant consciousness could have detected in the speed of such a movement and in the darkness of the night." (177: p. 80)

Lama Govinda visited a *lung-gom* training center where *lung-gom-pas* in training entered meditation cubicles, which contained the necessities of life. Once they entered, the doorway was sealed. The briefest period a monk remained in a cubicle was one to three months, the longest nine years. While the *lung-gom-pa* was sealed up, no one was allowed to see or speak to him. Alms, often in the form of food, were received by the *lung-gom-pas* through a 9 by 10 inch opening:

> The same small opening . . . is said to be used as an exit by the *lung-gom-pa* after completion of his nine years' practice in uninterrupted seclusion and perfect silence.

It is said that his body by that time has become so light and subtle that he can get through an opening not wider than a normal man's span, and that he can move with the speed of a galloping horse, while hardly touching the ground. (177: p. 91)

This improvement in running ability was said to occur in the absence of any physical practice, with the exception of minimal exercise in the form of walking on a terrace (in seclusion) provided for that purpose. If these reports are true, then a whole new dimension of physical capacity was tapped in the *lung-gom* training, through purely mental means.

Mountain climber Gaston Rebuffat has described an experience that resembled the *lung-gom* running. In steep terrain he was threatened by an impending storm:

Horrified at the thought of a storm in this fissure, where the sheet of water would so soon be transformed into a torrent, I climbed fast, very fast, and rather roughly. Behind me the ropes were heavy with moisture. Above, the cleft was barred by vertical walls forming a difficult obstacle, demanding care and attention. Meanwhile the rock grew greasy under its film of water. It began to rain, but we seemed to be making our way through a curtain of vapour, frigid, almost tangible and hard to penetrate. There was nothing ethereal about these regions, and yet I felt myself as light as if I had abandoned my human frame; I almost ran up the rocks. (397: p. 102)

Most of us would probably say that what Rebuffat did on that climb did not involve any unusual powers. His actions could be explained by extra adrenalin produced by his fear of being caught in the fissure. Then his climbing faculties were so aroused that timing, muscles, and judgment were functioning at a high level. But Rebuffat himself seems to think what he did that day was exceptional. How often does a climber feel that he has abandoned "his human frame"? Could it be that there is a level of functioning *beyond* the best of "ordinary" climbing ability—a higher gear, as it were—and did Rebuffat somehow get into that gear on that special day?

Extraordinary Balance

Peter Furst, anthropologist, tells of a shamanistic demonstration he and some students witnessed in 1966 while studying the Huichol Indians of North Central Mexico. The shaman, Ramon Medina Silva, took the anthropologists and members of the tribe to a "spectacular waterfall" that he said was "specially for Shamans." He then took off his sandals and proceeded to demonstrate the meaning of balance to a shaman. Furst writes that he "proceeded to leap—'fly' might be more appropriate—from one rock to another with arms stretched wide, often landing but a few inches from the slippery edge . . . Or he would stand motionless at the extreme limit of a massive rock, wheel about suddenly and make a great leap to the other side of the rushing water, never showing the slightest concern about the obvious danger that he might lose his balance and fall into space." (162: p. 153)

In *Tales of Power* Carlos Castaneda describes a very similar demonstration put on by don Genaro. On one occasion, standing on a ledge, Genaro called to Castaneda and then jumped to the ground. Castaneda says "I saw him plummeting down from a height of fifty feet or so. . . ." (77: p. 94) These feats of don Genaro could be viewed as variations of a form of kung fu known as "leaping kung," which enables one to "leap over a car or jump across a fifteen-foot-wide mountain stream." (80: p. 154) [Richard DeMille, in *Castaneda's Journey*, suggests that Castaneda got the idea for don Genaro from Peter Furst's lecture on Ramon Medina, which Castaneda attended as a student. (110: p. 189)]

Martial arts student John Gilbey once witnessed a similar feat. An adept named Chou called to him from an open window on the third floor of a building, telling Gilbey he would leap down beside him. Gilbey says:

> The next moment his small body was in flight. The next is incredible. Of course he landed on the wooden surface without injury, but this I had seen Japanese and Thai nonboxers do previously. But Chou landed not only without injury but also without sound! I swear it—I saw it but I did not hear it. A physicist may be able to explain it. I own that I cannot. (72: p. 129)

One of the presently inexplicable abilities reportedly practiced in the martial arts is that of being able to walk up perpendicular walls. This form of kung fu is sometimes called the "lizard technique." It

> . . . enables a student to scale a wall with nothing more than his hands and feet. Training starts with a pole inclined against a wall for assistance. Gradually, the angle of the pole against the wall is reduced until the student can scale the wall without the pole. In another version of this technique, the student stands with his back against the wall and using only his heels and hands mounts the wall. (80: p. 44)

It is also called wall climbing kung, or "gecko crawling," the gecko being a small lizard. Here is another account of this remarkable feat:

> . . . anyone well versed in this art can, with his back against a wall, move freely on and along the surface, horizontally and vertically, by using the controlled strength of his heels and elbows. While perfection of this *Kung* is indeed similar to a Gecko darting as a matter of routine up virtually any wall, it certainly is not easy for humans to master precarious wall climbing, which often threatens to create great insecurity or instability. Generously estimating, one out of a hundred students might consummate this *Kung* (80: p. 155)

Extraordinary Ease

A culminating experience in sport is the state of effortlessness that athletes achieve at special moments. Feats that are usually demanding and taxing—even exhausting—are accomplished with ease. This seeming effortlessness is a feature often noted by spectators. Grantland Rice described Red Grange's running ability on the football field as follows: He "runs . . . with almost no effort, as a shadow flits and drifts and darts. There is no gathering of muscle for an extra lunge. There is only the effortless, ghostlike, weave and glide upon effortless legs. . . . " (178: p. xi)

But the case for effortlessness in peak sports performance need not rest on secondhand observations, which are often made with the proviso "He makes it *look* easy," implying that although it may look simple enough, for example, to hit a golf ball 350 yards, it's not really easy to do it. But firsthand accounts from many athletes suggest that at certain moments it actually *is* as easy to perform as it looks.

Warren Spahn, after pitching his first no-hitter, said, "It was one of the easiest games I ever pitched. . . . Everything seemed easy. I didn't think about it until after the fifth and then I figured I'm over the hump and it's downhill." (315: p. 26) Bobby Jones, who impressed spectators by the ease with which he hit a golf ball, insists:

> Of all the times that I have struggled around the golf course, there are a few easy rounds that stand out in my memory. . . . Strangely, perhaps, one thing stands out about all these rounds: I had precisely the same feel on each occasion; I was conscious of swinging the club easily and yet without interruption. . . . I had to make no special effort to do anything.
> (237: pp. 184–185)

Although one might assume that to a great extent sensations of effortlessness and ease are the result of training and practice, the answer seems to be more complex. Mountain climber Lionel Terray writes of his experience after weeks of climbing:

> By this time we were so fit and acclimatised, both mentally and physically, to living in high mountains, that we had virtually overcome the normal human inadaptation to such surroundings. Our ease and rapidity of movement had become in a sense unnatural, and we had practically evolved into a new kind of alpine animal, half way between the monkey and the mountain goat. We could run uphill for hours, climb faces as though they were step-ladders, and rush down gullies in apparent defiance of the laws of gravity. The majority of climbs seemed child's play, which we could do without any particular effort in half or a third of the time taken by an ordinary good party. (487: p. 124)

By themselves, these accounts of extraordinary strength, speed, balance, and ease are too few to merit acceptance as fact. However, they are internally consistent enough to suggest that similar abilities are being described. If such abilities do exist, we would be foolish to reject them just because they fly in the face of what we have been conditioned to expect. If the experiences in this book demonstrate anything, it is that we must not set limits on what is possible.

Energy Reaching Out: Psychokinesis

In the 1970s a number of psychics have come to public attention with claims that they can perform feats of psychokinesis (PK), that is, the power to affect objects directly by purely mental means. One of the best-known psychics with PK abilities today is Uri Geller, noted for his supposed spoon-bending and watch-stopping abilities. Unfortunately Geller's abilities have not been adequately observed under strict laboratory conditions, although some reports of research with him have been published. (127, 372) Whether or not Geller's ability is genuine does not alter the fact that the *existence* of psychokinesis has been scientifically verified in many laboratories to the satisfaction of many reliable witnesses. Theoretically, PK ability can provide that extra edge which might explain some otherwise inexplicable athletic feats. But is there any evidence that PK occurs in sport?

Most PK laboratory experiments involve influencing the throw of dice. Subjects "will" specific die faces to turn up, or to fall to the left or the right. Willing is often mentioned by athletes. They often make many statements to suggest that at times they can actually "will" things to happen. There are many golf stories about changing the flight of the ball through the power of mind. Don Lauck notes that for years golf galleries had believed that Jack Nicklaus, "could win whenever he wanted, could *will* the ball into the cup if he needed a birdie at the 18th." (274: p. 3) Nicklaus' own words about Arnold Palmer show that he too prizes the power of willing. He insists that although Palmer possessed a fine putting touch when at his peak, it wasn't this skill that enabled him to sink so many pressure putts. "More than anything else you get the feeling that he actually *willed* the ball into the hole." (356: p. 41)

Another golfer, Johnny Miller, writes in his book, *Pure Golf:*

If you follow golf at all, you'll know that Bobby Nichols has a knack for holing putts in "clutch" situations to win big money tournaments. At the Dow Jones a few years back, I was playing with him in the final group, and he needed a long putt on the last green. I remember watching his actions as he moved in to make his stroke. Everything was positive. It was apparent that there was no doubt in his mind that he'd make the putt. When he hit the ball I thought to myself, "There is no way that ball will get to the hole," it was going so slowly, it looked as if it would be a foot short. Then I heard Bobby say, "Get in," and it did. He almost willed it into the hole. (325: p. 145)

These examples cannot be attributed definitely to PK, of course. After all, we cannot say that they succeeded in getting the ball to move by any but normal means. Yet these athletes seem to feel there was an additional, psychological factor involved, one connected with the act of willing. That there is a connection in Johnny Miller's mind, at least, between what happens in golf and what parapsychologists call PK is unmistakable from the following observation: "I have a premonition that in maybe five hundred years if you want to move, say, a lamp from one part of a room to another, all you'll have to do is think of this happening and it will . . . in fact." (325: p. 179)

John Brodie once discussed a touchdown pass he threw to the 49'ers' end, Gene Washington.

Murphy: When the play began it looked for a moment like the safety would make an interception. But then it seemed as if the ball went through or over his hands as he came in front of Washington. . . .

Brodie: Pat Fischer, the cornerback, told the reporters after the game that the ball seemed to jump right over his hands as he went for it. When we studied the game films that week, it *did* look as if the ball kind of jumped over his hands into Gene's. Some of them said it was the wind— and maybe it was.

Murphy: What do you mean by *maybe?*

Brodie: What I mean is that our sense of that pass was so clear and our *intention* so strong that the ball was bound to get there, come wind, cornerbacks, hell or high water. (343: p. 20)

In a *New York Times* article, William N. Wallace says New York Giants' tight end Gary Ballman "remembers a pass coming at him overthrown so far there was no way he could catch it. So heavy was his energy flow, so intense his aspirations, that he willed the ball to hang and come down into his hands." (506: p. 3) Later in conversation, Ballman told Wallace: "But it happened. It was a strange feeling, I'll tell you." (506: p. 3)

In the 1976 playoffs with the Oakland Raiders, tight end Russ Francis of the New England Patriots made a one-handed catch that seemed far beyond his reach to set up the Patriots' first touchdown. To Francis, however, the play was not difficult. He says, "The ball just seemed to slow down and crawl through the air. . . . As it hit my hand, I looked down and watched it dimple my skin. It's funny, but I sometimes think I can make something happen on the football field just by picturing it in my mind." (145: p. 76)

There are also hints of possible PK in baseball. Richard Grossinger describes what should have been a home run hit by Pittsburgh Pirate rookie Dave Augustine at Shea Stadium in 1973. It should have won the National League pennant. "But," Grossinger says, "the ball did not leave the field; its flight broke just above the grandstand and it dropped onto the railing, then bounced, not in the direction momentum should have taken it (into the stands for a home run anyway), but back into the glove of Cleon Jones, who threw out the lead run at home plate. . . . The Mets won the 1973 pennant." (185: p. 35)

If PK is a fact, there is no reason why fans cannot exercise it as well as players. Could PK be one of the many factors involved in the well-known phenomenon of the "home court advantage"? In several countries in East Africa, soccer teams pay for the services of a soothsayer. One in particular demand is Seriff, who casts spells on the opponents of the teams who hire him. Seriff notes that even if the opposing team has better players, still the ball "can be made to behave strangely—go wide, or go over or fall short of the goal." (514: p. 23)

John P. Brown, in his book on dervishes, tells of a sufi who, while watching a wrestling match, agreed with his companion that together they would try to aid one of the contestants by means of willpower. They also agreed that, having helped the first wrestler subdue his opponent, they would then concentrate on aiding the other man to overcome the first wrestler in turn. They succeeded both times. Brown also tells of two persons at another match who decided to help the weaker of the two wrestlers. "Immediately a wonderful occurrence took place; the thin, spare man seized upon his giant-like opponent, and threw him upon the ground with surprising force. The crowd cried out with astonishment, as he turned him over on his back, and held him down with much apparent ease. No one present, except ourselves, knew the cause." (67: p. 148)

Psychokinesis in the Martial Arts

The growing literature on the martial arts is packed with stories that to Western ears are unbelievable, yet an increasing number of observers testify to the truth of at least some of them.

In some feats performed by martial artists, physical contact is made with a person or object, but the influence exerted seems greater than the degree of contact made. It appears that the "real" work is done by a force much more powerful than any that the muscles alone provide. We will mention instances in which this is only a slight possibility, then work up to cases where an unknown force is the only likely explanation.

In the *Tameshiwari,* or breaking aspect of karate, "trained karateka can smash boards, bricks, cement blocks, ice, and roofing tiles with various parts of their body including the fists, open hands, and even their heads and fingers." (529: p. 77) In some of these breaking techniques, the effect seems to go beyond the immediate physical contact made between mere flesh and rocks, tiles or glass. Chow and Spangler (80) observed and photographed a master who said he would strike five bricks piled on top of each other, splitting each in two except for the second from the top. He did as he promised.

The populizer of kung fu, Bruce Lee, demonstrated in public, before photographers, his capacity to deliver a punch of tremendous impact, standing right foot forward, with his almost fully-extended right arm an inch away from his partner, who held a heavily-padded glove against his chest for protection. In this position, from which it is physically impossible to generate enough power to hurt an opponent, Lee knocked his partner flying into a waiting chair, several feet behind him. (33: p. 72)

A variant of Lee's technique is the "delayed death touch."

This refers to the ability, reported though difficult to prove, to strike a person in a vital spot and for the effect to be delayed, by hours, days or even months. In carrying this out, the "attacker" strikes the "victim" in a certain spot, at a certain time, in a certain way. Instead of dropping on the spot the victim goes on his way. Through some unknown process his vital energy is affected and at a certain point in his inner cycle the effect of the "touch" is felt and he dies or is seriously ill. (98: p. 37)

There are, in fact, eyewitness accounts "of men struck in the abdomen, by blows that barely marked the skin, who died later of ruptured spleens or kidneys, destroyed by the shock wave of energy dispatched by fist or foot." (233: p. 95)

This "death touch" can be explained by suggestion, if in fact complicity is not involved. American psychologist Martin Seligman (443) has studied voodoo deaths among Caribbean people and concluded that the victim's faith is the cause of death. Aware of a hex and sure of its power, the victim falls into a kind of learned helplessness and slides into submissive death.

But what about cases in which the victim is unaware of his intended fate? Then, if it is suggestion, it must operate by telepathy, a possibility that's not as far-fetched as it sounds at first. According to certain reports (74, 520), it is hinted that Russian researchers are working on techniques to influence people at a distance by telepathy. Some writers (98, 326) suggest that the delayed death touch is an application of the principles of acupuncture. One writer says, "It stands to reason that a powerful medicine (or medical technique) can just as easily kill or cripple [as cure]." (326: p. 42)

Another technique is the apparently simple but powerful matter of expelling the breath. This has such a tenuous physical basis that it can hardly account for the results it is claimed to produce. A famous Chinese boxer, Yang Lu-ch'an, is said to have "knocked a young challenger thirty feet across a room simply by expelling his breath with a laugh when the young man let fly a punch at the famous boxer's stomach." (123: p. 38)

Finally, two techniques in the martial arts seem to make sense only in terms of some kind of PK. One is the "spirit shout art," or "*kiai* shout." E. J. Harrison tells of a master who saw "a few sparrows perched on the branch of a tall pine tree, and fixing his steadfast gaze on the birds, gave utterance to the *kiai* shout, whereupon the birds fell to the ground insensible. When he relaxed the *kiai* the birds regained consciousness and flew away." (193: p. 169) Harrison says the shout was also employed for the opposite effect—that of restoring to consciousness persons that doctors had given up for dead.

Martial artist Robert Smith tells many anecdotes about the renowned Chinese boxer, Li Neng-jan. One concerns a young man who—on the pretext of offering tea to Li—planned to attack him, as in spite of his reputation he appeared to be a harmless old man. When he did so, says Smith, "Li merely used a spirit-shout . . . that knocked the [young man] out—without spilling his tea or interrupting his conversation with another man. When asked about it, [the young man] replied with: 'I heard thunder, his hands had eyes, I fell unconscious.' " (462: p. 14)

A last technique, inexplicable in ordinary physical terms, is *noi cun,* which Michael Minick describes as follows:

> More commonly known as the divine technique, this is a very rare form of kung fu practiced by only a handful of adepts. It is not widely taught or particularly popular because it takes the better part of a lifetime to master. And, quite frankly, it strains the credulity of those who are asked to believe that it exists. Simply put, it is a means of generating internal power so enormous one can fell an opponent without actually touching him. As fantastic as this sounds, most kung fu masters insist that such an art exists, and many claim to have witnessed it. One modern master writing in *Karate Illustrated* stated:
>
> Here in San Francisco lives a one-hundred-seven-year-old master who is still able to use *noi cun* (the use of internal power)

despite his age and the frailty of his body. I personally have seen him demonstrate. In one of his demonstrations, he asked a young man to step to the center of the room. Then, placing himself a few yards away, he stretched forth his arm, palm pointed outward, and concentrated deeply, drawing from within that great force of his *chi,* and within a few moments the lad was staggering backward, pushed off balance by the unseen force radiating from that outstretched hand. (326: p. 41)

Minick adds that the same master gave other examples of *noi cun,* including that of a "man in Hong Kong who broke a glass vase from across a room." (326: p. 41) Chow and Spangler give a variation of it known as "red sand palm." In this variation, "without touching an assailant's body, the adept merely makes signs of rubbing or striking at him with the palm of one's hand from a distance and the receiver will be injured. The wound will cause irreparable damage. Death usually follows in ten to fifteen days." (80: p. 145) They also describe "one finger Kung," in which "should the forefinger be aimed at an opponent, even though separated by a door, he still could be injured or destroyed." (80: p. 147)

Chow also witnessed a student who held a washboard with the corrugations facing his stomach, the skin of which was unblemished. A master, standing four feet away, meditated for half a minute and then flicked his wrist toward the board, but without touching either it or the student. When the student lowered the washboard and raised the sweater, the lines from the washboard were outlined in red across his stomach.

In all the examples given here, it is difficult or even impossible to see how ordinary physical principles could account for the feats accomplished. In cases such as expelling breath and the red sand palm and possibly even the hand smashing of karateka, the same principle may be acting as in the spirit-shout art, about which E. J. Harrison noted: "It is not the shout itself, but the force behind dictating it, that is really responsible for the phenomenon." (193: p. 120)

Another indication that the mind plays an essential role in the feats described is the stress that athletes both East and West place on confidence. Arnold Palmer told George Plimpton: "When I'm working well, I just don't think I'm going to miss a shot or a putt, and when

I do I'm as surprised as hell. I can't believe it. A golfer must think that way. . . . I don't mean to suggest that it's easy. In fact, the hardest thing for a great many people is to win. They . . . *doubt.* Which gets them into trouble." (384: p. 248) Masutatsu Oyama says, "The most important thing in the stone-breaking techniques is psychological self-confidence." He adds that if you try to break a stone, no matter how small, when you are not feeling confident, "In nine cases out of ten, you will break a bone, dislocate something, or injure yourself in some other way." (370: p. 224) Yet in a confident state one can break many stones without a single bruise. If it is purely a matter of physics, why should it matter whether or not one feels confident?

Elusiveness

Another aspect of these powers is an uncanny elusiveness that in extreme cases gives the impression of downright invisibility. The religious traditions of the East and Middle East consider the art of invisibility to be one of the siddhis, or extraordinary powers, that may develop in following a spiritual path. Morihei Uyeshiba, the founder of aikido, often demonstrated his ability to elude attack in this way. George Leonard writes:

> Scores of reliable witnesses have testified to demonstrations by Morihei Uyeshiba, in which he seemed to go beyond the limitations of known physical law. On one occasion, completely surrounded by men with knives, Uyeshiba reputedly disappeared and reappeared at the same instant, looking down at his attackers from the top of a flight of stairs. Uyeshiba refused to repeat this feat, saying that the effort involved might take several months from his life. (279: p. 252)

Leonard also quotes his teacher, Robert Nadeau, a former student of Uyeshiba. On one occasion, the Master invited Nadeau to attack him, which he did with all his strength, wanting to make a good impression.

> But when I got close to him, it was like I'd entered a cloud. And in the cloud there's a giant spring that's throwing me out of the

cloud. I find myself flying through the air and I come down with a hard, judo type slap-fall. Lying there, I look around for [Uyeshiba], but he isn't to be seen. Finally, I turn all the way around, the one place I wouldn't have expected him to be, and there he is, standing calmly. (279: p. 253)

Leonard also describes a film taken of Uyeshiba as he was attacked by two men. It shows him facing his attackers, apparently trapped. But in the next frame he has moved two feet away and is facing in the opposite direction. According to Leonard:

While Uyeshiba appears to shift from one position to another in a fraction of a second (or in no time at all!) the oncoming movement of the attackers proceeds sequentially, a fraction of a step at a time, until the two collide and are pinned by the Master.

Whether or not Uyeshiba's feats can be scientifically validated, the fact remains that those who were best acquainted with the Master are convinced that he was operating "in another dimension," especially in his last years. Again and again he seems to have "just disappeared," or to have created "a warp in time and space." Such terms as these recur repeatedly in descriptions of Uyeshiba's work, and may serve to remind us of possibilities that lie beyond the rather rigid strictures of this culture. (279: p. 253)

In a provocative article on running back Mac Lane of the Kansas City Chiefs, Robert F. Jones says, "There has to be some quality of magic in the elusiveness of the best running backs. Mere physics can no more explain the missed or broken tackles that mark every long run from scrimmage than mere chemistry can explain the excitement such a performance arouses in the spectator." (236: p. 25) A number of ball players are credited with the ability to make the ball "disappear." It has been said that the great Satchel Paige was able to actually dematerialize the ball. Biz Mackey, a great catcher, says of Paige's fastball:

A lot of pitchers have a fastball, but a very, very few—Feller, Grove, Johnson, a couple of others besides Satchel—have had that little extra juice that makes the difference between the good and the great man. When it's that fast, it will hop a little at the end of the line. Beyond that, it tends to disappear. Yes, disappear. I've heard about Satchel throwing pitches that wasn't [sic] hit but that never showed up in the catcher's mitt nevertheless. They say the catcher, the umpire, and the bat boys looked all over for that ball, but it was gone. Now how do you account for that? (379: p. 141)

Pele, the soccer great, confided that, on a day when everything was going right, suddenly he felt "a strange calmness I hadn't experienced in any of the other games. It was a type of euphoria; I felt I could run all day without tiring, that I could dribble through any of their team or all of them, that I could almost pass through them physically. I felt I could not be hurt. It was a very strange feeling and one I had not felt before. Perhaps it was merely confidence, but I have felt confident many times without that strange feeling of invincibility." (378: p. 51)

Were all these athletes and spectators deluded? Perhaps. But it is also possible that they were keying into what may be the deeper reality of what we have mistakenly assumed was an impenetrable universe but which in fact is much more mutable and diaphanous. That the worlds of the mystic and the physicist are very alike has been pointed out in recent books by Capra (76) and Leshan (280), among others.

Uncanny Suspension

At certain moments, as we have seen, athletes have feelings of floating and weightlessness. Sometimes, in fact, they even have out-of-body experiences. Now we would like to consider the possibility that the athlete is literally able to suspend himself in midair. In the earlier chapters we discussed the athletes' subjective feelings that they were floating or outside themselves. But is there an objective reality involved, something that can be verified by others? We think that there is. We have collected many statements by sportswriters, coaches, and other observers that attest to the fact that some athletes actually can, for brief moments, remain suspended in the air. Basketball players and dancers, especially, seem to demonstrate this amazing ability.

Referring to the ability of the Denver Nuggets' David Thompson to remain suspended in air, Marshall Frady used the term, "the uncanny suspension." (155: p. 30) Witnessing an instance of this deeply affected author James Michener. He describes a 1941 basketball game and player Hank Luisetti in his *Sports in America:*

Somehow, Luisetti stayed up in the air, faked a shot at the basket, made the Denver center commit himself, and with a movement I had never seen before, simply extended his right arm an extra foot and banked a one-handed shot gently against the backboard and into the basket. It seemed as if he had been in the air a full minute, deceiving three different players, and ending with a delayed shot that was staggering in its beauty. (322: p. 446)

An article in *Time* describes a performance by premier danseur Mikhail Baryshnikov:

. . . when he launches his perfectly arched body into the arc of one of his improbably sustained leaps—high, light, the leg beats blurring precision—he transcends the limits of physique and, it sometimes seems, those of gravity itself. If one goes by the gasps in the theater or the ecstasies of the critics, such moments turn Mikhail Baryshnikov, if not into a minor god, then into a major sorcerer. . . .

He is an unbelievable technician with invisible technique. Most dancers, even the great ones, make obvious preliminaries to leaps. He simply floats into confounding feats of acrobatics and then comes to still, collected repose. He forces the eye into a double take: did that man actually do that just now? Dance Critic Walter Terry says that "Baryshnikov is probably the most dazzling virtuoso we have seen. He is more spectacular in sheer technique than any other male dancer. What he actually does, no one can really define. His steps are in no ballet dictionary. And he seems to be able to stop in mid-air and sit in space." (34: p.44)

If these athletes and danseurs really can remain in the air longer than is normally possible, how do they do it? Again, a possible answer may be found in the literature of the world's religions, all of which mention levitation, or the ability to rise and remain in the air. Some suggest that levitation is a symbol of spiritual emancipation. Ernest Wood observes, "Levitation is a universally accepted fact in India. I remember one occasion when an old yogi was levitated in a recumbent posture about six feet above the ground in an open field, for about half an hour, while the visitors were permitted to pass sticks to and fro in the space between." (466: p. 21)

Levitation in the West figures prominently in two classic volumes by two scholars, Herbert Thurston (492) and Montague Summers (477), in independent works with the same title: *The Physical Phenomena of Mysticism*. Both give examples of levitation by Christian saints, such as Teresa of Avila and Joseph of Copertino. James Webb, in a scholarly history of nineteenth century occultism, notes a surprisingly large number of accounts of levitation which were said to have occurred during that century. In a discussion of unusual physical phenomena associated with mysticism, the mathematician and parapsychologist A. R. G. Owen says, "The evidence is not conclusive, but it strongly suggests that levitation occurs only in ecstasy." (368: 2703) This fits in nicely with the view that levitation is a logical extension of the experience of being "beyond," "beside," or "outside" one's self. However, it is difficult to reconcile it with another large body of data, that gathered by spiritualists and psychical researchers. Here the evidence for levitation centers on the feats of physical mediums, two of the best known being Daniel Dunglas Home and Eusapia Palladino. Sometimes, in the presence of such mediums, objects were seen to rise in the air, while on other occasions the mediums themselves levitated. A good review of the highlights of physical mediumship by a skeptical parapsychologist, J. Fraser Nicol, may be found in the *Handbook of Parapsychology*, compiled by psychiatrist Benjamin Wolman. Nicol concludes: ". . . the overwhelming number of reports on mediumistic physical phenomena offer no valid evidence. Fortunately, there are a few cases which the majority of critically minded students find it unreasonable to dismiss." (357: p. 311) He names the exceptions, which include Home and Palladino. Another skeptical parapsychologist, E. J. Dingwall, has written excellent surveys of the lives and phenomena of these two famous mediums. (117, 118)

Levitation, if it occurs, would be a form of psychokinesis. It is of the utmost importance that any current instances of levitation be studied scientifically. (Some of those involved in the transcendental meditation movement currently claim to be able to teach meditators how to levitate, but demonstrations are prohibited.) In the meantime, we must be content with traveler's tales such as those included in this book, bolstered by laboratory evidence that at least small psychokinetic effects do occur. [For a review of the evidence for laboratory PK, see the surveys by Rush (416), Schmeidler (429), and Stanford (471).]

If, for purposes of discussion, we assume that levitation does occur, it is possible that the seemingly inexplicable ability of a Julius Erving or a Mikhail Baryshnikov may be rudimentary and spontaneous occurrences of it, not entirely due to muscular exertion. The athlete's extreme effort to remain airborne may be necessary for the occurrence of a nonphysical factor.

Have we any clues as to how this amazing ability is induced? Danseur Vaslav Nijinsky, when asked if it was difficult to remain suspended in the air, "did not understand at first, and then very obligingly [replied]: 'No! No! not difficult. You have to just go up and then pause a little up there.' " (68: p. 203) Nandor Fodor, a psychoanalyst and psychical researcher, asks whether Nijinsky's ability is a rudimentary form of levitation or only an illusion. He concludes it is indeed levitation, and suggests that Nijinsky—perhaps unconsciously—used a special technique that incorporated aspects of yoga. He was able to see himself from outside during a performance, and this suggested to Fodor that he was in a form of trance during peak performances. Also, his technique apparently involved both breathing and muscular control. Fodor, who knew Nijinsky's widow, asked her if her husband knew how he did it. Romola Nijinsky replied, "I often asked him how he managed to stay up in the air. He never could understand why we could not do it. He just took a leap, held his breath, and stayed up. He felt supported in the air. Moreover, he could control his descent, and could come down slower or quicker as he wished. I know he had extraordinary thigh muscles, and I know that in the matter of filling his lungs with air he has, in a friendly contest, easily beaten Caruso and Erich Schmedes." (151: p. 26)

Fodor learned that it was standard technique in ballet to breath in before a leap, to hold the breath while in the air, and to breath out after landing. With this technique dancers would unconsciously acquire a control over their breathing similar to that practiced by yogis to achieve buoyancy.

Unlike saints, yogis, and shamans, athletes are not aiming at spiritual emancipation. Unlike physical mediums, they are not trying to levitate just for the sake of levitation. But the discipline and training of sport and dance, plus situations calling for rising in the air—as in basketball, ballet, or the broad jump—combined with conscious or unconscious breathing exercises, may trigger a rudimentary form of levitation.

The Invisible Barrier

John Gilbey once saw a marital arts master take a sword and slice through a piece of wood six inches thick, four inches wide, and a foot and a half long. This was to demonstrate the sharpness of the sword. Next he said that "by concentration I will isolate various components of my body so that a sharp sword will not penetrate the skin." He then had an assistant place the sword against his bicep and put all his weight on it. No skin was broken. "There was only a slight red line caused by the pressure of the blade." Finally, he asked Gilbey himself "to strike *with all my strength* at his left forearm. He enjoined me to focus well since, if I hit his upper arm inadvertently, it would be unfortunate.

"I took the sword from the assistant, focused on Hirose's arm, and brought the sword down sharply. . . . In an unbelieving trance I held his arm and gazed at it. A red line creased the skin, but that was all." (172: p. 143–144)

This form of mind over matter may also be operative in sport—a state of invulnerability in which the athlete cannot be harmed. Sometimes it seems as if an invisible physical curtain or wall is protecting him, preventing the athlete from being touched by anyone or anything harmful. In fact, the barrier appears to be mental, and if the religious texts are to be relied on, its presence is due to the athlete's having achieved the right attitude toward his opponent and, indeed, toward life itself.

Photographs in the book by Chow and Spangler (80) illustrate the form of *Ch'i Kung* that John Gilbey witnessed. In one case Grand Master Lung Chi Cheung allowed the wheel of an automobile to run over his stomach, yet he was not hurt. In another instance, five bricks were placed on the head of Northern Shaolin Master Lung Kai Ming; his brother then broke the bricks with a blow from a sledge hammer, but Lung was not hurt.

Although Western athletes do not actively cultivate invulnerability, there are scattered accounts of individuals who seem ·to be unusually free from injury. This is usually attributed to exceptional speed and reflexes that enable one to avoid harm—or simply to good fortune. It may be, however, that abilities like the ones just reviewed could occur spontaneously, as a natural outgrowth of the attitude and discipline of the athlete.

Dr. Ferdie Pacheco, Muhammad Ali's fight doctor, says Ali "has a God-given great body. . . . Take his ability to take body shots. Why do his ribs not break when he allows someone like George Foreman to pound him? I don't know why, but they don't. . . . And take his facial tissue. He's hardly ever marked." (7: p. 5)

Another variation on the theme of invulnerability involves a kind of hypnotic ability some athletes can exercise. Ratti and Westbrook point out that *ki* can be channeled by means of a magnetic personality which enables one to

> . . . call upon strong powers of projection and suggestion, and these can often be used to prevent combat, or to win it. There is an episode . . . said to have involved a samurai who was set upon in the woods by a pack of wolves. . . . He merely kept walking straight ahead, his countenance so stable, aware, and potentially explosive that the animals were frozen in their tracks, while he passed safely through their midst. Other episodes mention men lying in ambush only to confront a victim who, simply by gazing at them, terrorized them so effectively that they were immobilized. (394: p. 370)

Bobby Orr seems to have exercised a similar influence on the Chicago Black Hawks when the Bruins defeated them in four straight games in the 1970 Stanley Cup. In trying to account for the Hawks' poor showing, sportswriter Gary Ronberg says:

> Admittedly, Orr is the finest player in the game today. Does he also have hypnotic powers? In the past, respect for excellence never prevented opponents from breaking lances with a Rocket Richard or a Gordie Howe. Yet there was Orr, gliding along as if shielded by an invisible barrier as the Hawks sleep-skated sheep-like in his wake. One of the most amazing moments of any cup series came in the third game when Orr skated behind the Chicago

net with three Hawks chasing after him and then leisurely set up the easiest kind of goal. (413: p. 18)

Ronberg also quotes a teammate of Orr's who marveled that only a couple of Black Hawks had been willing to "mix it. . . . Hell, everybody else was just standing around watching Bobby fly, like they were in awe or something." (413: p. 21)

Something unusual may have been happening in these cases, something related more to attitude and state of mind than to reflex and muscle. We cannot say that psychokinesis was definitely involved. But we do suggest that these events might not be due to physical abilities as we normally perceive them. To understand why other possibilities may be involved, we must first open our minds to other explanations.

Mind Over Matter

Does mind directly influence matter in sports situations? Only those whose minds are completely closed would definitely rule it out. If we assume only the *possibility* that PK occurs in sport, then do we have any clues as to how it can operate?

Sport constantly shows us how the mind imposes barriers on what the body can do. This mental barrier, this tendency to set a limit on what humans can or cannot do, is what needs to be overcome. Time and again it has been shown that once one athlete breaks through a barrier, other athletes will soon follow, thus showing that the barrier, all along, was not physical but mental. French mountaineer René Dittert observes, "It is a strange fact, but one that has always proved true, that where one man has imposed his domination over the elements another man can pass. The way is open, because the forces of nature have waited for man to prove himself master before submitting." (215: p. 121) Arnold Beisser notes, after discussing barriers to breaking records in sport, "The final striking impression is that when a record is finally broken by one man it opens the way for others to do the same." (39: p. 155) In this connection sportswriter and runner Kenny Moore makes an interesting point in his article on Henry Rono, Washington State track star. He says that in Rono's native Kenya, the living conditions demand a "realism, a clarity of judgment about such things as pain and effort, that is difficult for Westerners to share." (332: p. 42) Moore considers that this cultural factor has important implications as far as Rono's capacity to break records is concerned: "Rono has no illusions, which is good, because the case has been made that it is our illusion that we can go no faster that holds us back." (332: p. 42)

Perhaps the biggest barrier of all is the belief that although we can move our bodies directly, we cannot move anything beyond their reach. But what if we are viewing the problem through the wrong end of a telescope? Thirty years ago a psychologist, R. H. Thouless, and a mathematician, B. P. Wiesner, put forth an hypothesis that, if true, would provide an explanation for some of the unusual feats described in this chapter: *"I control the activity of my nervous system (and so indirectly control such activities as the movements of my body and the course of my thinking) by the same means as that by which the successful psychokinetic subject controls the fall of the dice or other object."* (491: p. 197)

That this notion is not outdated is underlined by the fact that the world-famous physiologist Sir John Eccles recently suggested much the same idea. In an invited address at the 1976 convention of the Parapsychological Association, he proposed that the simple act of saying a word was actually a form of psychokinesis: "The mind has been able to work upon the brain cells, just slightly changing them. . . . The mind is making these very slight and subtle changes for hundreds of millions of cells, gradually bringing it through and channeling it into the correct target cells to make the movement. And so there is psychokinesis, mind acting upon a material object, namely brain cells. It's extremely weak, but it's effective, because we've learned to use it." (128: pp. 257-258) We are suggesting that athletes are learning in a similar way—haphazardly, if not by design—to extend the reach of the body beyond the confines of the flesh.

What if it is really the mind that is accomplishing these physical feats? What if an athlete can control his muscles the same way that a PK subject in the laboratory can control the throw of a die? If this hypothesis is correct, it removes a mental barrier for if it is the mind that is the prime mover, then the muscles are just as much "outside" the mind as is a die face or the table lamp that Johnny Miller feels we will one day be able to move by mind alone. Or put the other way, the die face or lamp are no more outside the reach of the mind than one's muscles. The literature suggests that a few individuals who are able to perform mind-boggling feats view reality in just this way. Baseball enthusiast Richard Grossinger observes:

> Pitchers have torn muscles, broken bones, been operated on, had ligaments grafted; they have altered everything about their delivery and rhythm that made them a pitcher in the first place. They have come back from rotary cuff surgery, from not being able to lift their arms for a year and a half, and they have won ball-games. Occasionally, like Jim Palmer and Luis Tiant, they have pitched the best baseball of their lives after the actual physical equipment was seemingly taken away. It is almost as though the outer throwing form is an illusion. If you learn how to do it in terms of a strong healthy body, the skill remains, the ability to put it over, long after the body ceases to back it. An inner image of the entire pitching sequence is regenerative, like a reptile limb. (185: p. 32)

The abilities reviewed in this chapter suggest that some of us are demonstrating, in sport, that we can extend our boundaries beyond the confines of our bodies. It appears that the body is not so much the end of sport as the beginning. It is a centering point, a place to start from, but from this sturdy base we are capable of reaching beyond—of fleshing out the spirit in areas where the body cannot reach, initiating movements the eye cannot see, revealing strengths that transcend mere muscles, and exerting energies that can no longer be considered physical in the ordinary sense. In similar fashion, sport may not only be an end in itself, but the beginning of a human unfoldment that will eventually extend the boundaries in all areas of life.

**5
Sport
and
Mysticism**

While reading the stories we have presented so far, you may have wondered about their authenticity. How many of these accounts are like the fisherman's tale in which the fish grows larger with each telling? Does Patsy Neal, for example, exaggerate and sentimentalize her religious experience? (See pp. 133–134.) Did Morehei Uyeshiba's students gradually embellish their teacher's legend through the years? Did Babe Ruth really point to those centerfield bleachers? Sometimes exaggeration is apparent in the storyteller's style, as when mountaineer Frank Smythe exclaims: "Physically you may feel but a cosmic speck of chemicalised dust, but spiritually you will feel great. For is not your vision capable in one glance of piercing the abysses of space? Is not your hearing attuned to an immortal harmony? . . . On a mountain-top a man feels himself to be an entity whose span is timeless, whose scope is magnificent beyond conception, whose birth, whose death are incidental milestones on a splendid road without beginning and without end." (464: p. 12)

Accounts of spiritual awakening, or opening, can be exaggerated through inflated memory after the fact, through sentimentality, through sheer bad writing (there are volumes of purple sporting prose!). But from our many interviews with sportspeople during the past six years, we have learned that the mystical aspects of sport are also deflated and suppressed. The repression of the extraordinary moment, we suspect, is just about as common as its embellishment. In spite of the growing interest in meditation and religion among amateur and professional athletes, in spite of the magazine articles about "sport highs" and the "inner game," people are often apprehensive about the sublime and uncanny aspects of sport.

We believe that people in many fields of activity have trouble accepting such experience—in the modern West at least—because they have no context, no language or philosophy to support it. The world of sport shares this general lack of understanding. Many powerful incidents slip away like Brigadoon because they find no place in the experiencer's ordinary frame of reference.

We have kept this problem in mind during our interviews and literature search. But though we are generally dealing with subjective reality—with stories that may be distorted by denial, exaggeration, or faulty memory—we do have a good deal of objective corroboration of these exceptional events from teammates, spectators, and sportswriters. What emerges from this wealth of material is clear: a large number of participants in a wide variety of sports have reported events remarkably similar to the ones we have described in the preceding chapters.

The Spiritually Evocative Elements of Sport

What is it, then, that evokes this range of experience? What happens on playing fields, mountain heights, or ocean wilderness that doesn't happen (at least as often) in office, classroom, or subway? We think there are certain intrinsic elements in sport that make it a vehicle for spiritual awakening. Let's look at some of these factors.

The Physical and Mental Demands of Sport

As in any discipline, athletes must submit to the rules, requirements and ordeals of their particular sport. To do this, they need to relinquish old patterns. In perfecting their skills, they have to give up habits and responses that impede their performance. To some extent they must acquire (or open to) another nature. And when they do, new powers emerge, new energies are brought to play, new vistas begin to open before them. As we have seen, many people say they are renewed, even reborn, though the old self may return when the sporting event or the season is over.

Giving up old patterns—both mental and physical—is required of the sports participant from the very beginning. Most joggers, for example, have to resist the urge to quit as they exercise lungs, heart, and legs beyond their ordinary capacity. The impulse to stop arises after you have gone only a few hundred yards. But the compensating pleasure of exceeding a limit, the glow of fitness, the sense of pride in overcoming resistance come into play as well. Many will testify to both the pains and the joys that every sport brings from the start.

The pains of runners come in part from the breaking down of fat, muscle, and capillaries so that the body can reform itself for more efficient movement. Thousands of miles of blood vessels are developed on the way to fitness, the balance of hormones is changed, and if you persist, whole groups of muscles are gradually restructured. Attitudes toward fear and discomfort change too. Runners, like most dedicated sports participants, learn to push beyond limits and recognize the unexpected second energy, learn how to endure the nay-saying voices until a newfound strength arrives. "Break-down and build-up"—whether physical, emotional, mental, or spiritual—is the rule in running as it is in most sports.

Sometimes the relinquishment of old patterns involves one's entire sense of self. Mike Spino, the innovative running coach and former distance runner, described such a crisis:

> In the winter of 1967, I was training on dirt and asphalt, paced by a friend who was driving a car. I had intended to run six miles at top speed, but after the first mile I was surprised at how easily I could do it. I had run the first mile in four and a half minutes with little sense of pain or exertion, as if I were carried by a huge momentum. The wet pavement and honking horns were no obstacle at all. My body had no weight or resistance. It began to feel like a skeleton—as if the flesh had been blown off of its bones. I felt like the wind. Daydreams and fantasies disappeared. The only negative feeling was a guilt for being able to do this. When the run was over conversation was impossible, because for a while I didn't know who I was. Was I the one who had been running or the ordinary Mike Spino? I sat down by the roadway and wept. Here I was, having run the entire six miles on a muddy roadside at a four-and-a-half minute pace, which was close to the national record, and I was having a crisis deciding who I was.

Spino's dilemma that day was like the problem the football player on the San Francisco 49'ers had when he admitted his uncanny experiences into consciousness (see Chapter 1). A new self, as it were, had appeared before them, and their old markers of self-identification had suddenly become less certain. When this happens, in sport or anywhere, it is as if pins are pulled loose and floorboards begin to give way. For a while, then, sport is like profound artistic discovery or falling in love or religious awakening. Not only are particular attitudes or bodily structures stretched but the entire self is turned over. Such openings can lead to a fuller life if the athlete understands and accepts what is happening. It's possible to resist the opening, however, especially if there is no one to guide or help you understand the possibilities that beckon.

Sport's Sacred Time and Space

Johan Huizinga, in his classic study of play, *Homo Ludens,* has described the role of boundaries in sport—the arena or magic circle, and the fixed duration in which a game or contest is set.

> Into an imperfect world and into the confusion of life [these boundaries] bring a temporary, a limited perfection. Play demands order absolute and supreme. The least deviation from it "spoils the game," robs it of its character and makes it worthless. The profound affinity between play and order is perhaps the reason why play, as we noted in passing, seems to lie to such a large extent in the field of aesthetics. Play has a tendency to be beautiful. It may be that this aesthetic factor is identical with the impulse to create orderly form, which animates play in all its aspects. The words we use to denote the elements of play belong for the most part to aesthetics, terms with which we try to describe the effects of beauty: tension, poise, balance, contrast, variation, solution, resolution, etc. Play casts a spell over us; it is "enchanting," "captivating." It is invested with the noblest qualities we are capable of perceiving in things: rhythm and harmony. (219: p. 10)

Games often create an order that resembles the cadenced life of ashrams and monasteries, and sporting expeditions are in certain respects like religious pilgrimages. The acts they comprise are invested with special meaning and are pointed toward perfection. Athletes feel the effect of a playing field in their bones. Fenway Park or an Olympic stadium or a famous golf course like St. Andrews can bring a quickening of the spirit, a concentration of energies, a connection with heroes past and future that give performances in these places a heightened quality. And even when there is no stadium or arena involved, sport implicitly creates a sacred time and place. A mountain to be climbed, an ocean to be crossed, or a stretch of countryside to be raced on can summon up significance and power for us simply by being designated the field of adventure. The spatial and temporal boundedness of sport, by ordering and sublimating our energies and by closing off the world's drudgery and confusion, can evoke our spiritual depths like a work of art or a monastic discipline.

Sustained and Focused Attention

Every sport requires concentration, freedom from distraction, and sustained alertness. The development of athletic skill depends on one's ability to focus unbroken attention on the space, objects, and other people involved, and on one's own kinesthetic sense of the body. A wandering mind diminishes ability, whether you are running or bowling, playing football or chess, climbing mountains or skydiving. Success depends on your being wholly present in the action. The greatest athletes are legendary for their powers of concentration. The literature and gossip of every sport is filled with tales about the playing trances of its stars. Billie Jean King writes that when she is playing,

> . . . it's like I'm out there by myself. I've talked with Laver and Rosewall about this, and even Court a little, and on their great days their attitude is exactly the same. I concentrate only on the ball in relationship to the face of my racket, which is a full-time job anyway, since no two balls ever come over the net the same way. I appreciate what my opponent is doing, but in a detached, abstract way, like an observer in the next room. I see her moving to her left or right, but it's almost as though there weren't any real opponent, as though I didn't know—and certainly didn't care— whom I was playing against. (251: p. 197)

British golfer Tony Jacklin describes the "cocoon of concentration" he sometimes finds himself in: "When I'm in this state, this cocoon of concentration, I'm living *fully* in the present, not moving out of it. I'm aware of every half inch of my swing. . . . I'm absolutely engaged, *involved* in what I'm doing at that particular moment. That's the important thing. That's the difficult state to arrive at. It comes and it goes, and the pure fact that you go out on the first tee of a tournament and say, 'I must concentrate today,' is no good. It won't work. It has to already *be* there." (120: p. 30)

Most athletes make a distinction between their usual efforts at concentration and this special kind of playing trance. Call it the "zone," a "cocoon of concentration," a "white moment," or whatever, it brings extraordinary integration and power. The distinction these athletes make between ordinary concentration and such a state resembles the distinction religious teachers make between different levels of meditation.

For instance, in Patanjali's yoga sutras, four levels of attention are described. The first, *pratyahara* (377: p. 171), is the deliberate withdrawal of attention from external objects, drawing the senses with it. (Billie Jean King's blocking everything but the ball from her focus.) In the second state, *dharana* (377: p. 173), the yogi holds his mind steady upon a center of consciousness within the body or upon a particular form outside him. (A runner focusing on his stride or a golfer concentrating on the ball.) The third stage, *dhyana* (377: pp. 173-174), is "an unbroken flow of attention toward the object of contemplation," an effortless absorption beyond "brute will." This resembles the playing trance described by Tony Jacklin and Arthur Ashe. Many athletes, like Jacklin, distinguish ordinary concentration from this seemingly effortless state. In the fourth stage, *samadhi,* "the true nature of the object held in contemplation shines forth, undistorted by the mind of the perceiver." (377: p. 175) Here there is perfect clarity and an effortless sense of unity with whatever is perceived. (Yuri Vlasov's "white moment"? See page 127.)

Many experiences described by athletes share these qualities. The withdrawal of attention from distractions, the deliberate holding of a constant focus, the effortless absorption, the sense of unity and rightness of movement that Jacklin, King, and others describe are not unlike these stages of yogic meditation. The playing trance in sport may not have the stability, penetration, and pervasiveness of the dedicated contemplative's realizations, but there are striking similarities between the two kinds of experience and between the stages in which they develop.

Another way to characterize these deepening levels of concentration is by the amount of time the mind can remain undisturbed by inner or outer distractions. According to the yoga sutras:

It has been said that if the mind can be made to flow uninterruptedly toward the same object for twelve seconds, this may be called concentration. If the mind can continue in that concentration for twelve times twelve seconds (i.e., two minutes and twenty-four seconds), this may be called meditation. If the mind can continue in that meditation for twelve times two minutes and twenty-four seconds (i.e., twenty-eight minutes and forty-eight seconds), this will be the lower *samadhi*. And if the lower *samadhi* can be maintained for twelve times that period (i.e., five hours, forty-five minutes, and thirty-six seconds), this will lead to *nirvikalpa samadhi*. (The profoundest state of ecstasy.) (377: p. 179)

Like yoga, sport invites and reinforces an ever deepening attention to the task at hand. The thousands of miles a distance runner covers, all the shots a golfer makes in practice, the hours each day a gymnast spends perfecting each maneuver lead to moments that resemble religious ecstasy.

But why does focusing our mind and energies do this? Again we turn to the yoga sutras: Ignorance and suffering come, they say, from a false identification with the passing objects of experience, through a distraction from our deepest source. By quieting the surface mind, however, by withdrawing our assent to the world's random turning, we can perceive our true identity with spirit. This identity with spirit, though, need not be named as such to be effective. It is an experience that transcends naming, something we intuitively recognize even if we don't have words or concepts to describe it. An old Indian story tells about a thief who, while pretending he was a yogi in order to avoid arrest, became enlightened. It didn't matter how his meditation got started, only where it ended. It is like that with some athletes who concentrate simply for the sake of their sport: they catch glimpses of spiritual freedom through their discipline and feel the call of the interior life.

Detachment from Results

Because the gathering of energies we have just described takes place in the heat of competition, in the midst of all the ups and downs that come with winning and losing, the sports participant often acquires a certain detachment from results. If an athlete cannot bear to lose or gets overinflated from winning, he or she is less likely to succeed. So games and contests teach a centeredness in action, a grace under pressure. Such inner poise and disinterest are fundamental to every spiritual teaching, for without them the richness of awareness is impeded. Detachment from the results of one's actions facilitates a quieting of the mind that makes way for the kinds of experience we examined in the preceding chapters. If the mind is agitated and the emotions in turmoil, there is no room for the extraordinary peace, the sense of power, and the joy that so many sports participants report.

The concentration of energies and awareness demanded by sport is heightened, we believe, because it takes place in the midst of winning and losing, in the midst of dramatic ups and downs. The participant who perseveres in a sport has to learn the poignant lesson—at some level at least—that there is an interior grace that transcends the world's uncertain results. Sport is likely to instruct us in the ancient wisdom that by losing our lives we gain them. A famous spiritual teacher writes: "You may take this for the truth, that when a free mind is really disinterested, God is compelled to come into it." (129: p. 84)

Sport's Creative and Integrative Power

Whether you're learning to run the mile, lower your golf score, or scale a mountain, sport demands a creative joining of skills and capacities. Willpower, awareness, imagination, emotion, the senses, the intellect, and motor control must all be harmonized for top performance. Dreams and reveries come into play too. New alignments of body and mind seem to take place in the middle of the night, and the process becomes continuous through waking and sleeping. (17: pp. 81-82; 46: p. 60; 89: p. 11) Successful athletes make an enormous number of psychological and physiological connections that lie beyond the scope of verbal awareness. Their creativity is very close to creativity in art, science, and religion in this regard. (66: pp. 155-162) For example, Olympic hurdle champion David Hemery writes, "In the course of any season, the athlete will face all of the following: defeat and victory; sickness and health; tension and relaxation; degrees of pain, doubt, disappointment and despair, as well as satisfaction and even ecstasy." (200: p. 186) In his book *Another Hurdle* he describes the way his sport obsessed him day and night, through winning and losing, pain and health. He found himself perfecting his ability at home as well as on the track, in his dreams and in his training sessions.

Lee Evans, the 400 meters Olympic champion and world record holder, has talked to us about the power of the subconscious mind to search out flaws in racing style and correct them. Working with Bud

Winter, the great sprint coach at San Jose State College, in the late 1960s Evans used self-hypnosis and mental practice for several years while on his way to championships and world records. In practicing for the 1968 Olympics, he visualized every step of the 400 meter race until he saw "each stride he would take." By repeating this exercise again and again, he says, his style and pacing got better and the overall flow of his performance was perfected. The world record he set in that race still stands, ten years later. In conversations with me (Murphy), he has talked about dreams and waking reveries in which new ideas, images, and feelings about his running would appear, sometimes unexpectedly. As I listened to Evans describe this process I couldn't help thinking about descriptions that certain artists and scientists have given of their discoveries. The French mathematician Henri Poincare, for example, discovered part of the Fuchsian functions as he stepped onto a bus: in the time it took his foot to pass from the ground to the first step a whole field of mathematics appeared before him. Kekule discovered the formula for the benzene molecule in a dream. Coleridge wrote *Kubla Khan* after hearing it in a sleep that was stimulated by the opiate laudanum. The history of artistic and scientific discovery is filled with sudden insights of this kind, delivered like lightning from unconscious levels of the mind. (171, 257) The world of sport is filled with similar stories, because like art and science it can engage the imagination and the will down to their deepest roots. For David Hemery, Lee Evans, and other athletes, this all-involving process is part of sport's fascination.

But psychological integration is more than *intra*-personal, for it always involves others. Even in the most individualistic sports like running or mountaineering, friendship and teamwork are involved. Without them sport loses part of its beauty. Just as it is fundamental to all religious life, cooperation with others has been one of the most honored of sporting virtues. Football player Bill Curry told George Plimpton:

> I always knew that if I quit, my relationship with those friends would be different. Football is a very exclusive fraternity. Every retired player I've talked to, without exception, has said, when I asked if he missed it: "No, I don't miss it at all. Who wants to go out there and sweat?" Then they get a funny look on their face and they say, "But I tell you what, I miss the guys." (387: p. 93)

Sport's Exploration of Human Limits

Sport proliferates, one can argue, out of a drive in the human race to realize more and more of its bodily possibilities. One of our most fundamental drives is to know and dramatize the richness of physical life. So people run, jump, swim, and fly, surf on 20-foot waves, dive to the ocean depths, glide on wings grown smaller and smaller, or climb into dangerous caves or up the most precipitous mountains. Where will this proliferation of athletics end? To what adventures and extremes will it lead us?

In this, sport is like spiritual adventure the world over. When you read the Indian and Tibetan scriptures, for example, you find an immense variety of ways for self-exceeding. Thousands of mental states, endless varieties of love, and countless supernormal powers are dramatized in the lives of the saints. Both sport and the spiritual life grow out of our human urge to express the richness of existence.

The demands our games make on us take many forms, for each has its own particular set of archetypes, or ideals. Mountaineering and race car driving, for example, require very different sets of capacities. Each stretches us in a special way and aligns us with particular dimensions of experience. And in no other field of human activity is there such a proliferation of specialized physiques. For as athletics have developed in the modern world, they have required an ever greater variety of skills and body structure to support them—whether it is the muscular frame of a 270-pound defensive tackle, the elastic joints of a gymnast, the prodigious cardiopulmonary system of a marathon runner, or the steady hand of an archer. Never before have there been so many experiments with the body's limits.

This vast cultivation and redesign of the body—if we may call it that—provides an unprecedented laboratory for exploring the limits of human possibility. In this, we think sport points beyond itself. For it is possible to imagine an historic adventure in human transformation that might arise in part from the experiments and achievements of athletics. We will say more about this possibility in our concluding chapter.

Sport's Ability to Command Long-Term Commitment

The long-term involvement that sport commands from so many people provides a unique basis for spiritual adventure because without sustained commitment the intricate, far-reaching changes of mind and physique that such an enterprise requires are simply impossible. In most religious teachings it is said that no lasting realization can be achieved without many years of steady practice. Most teachers have said that enlightenment costs no less than everything. Many athletes make that kind of commitment to their sport, at least for a part of their lives.

The spiritually evocative elements we have discussed—long-term commitment, sustained concentration, creativity, self-integration, being in sacred times and places, and stretching to the limits of one's capacity—are common to both sport and religious discipline. These similarities between the two kinds of activity often lead to the same kinds of experience. In the pages that follow, we will explore the similarities between spiritual and athletic experience more closely.

The Perennial Philosophy

In the lore of Eastern philosophy and yoga, in the writings of mystics from every great religion, and in the accounts of modern seers there exists a coherent body of insight that often corresponds with the spiritual experiences of sports participants. The resemblance between this ancient, well-established knowledge and the stories sportspeople tell are sometimes dramatic and compelling.

Aldous Huxley, borrowing from the philosopher Leibnitz, called this ancient knowledge the Perennial Philosophy, because it has arisen repeatedly in almost every society for the past three thousand years and because rudiments of it exist even in stone-age cultures. It appears in the writings of Taoist, Hindu, Buddhist, Greek, Moslem, Jewish, and Christian mystics. And in modern times it reappears each century, surviving every period of skepticism and despair. Everywhere and always in human history it has possessed a core of fundamental agreement, though the intellectual forms, the language, the ritual and practices in which it has appeared have differed.

Let's look at some of its central tenets, for they help us understand the extraordinary aspects of sport we are examining. This is not a complete summary of the perennial philosophy, but it is adequate, we think, to show some of the parallels that exist between the two fields of experience.

The Fundamental Reality

The central perception of the perennial philosophy is that there is a fundamental reality, godhead, or ground of existence that transcends the ordinary world, yet exists in it. However separate in appearance they may be, the individual, the universe, and the transcendent divinity are essentially one. This spiritual reality is the source of all consciousness and can be known directly—either spontaneously as in sports or through deliberate practices like prayer and yoga—because we are secretly joined with It already.

> That moves and that moves not,
> That is far and the same is near.
> That is within all this and
> That is also outside all this.
>
> —*Isha Upanishad*

> One Nature, perfect and pervading, circulates in all natures,
> One Reality, all-comprehensive, contains within itself all
>   realities.
> The one Moon reflects itself wherever there is a sheet of water,
> And all the moons in the waters are embraced within the one
>   Moon.
> The Dharma-body [the Absolute] of all the Buddhas enters
>   into my own being.
> And my own being is found in union with theirs. . . .

> The Inner Light is beyond praise and blame;
> Like space it knows no boundaries,
> Yet it is even here, within us, ever retaining its serenity and
>   fullness.
>
> —Yung-chia Ta-shih
>
> (221: p. 8)

These statements from Hindu and Buddhist teachers point to the eternal Reality that is all things and transcends all things. See how they resemble this account of Charles Lindbergh of his epic flight to Paris:

While I'm staring at the instruments, during an unearthly age of time, both conscious and asleep, the fuselage behind me becomes filled with ghostly presences—vaguely outlined forms, transparent, moving, riding weightless with me in the plane. I feel no surprise at their coming. There's no suddenness to their appearance. Without turning my head, I see them as clearly as though in my normal field of vision. There's no limit to my sight—my skull is one great eye, seeing everywhere at once. . . .

All sense of substance leaves. There's no longer weight to my body, no longer hardness to the stick. The feeling of flesh is gone. I become independent of physical laws—of food, of shelter, of life. I'm almost one with these vaporlike forms behind me, less tangible than air, universal as aether. I'm still attached to life; they, not at all; but at any moment some thin band may snap and there'll be no difference between us. . . .

I'm on the border line of life and a greater realm beyond, as though caught in the field of gravitation between two planets, acted on by forces I can't control, forces too weak to be measured by any means at my command, yet representing powers incomparably stronger than I've ever known. . . . .

Death no longer seems the final end it used to be, but rather the entrance to a new and free existence which includes all space, all time.

Am I now more man or spirit? Will I fly my airplane on to Europe and live in flesh as I have before, feeling hunger, pain, and cold, or am I about to join these ghostly forms, become a consciousness in space, all-seeing, all-knowing, unhampered by materialistic fetters of the world? (293: pp. 389-90)

"My skull is one great eye, seeing everywhere at once"—what a vivid image of his experience. "Am I about to . . . become a consciousness in space, all-seeing, all-knowing, unhampered by materialistic fetters of the world?"*

---

* Lindbergh did not describe his experience in his first book, *We, Pilot and Plane,* published in 1927. *The Spirit of St. Louis* was published in 1953, 26 years later. Like several athletes we have talked to, it took him many years to acknowledge and appreciate the mystical dimensions of his adventure. His posthumous book *Autobiography of Values* (291) reveals more of his feelings and insights regarding these matters.

Lindbergh's description of his experience could almost be a paraphrase of certain religious scriptures. The apprehension of a greater realm beyond this one, the feeling of independence from his body and physical laws, and the sense that he is acted upon by "powers incomparably stronger than I've ever known" arise from the same realization that pervades the perennial philosophy.

Figure skater Toller Cranston described a performance when "the audience was still, watching intently, anticipating. [At one point] . . . I felt an electric shock run through the crowd. They understood. In that brief instant we fused. Reality no longer existed and time became suspended. We opened the gateway to tomorrow that night and passed through. We could feel it; we could feel the birth pangs. It was something beyond love, beyond reality." (365: p. 10)

The Provisional Reality of the Ordinary World

Cranston's experience that night was more real, he said, than everyday existence. It was something *beyond reality*.

This shift in one's apprehension and assignment of reality occurs in sport, sometimes for fleeting moments, sometimes for hours or days following an experience like Cranston's. Several people have told us that the world "seemed like a dream" after a particularly uplifting game or sporting expedition. For a while after these events, they say, everything seemed unimportant compared to their spiritual realizations. Listening to their accounts, we have been reminded of statements by mystics that the world seems illusory after illumination.* This sense of illusion comes in part from a spontaneous reordering of priorities and attachments: suddenly God or Spirit is more important than one's ordinary worldly concerns.

But as spiritual insight develops, the world comes to be seen as an aspect or manifestation of the Reality that once seemed to transcend it. In the language of Buddhism, "Samsara [the ordinary world] *is* nirvana." In order to arrive at this sense of the Divine in everything, however, one must live the right kind of life.

---

* William James, *The Varieties of Religious Experience* (227); see especially "The Sick Soul," pp. 125–163, and "The Divided Self," pp. 163–186. In *The Collected Works of Sri Aurobindo* (20), vol. 22, pp. 39–69, Sri Aurobindo's letters describe the shifting sense of reality in the practice of yoga.

The Need for Discipline

Many athletes have trouble recapturing peak moments because they have trouble incorporating the meaning of these experiences into the rest of their lives. Former quarterback John Brodie describes this problem succinctly:

> Football players and athletes generally get into this kind of being or beingness—call it what you will—more often than is generally recognized. But they often lose it after a game or after a season is over. They often don't have a workable philosophy or understanding to support the kind of thing they get into while they are playing. They don't have the words for it. So after a game you see some of them coming down, making fools of themselves sometimes, coming way down in their tone level. But during the game they come way up. A missing ingredient for many people, I guess, is that they don't have a supporting philosophy or discipline for a better life. (343: p. 22)

To hold these realizations, this "being or beingness," we must live in tune with their truth and practice some kind of spiritual discipline. St. John of the Cross (1542–1591), wrote:

> He who interrupts the course of his spiritual exercises and prayer is like a man who allows a bird to escape from his hand; he can hardly catch it again. (221: p. 292)

Saint Francis de Sales (1567–1622):

> I am glad you make a fresh beginning daily; there is no better means of attaining . . . than by continually beginning again. (221: p. 293)

And the German mystic Meister Eckhart (1260–1328):

> I tell you that no one can experience this birth of God in the soul without a mighty effort. No one can attain this birth unless he can withdraw his mind entirely from things. (221: p. 292)

These statements are not unlike the passionate praise of discipline that comes from many athletes. Yuri Vlasov, champion Russian weightlifter, told reporter Robert Lipsyte:

> At the peak of tremendous and victorious effort . . . while the blood is pounding in your head, all suddenly becomes quiet within you. Everything seems clearer and whiter than ever before, as if great spotlights had been turned on.
>
> At that moment you have the conviction that you contain all the power in the world, that you are capable of everything, that you have wings. There is no more precious moment in life than this, the white moment, *and you will work very hard for years just to taste it again.* (295: p. 280)

Surfing champion Midget Farrelly described his passion for perfection:

> That is what I'm after—perfection. Give me perfect timing, perfect balance, perfect co-ordination, perfect movement, and the perfect wave to try them on—as big a wave as possible, as long a wall as possible, the surface as smooth as possible, the wave as hollow and as cleanly peeling as possible, and so fast that I would be just able to ride it. That would be perfection.
>
> Maybe perfection can never be reached. But I hope that by practicing continually and by gaining more and more experience I'll get to know enough about waves to leave me free to concentrate on the board. And if I know the board, I'll be able to concentrate on what I want to do on it. And by the time I've reached the peak of my surfing life I should be able to make one movement on the board instead of two—drop down the waveface once instead of twice.
>
> You've got to regulate, moderate, and keep refining everything you do. And all the time you keep pushing yourself, trying to push yourself right up to the limit, and beyond it. (141: pp. 27–28)

Knowing and Expressing the Deeper Perfection

"You will work very hard for years just to taste it again"—athletes often give this reason for training hard and long. And work hard they must, to achieve the prodigies of physical excellence we have described. An old Buddhist story has it that one cannot achieve enlightenment until he wants it as badly as a person held under water wants air. Some athletes train as arduously as religious monastics. Topflight gymnasts practice eight hours a day for decades. Distance runners run up to 200 miles a week. Many swimmers live through agonies, both in practice and in competition, and weightlifters often measure their progress by the amount of pain they can endure.

This willingness to suffer so much for their sport can be understood as a concentrated expression of the universal human drive to know and express the deeper perfection and beauty we secretly sense. That deeper perfection is more important to many athletes than prizes or applause. Billie Jean King writes in her autobiography:

> It's a perfect combination of . . . violent action taking place in an atmosphere of total tranquillity. . . . When it happens I want to stop the match and grab the microphone and shout, '*That's* what it's all about.' Because it is. It's not the big prize I'm going to win at the end of the match, or anything else. It's just having done something that's totally pure and having experienced the perfect emotion, and I'm always sad that I can't communicate that feeling right at the moment it's happening. I can only hope the people realize what's going on. (251: p. 201)

William Willis expressed a similar feeling when he tried to account for his sailing alone on a raft across the Pacific Ocean:

> This was not a stunt—not merely an adventure. And I did not want to prove any scientific theory, or discover and set up any new course of any kind for others to follow. To me, this voyage was something much more—it was a pilgrimage to the shrine of my philosophy. Call it an adventure of the spirit. On this voyage I wanted to prove—had to prove to myself—that I had followed the right star throughout my life. (524: p. 15)

Ben Hogan's devotion to practice is a legend among golf professionals. His friend and fellow player, Jimmy Demaret, describes an episode that typified Hogan's discipline:

He'll practice like no one else I've ever known. He loves to just stand there and hit golf balls. No man ever lived who has hit as many golf balls as Hogan. He won't think of going out for a round, even a meaningless one with friends, unless he's hit some practice shots. And practice for Hogan may mean hitting as many as a thousand balls in five or six hours. . . .

In the first round of the Rochester Open in 1941, Hogan burned up the course, shooting a record 64. He had ten birdies in that score, but the poor guy took a six on the par four seventeenth. I had a 69, which I thought good enough, and I sat around with the fellows in the clubhouse until it was almost nighttime, gabbing and having a drink or two.

When I went out to the car to drive home, I noticed a late evening eager beaver all alone on the practice tee hitting wood shots. I didn't have to be told it was Hogan. I walked over to him.

"What are you trying to do, man?" I asked. "You had ten birdies today. Why, the officials are still inside talking about it. They're thinking of putting a limit on you."

Ben gave me that dead-serious look of his. "You know, Jimmy, if a man can shoot ten birdies, there's no reason why he can't shoot eighteen. Why can't you birdie every hole on the course?" And then his face took on a look of real anguish and he wailed, "And how about that terrible seventeenth?" (109: pp. 159-160)

The Essential Ecstasy

To the eye of the spiritually awakened, the world is filled with beauty and adventure. In the words of the yaqui sorcerer Don Juan, ". . . it is brimming with possibility every minute." This in spite of suffering and discord, in spite of ignorance and general human failure.

Sri Aurobindo, the modern Indian mystic and philosopher, reflects the vision of seers throughout history when he writes:

There must be something in us—much vaster, profounder, truer than the superficial consciousness—which takes delight impartially in all external being and enables it to persevere through all labours, sufferings and ordeals. . . .

In our ordinary life this truth is hidden from us or only dimly glimpsed at times or imperfectly held and conceived. But if we learn to live within, we infallibly awaken to this presence within us which is our more real self, a presence profound, calm, joyous . . . of which the world is not the master. (22: pp. 96–97)

This idea that there is something profounder in us fits many athletes' reports of inward knowing and transcendence—they sense something that "secretly supports the superficial being and enables it to persevere through all labours, sufferings and ordeals." Vlasov's statement that there is no more precious moment in life than the "white moment"—and that a person will work for years to achieve it—points toward the essential inner joy Aurobindo describes.

At the same time, sport is filled with a sense of play and adventure. More than anything, we think, this mix of ecstasy and playfulness gives sport its hold on so many people. More than many other human activities, sport reveals this essential truth of existence as it is perceived in the perennial philosophy. As one of the Indian scriptures says, "From Delight all these creatures are born; In that Delight they live and move; to that Delight they will return." Ernest Hemingway thought the bullfight dramatized this truth. He tells us of the "complete faena [the final part of the fight]; the faena that takes a man out of himself . . . that gives him an ecstasy that is, while momentary, as profound as any religious ecstasy." (201: p. 212)

The essential joy of sport, so closely allied to that secret delight which "supports the superficial being," often emerges in the ordeal of athletic training and performance. A friend told us about a time he ran for five hours around the deck of a ship—a distance he later estimated to be more than 30 miles.

The discomfort grew extreme, grew into pain, but I stayed with it, said that it was all right, wondered if there was anything on the other side. After awhile the pain subsided. . . . Then it returned as before, and I climbed into it again, allowed it to be OK. Then once again it slipped away. By this time I must have run at least three hours in circles on the deck of the ship. I was beginning to lose touch with my body, floating away to distant places. . . . There were thoughts of grandeur and supreme power; I could do anything. Then after a long time I began to encounter a new experience, a kind of vibrant numbness. A dull tingling throughout my whole body as if one of my limbs were coming awake after the circulation had been cut off. *There was great pain but also ecstasy.* I knew that I should stop but I couldn't: I couldn't let go of that power and joy.

Athletic ordeals like this, in which pain is consciously invited so that it might turn into strength and joy, resemble the ordeals of religious contemplatives. In Zen Buddhism there are periods of practice that last for weeks, during which a monk might sit in meditation for twelve hours a day or more. The pain and distraction that arise during these sessions are sometimes overwhelming, but depths of knowing, joy, and freedom emerge from the experience to overcome the agony. Dervish dancing rituals sometimes last for many days without stopping. Yogis may sit in the same place for months. Sport and religious practice both embrace ordeal in the service of illumination and freedom. By consciously transforming pain into delight, the athlete begins to awaken to the inner presence "of which the world is not the master."

Distance runners are notorious for the pains they put themselves through. Champion miler Herb Elliot says that his coach, Percy Cerutty, helped him to world records "not so much by improving my technique, but by releasing in my mind and soul a power that I only vaguely thought existed. 'Thrust against pain,' Percy told me. . . . He introduced me to every book about Francis of Assisi and said, '*Walk towards suffering. Love suffering. Embrace it.*'" (133: p. 38) (Italics ours.)

It's easy to see the love of play and adventure exemplified in sport. But the athlete's love of pain and ordeal is more mysterious. One key to the mystery comes with the ancient mystical insight that a fundamental delight exists within or behind all suffering.

Knowledge by Identity

In the *Tao Te Ching*, the founding scripture of Taoism, it is said that the wise man can know the whole world without leaving his room. Teachers in many religious traditions have insisted that this is the case, that the discovery of our spiritual depths is a doorway to knowledge of the world at large. In a famous Indian metaphor, the universe is compared to the god Indra's "net of jewels," in which each jewel—that is, each person or facet of existence—is present in every other.*

> One Reality, all-comprehensive, contains within itself all realities.
> The one Moon reflects itself wherever there is a sheet of water.
> And all the moons in the waters are embraced within the one
>   Moon.
> The Dharma-body [the Absolute] of all the Buddhas enters into
>   my own being. . . .Yung-chia Ta-shih (221: p. 8)

The Roman mystic and philosopher Plotinus expressed it this way:

> Each being contains in itself the whole intelligible world. Therefore All is everywhere. Each is there All, and All is each. Man as he now is has ceased to be the All. But when he ceases to be a mere ego, he raises himself again and penetrates the whole world. (221: p. 5)

Because we are usually attached to ordinary appearances, we have little or no access to this fundamental order. We need to penetrate beneath appearances if we are to find the all-encompassing knowledge we secretly possess. Meister Eckhart wrote:

> When is a man in mere understanding? I answer, "When a man sees one thing separated from another." And when is a man above mere understanding? That I can tell you: "When a man sees All in all, then a man stands beyond mere understanding." (221: p. 57)

Every mystical tradition refers to a knowledge-by-identity that transcends all particular kinds of information to an integral insight

---

* The scientific equivalent today is the hologram. In every section of a hologram there exists a miniature duplicate of the entire picture. Stanford's Karl Pribram and other brain researchers believe that the brain operates largely on holographic principles. [See *The Silent Pulse*, by George Leonard. (278)]

through which one knows the world's essential secret. But there are more mundane kinds of knowledge that derive from it: some mystics, it is said, can read another person's mind and heart, can divine the secrets of nature, can sense what is happening in other times and places. To make this practical kind of knowledge accessible, however, the seer has to have a mind prepared to absorb these particular items. It takes the artist's trained sensibility or the scientist's immersion in the pertinent scientific data to translate the essential knowledge by identity into artistic or scientific discovery. Athletes, it seems, also reach into this knowing to accomplish extraordinary feats. D. T. Suzuki, the famous Japanese scholar and translator of Zen Buddhist texts, quotes a Japanese swordsman:

> When the identity is realized, I as swordsman see no opponent confronting me and threatening to strike me. I seem to transform myself into the opponent, and every movement he makes as well as every thought he conceives are felt as if they were all my own and I intuitively . . . know when and how to strike him. (479: p. 206)

In her book *Sport and Identity,* physical education professor Patsy Neal describes an experience she had competing in the Free-Throw Championship at the National AAU Basketball Tournament as a college freshman. She had practiced strenuously for the event and knew she was capable of scoring well, but was too nervous to do well in the early rounds of competition. On the night before the last round she prayed for help and tried to envision a sense of calm while surrounded by the spectators, but images of failure defeated her efforts. Finally, she fell asleep. She writes:

> But then a strange thing happened in my sleep. Sometime during the night, I had a dream. I was shooting the free-throws, and each time the ball fell through the goal, the net would change to the image of Christ. It was as though *I* was flowing into the basket instead of the ball. I felt endless, unhampered . . . and in some way I was connected to the image of Christ that kept flowing from the basket. The sensation was that of transcending *everything.* I was more than I was. I was a particle flowing into *all* of life. It seems almost profane to try to describe the feeling because words are so very inadequate.

The next day, I still had the feeling when I woke. I felt as though I was *floating* through the day, not just living it. That evening, when I shot my free-throws in the finals, I was probably the calmest I have ever been in my life. I didn't . . . see or hear the crowd. It was only me, the ball, and the basket. The number of baskets I made really had no sense of importance to me at the time. The only thing that really mattered was what I *felt*. But even so, I would have found it hard to miss even if I had wanted to.

. . . I know now what people mean when they speak of a "state of grace." I was in a state of grace, and if it were in my power to maintain what I was experiencing at that point in time, I would have given up everything in my possession in preference to that sensation. (350: p. 167)

She won the championship, missing only two baskets out of fifty. As a result of this and related experiences, she says, "I *know* God exists, regardless of the name we give Him, or the way we describe the way He works." (350: p. 169)

What a beautiful series of images!—all the more powerful, we think, because of Neal's youthful naiveté. She flowed into the basket, which had assumed the face of Christ, and performed miraculously well. Could there be a clearer, less embellished example of knowledge by identity? But we are stretching a point, you might argue. To find union with Christ shooting baskets! We might answer with Saint Francis de Sales:

God requires a faithful fulfilment of the merest trifle given us to do, rather than the most ardent aspiration to things to which we are not called.

Or with Saint Francis of Assisi that God can be served and known in our simplest act or loving gesture.

Athletes often communicate with one another in ways that seem to surpass ordinary connections, in ways that have the flavor of knowledge by identity. Pitching great Sandy Koufax tells us about the extraordinary rapport he had with catcher John Roseboro. He recalls it as his most vivid memory of the 1963 World Series:

As I got the ball back and began to look in for the sign, I thought to myself: I'd like to take something off my curve ball. . . .

Now why does a thought like that come to you? A change-up curve is exactly what you don't throw Mantle, particularly in a spot where it can cost you a ball game. Change-up curves are what Mantle hits out of ball parks. I hadn't thrown a change-up in the entire game, as far as I could remember. And at the same moment that the thought came into my mind, there flickered the answering thought: But how will I explain why I threw it if he hits it out of here?

I know it isn't brave, noble, or professional to worry about being second-guessed. It's just human.

And while the thought was still half formed in my mind, I was looking down toward the plate, and John Roseboro was putting down two fingers, the sign for the curve. He was putting them down hesitantly, though, so hesitantly that I had the feeling there was something more he wanted to tell me, something that couldn't be communicated by means of a sign. Normally he'd pull the fingers right back. This time he left the fingers there for a couple of seconds and then, slowly, still hesitantly, he began to wiggle them, the sign to take something off it.

As soon as I saw the fingers wiggle, I began to nod my head emphatically. I could see John begin to smile behind the mask, and then the fingers began to wiggle faster, as if he were saying to me, "Sandy baby, you don't know how glad I am that you see it this way too."

As it was, I copped out just a little. I did take something off my normal curve, but I didn't throw it real slow. It was a good pitch, though. It broke right down in there for a called third strike.

As soon as we hit the clubhouse, I grabbed Roseboro. "What was the matter, John?" I said. "You seemed a little hesitant about wiggling the fingers on Mantle." And he grinned back and said, "I wanted to call it, but I was thinking: How are we ever going to explain a change-curve if he hits it out?"

That's how close the rapport between us can get. Not only did we have the same idea at the same moment, we even had the same thoughts about what could happen back in the clubhouse.
(260: pp. 213-215)

There are enduring legends about the uncanny rapport among skiers and climbers lost in the mountains or wilderness, among basketball players, rowers, and participants in other sports. Certain rodeo riders even claim they achieve oneness with bucking bulls and horses. Many kinds of knowing that develop in sport clearly resemble the knowledge by identity that is a central tenet of the traditional mystic teaching.

The Richness of the Inner World

As we have seen, a wide variety of spiritual experience emerges in sport—moments of preternatural calm and stillness, feelings of detachment and freedom, states filled with invincible force. These experiences induce a wide range of extraordinary perceptions, including changes in time and space, apparent clairvoyance and telepathy, and glimpses of disembodied entities. This richness of experience is paralleled in the mystical traditions by the knowledge that ordinary human nature opens into a vast and complex inner world. Various metaphors have illustrated this fact of spiritual life. In the Greek myth of the Minotaur the path to transformation led through the labyrinth; the seeker, like Theseus, had to find his way with the help of Ariadne's golden thread (which symbolized a teacher's leading). The soul was often pictured as a mansion (Saint Teresa's *Interior Castle*) or as a Magic Theatre (in Herman Hesse's *Steppenwolf*), in which one space opened into many others. Hindu and Buddhist writings describe a multitude of inner worlds. As Sri Aurobindo writes, we

> . . . have not learned to distinguish the different parts of our being; for these are usually lumped together simply as "mind." . . . Therefore [we] do not understand our own states and actions. . . . It is part of the foundation of yoga to become conscious of the great complexity of our nature. (20: vol. 22, p. 233)

To the uninitiated, this complexity may increase the spiritual world's sense of strangeness. The 49'er lineman we described in Chapter 1 was estranged from his inner experience in part by its teeming unpredictability. There had been more than one uncanny event in his playing career—including a disembodied voice and a perception of other players' changing their size and shape! The multiplicity of these uninvited perceptions contributed to his confusion about them. But an experienced spiritual teacher might have told him that all this strangeness was a sign of inner richness, that perhaps he was gifted for the inner life.

Another veteran of the National Football League, former St. Louis Cardinal linebacker David Meggyesey (317), fell into the labyrinth of the interior life during his playing days, but he has boldy gone on to explore it. His adventure began during a practice game against the Minnesota Vikings when he received a blow to the head. In a semi-dazed state, he sat on the sidelines and watched the setting sun beyond the stadium. He felt "an eerie calm and beauty," and had an impression of "outlines wavering gently in the fading light." In this pervasive sense of the uncanny and marvelous, he began to see "auras around some of the players." The experience helped trigger other strange experiences that season. In another game he found himself playing in "a kind of trance where I could sense the movements of the running backs a split second before they happened." With this heightened sense of anticipation he played a brilliant game.

But this kind of brilliance was to lead him beyond football. His unusual experiences during that football season have opened into a more complete understanding and practice. One inner space led to another. The spontaneous richness of these events led him into yoga and other disciplines, and he has finally evolved his own path through the adventures of the inner life.

The Subtle Body

When David Meggyesey saw auras during that football game he was beginning to perceive something that has often appeared in the work of religiously inspired artists. The golden halos and mandorlas in Christian art, the flames that encircle Japanese deities, the explosions of light from the bodies of Indian saints are all renderings of something actually seen by religious artists and yogis. Sri Aurobindo writes:

> The lights one sees in yogic concentration are the lights of various powers or forces of the higher consciousness. . . . They are not hallucinations. They indicate an opening of the inner vision.

Lights are very often the first things seen in yoga. They indicate the action or movement of subtle forces belonging to different planes—the nature of the force depending on the color and shade of the light. (20: vol. 23, p. 936)

Athletes—especially in the martial arts—sometimes report perception of light and subtle energy. Denise McCluggage, in a book entitled *Centered Skiing*, describes an experience she had at a basketball game:

A few years ago I saw a basketball game that was a fascinating network of visible energy, thanks perhaps in equal part to my squinting eyesight and to an intervening haze between my seat and the playing floor. . . . Bright cords of varying width connected the Golden State Warriors at their middle. The lines all emanated from Rick Barry, making him look like something straight out of Castaneda. Rick was glowingly, obviously, the hub of the team that night. The changing thicknesses of the cords extending from him indicated where his next pass was going, even when he was looking in another direction. The ball followed a remarkably predictable path down shining corridors of energy. (302: pp. 20-21)

In the lore of the perennial philosophy in both the East and the West, auras, halos, filaments of energy, and similar phenomena are considered aspects of a subtle body we all possess. Hierocles of Alexandria, a fifth century philosopher, mentions this in commenting on Pythagorian mystical practice:

Together with the discipline (*askesis*) of virtue and the recovery of truth, he shall also be diligent in the purification of his radiant (*augoeides*) body, which the Chaldean Oracles also call the subtle vehicle of the soul. (316: p. 65)

Through the practice of a transformative discipline one can learn to sense this second body and can at times completely disengage it from the physical body. There is a large literature on the subject of disengagement or "out-of-body" experience. As we have seen in Chapter 3, this also happens in sport.

Another phenomenon related to the subtle body is the perception of disembodied entities. The stories of Estcourt and Scott about the

British ascent of Mount Everest in 1975 include encounters with phantom climbers. Joshua Slocum, the first man to circumnavigate the globe alone, saw a phantom during his epic voyage. The loneliness, fatigue, and intensity induced by voyages like Slocum's or climbs like Estcourt's and Scott's (see Chapter 3) often trigger such visions. They are, of course, generally brushed aside as hallucinations because our modern Western outlook denies their reality.

The strange energies some athletes feel in the midst of a game, the uncanny suspension, out-of-body experience, and perception of disembodied entities we described in Chapters 3 and 4 all can be understood as aspects of the subtle body as it is described in the contemplative literature. The awareness of this energy can be cultivated. Several martial arts teach us to feel and manipulate the *ki* (or energy) that is ordinarily unperceived by us. We will examine some of these disciplines in the next chapter.

Exceptional Powers

We have seen how sport evokes exceptional physical and mental control, mastery of pain, acuity of sense perception, apparent extrasensory ability, and feats of extraordinary strength and endurance. The range of these powers is immense, and it seems to be growing as more sports are invented or old sports are made more difficult. Mountain climbers, for example, are making ascents once considered impossible. Spelunkers are going into more inaccessible and dangerous caves. Skydivers make more and more perilous jumps. Everywhere in sport, participants are developing new and more advanced skills as technique improves and as more exact analysis is brought to bear on the structure of the human body and the dynamics of physical movement.

Biomechanics (the study of human motion), kinesiology, filmed studies of bodily movement, and physiological analysis have grown in recent decades to further our understanding of physical capacity and its development. But in spite of these new sciences certain powers are still poorly understood, among them the kinds of experience we have been examining. Once again, we believe that the spiritual traditions can come to our aid, for they have described and catalogued many of these exceptional powers. The Hindu and Buddhist scriptures are especially helpful in this regard.

The Sanskrit words *siddhi* and *vibhuti* are technical terms of Hindu and Buddhist spiritual practice that have been used in Indian teachings since the first millennium before Christ. The two terms are roughly synonymous—the first usually translated as "power," the latter as "perfection." Both refer to the wide range of capacities that spiritual practice can evoke, from realizations of various aspects of the Divinity to specific abilities like the mastery of pain or the ability to read minds at a distance. Taken together as they appear in the various Indian scriptures the *vibhutis* and *siddhis* provide the largest inventory of extraordinary human potentials the world has ever seen. They include all the sporting powers we have looked at and many, many more.

Several years ago, when I (Murphy) began to see how many strange things appeared in places as unlikely as a golf game, I began to play with the notion that sport had a genius for evoking the old yogic powers. By comparing lists of the traditional *siddhis* with lists of powers described to me by sports participants I came up with some striking similarities. In the pages that follow we present the same kind of comparative list to show how suggestive the *siddhi* idea can be for our understanding of exceptional athletic abilities. In some cases, just naming these powers can lead to their recognition. The *siddhi* or *vibhuti* idea must have stimulated a similar recognition of exceptional capacity in the yogic life. Here as everywhere, *a concept or metaphor can encourage recognition*. This has certainly been the case in several of our interviews with sports people.

Hundreds of other powers could also be listed in the following table, from both contemplative sources and from sport. The ones we have included are meant only to dramatize the similarities between these two fields of experience and the wide range of capacities they both evoke. We should mention that the terms *siddhi* and *vibhuti* refer not only to powers like the ones listed in this table, but also to cognitions of the fundamental aspects of Reality. These cognitions are sometimes called the *brahmasiddhis* (powers to apprehend Brahman) and are regarded as the highest of all powers that result from the practice of yoga. We do not include them in the table because they fall outside the general range of our inquiry.

For some of the powers listed in the table we have included a middle column headed "Equivalent Psychological Powers," because we are uncertain whether the *siddhi* as it has been described in Eastern scripture is meant to refer to a psychological transformation or to a bodily change. Invisibility, for example, may refer to the yogi's sense of ego-loss and his ability to blend with the environment; his supposed ability to dematerialize his body may only be a superstitious accretion of belief around his spiritual capacity. But maybe there are moments of physical invisibility too. We cannot absolutely rule that out. For instance, as we noted in Chapter 4, several witnesses have claimed that Morehei Uyeshiba, the inventor of aikido, disappeared before their eyes at times, and there is a movie in which he appears to do so. We think the question should be left open. The middle column, therefore, provides qualifiers for those powers that may not be physical in the ordinary sense.

Extraordinary Powers in Yoga and Sport

Siddhi	Equivalent Psychological Power	Accomplishments in Sport
• Exceptional control of bodily processes, feelings, thoughts, imagination and other mental functions.		Pulse, heartbeat, breathing, and other physiological processes come under extraordinary control when a runner does the marathon in a little over two hours (which means an average of better than a mile every five minutes for the entire 26 miles), or when underwater swimmers hold their breath for more than five minutes at depths of up to forty feet, or when a race driver makes the hairpin turns required in Grand Prix driving.
• Mastery of pain, both psychic and physical.		The transcendence of pain in football, boxing, wrestling and other sports often seems miraculous. Football players have gone through games with broken ribs, noses, toes and fingers. Boxers have finished fights with broken hands and wrists. Often there is no pain at all during the contest, so great is the player's concentration.
• Ability to survive with little or no oxygen, as when a yogi is buried alive.		The anaerobic abilities of ocean divers and distance runners.
• The Tibetan tumo (inner fire); the ability to generate heat from within the body with little or no muscular exertion.		Mountain climbers, sailors and ocean swimmers report similar abilities to withstand freezing temperatures.

Siddhi	Equivalent Psychological Power	Accomplishments in Sport
• Ability to change shape, size and mass.	Psychic mobility, altered consciousness.	Morehei Uyeshiba, the inventor of aikido, seemed to change his shape and size in the swirl of a free-form match. Drastic changes in body image have been reported by golfers, football players, ocean divers, skydivers, and mountain climbers. Sometimes these changes are perceived by onlookers as actual changes in body shape and size.
• Invisibility.	Ego-loss, blending, and harmonizing with the elements.	Uyeshiba, in a movie demonstrating aikido, seems to disappear for an instant then reappear in another place. His followers swear the film was never tampered with.
• Auras, halos, the odor of sanctity, emanations of extraordinary energy.	Acting as a channel for other levels of the universe, "manifesting the Divine," mystical and creative illumination.	A skydiver saw "forms of light tumbling down the wind around her" during a jump in which she was suspended on a thermal updraft for over an hour. For Bundini Brown, Muhammad Ali glowed in the dark in certain extraordinary moments. (386)
• Levitation.	The sense of being lifted up by other energies, by the *ki* or *prana* of the Eastern disciplines or by God's grace.	A form of levitation appears in some of the martial arts when the participant is taught to make himself lighter or heavier at will through the manipulation of *ki*. Lee Evans and other sprinters talk about "tipping," a spontaneous lifting sprint form that seems to carry the runner on the very tips of his toes as if he were hardly touching the track at all.

Siddhi	Equivalent Psychological Power	Accomplishments in Sport
• Bilocation, being in two places at once.	Out-of-body experience, and/or the power to impress others at a distance.	David Smith, in his unique pentathlon, described the sensation of "rising above his body" while he was swimming. (235: p. 50) Chapter 3 reports other out-of-body experiences.
• Stigmata, tokens of espousal, and other signs on the body.		It could be argued that the sometimes radical changes of body structure an athlete goes through to perform a particular feat or to play a particular position is like this *siddhi*. The same power of mind over matter often seems to be involved.
• Ability to pass through solids, porousness.	Inner emptiness and freedom. Loosening of ordinary psychic structures and boundaries. Mental and emotional fluidity.	Pele: "I felt that I could dribble through any of their team or all of them, that I could almost pass through them physically." (378: p. 51) In aikido and kung fu there is something called "mesh practice" in which the participant imagines—then becomes—a net through which an opponent's energy and body may pass. In karate, the power to split boards and bricks is ascribed as much to *ki* as to sheer muscular force.
• Incombustability, fire immunity and impassability.	Inner equilibrium and imperturbability; a sense of indestructibility; identification with the Eternal.	In firewalking and swordswallowing—which might be classified as sports—we see this *siddhi*. In the nineteenth and early twentieth centuries there was a game which involved the ducking of bullets. Some of the great heroes of this pastime, it was said, became refractory to bullets through the power of their minds.

Siddhi	Equivalent Psychological Power	Accomplishments in Sport
• Freedom from the aging process.	Contact with the ever-born, ever-renewed, self-existent being that is characteristic of higher states.	George Blanda, at 45 was starring for the Oakland Raiders. Sam Snead was a money winner on the PGA tour at the age of 65. Percy Cerutty, the famous track coach, was a physical dynamo until the day he died. Bernard McFadden parachuted into the Seine and the Thames on his 85th and 86th birthdays. Track and swimming records for people over forty are falling at an incredible rate.
• Androgyny; the 32 male and 32 female signs of the perfect Buddha. Balance of the "male" and "female" characteristics.		Many male athletes, even in the fiercest sports, have a strikingly feminine aspect, contrary to the old macho cliché. Freed from the need to prove themselves in this regard they can allow a wider range of feeling and perceptions. The same can be said for many female athletes who exhibit strong "male" characteristics. This expansion of awareness and behavioral repertoire through the dropping of defenses has been pointed out by various psychologists and sociologists.
• Precognition, prophecy, retrocognition, time travel.	Freedom from tyranny of the past, present, or future. Psychic mobility.	David Meggyesey claims he made many tackles because he could anticipate the moves of the other team's running backs: somehow he knew what they would do an instant before they did it. See Chapter 3 for more examples.
• Clairaudience.	Access to the inner worlds of music and rhythm; the "music of	Bobby Jones often heard a melody as he played and sometimes used it to give a rhythm to his

Siddhi	Equivalent Psychological Power	Accomplishments in Sport
	the spheres''; the Om-kar of Indian tradition (a realm in which the mystic sound of ''om'' never ceases).	golf swing. The sound of crickets or a subtle ringing sometimes comes to golfers and mountain climbers in the stillness of their concentration. Roscoe Newman, a retired Navy captain, tells about times when he was learning to fly, when he would ''climb over the haze into a different world above five thousand feet and roll and loop until pleasantly pooped.'' During these flights he would ''synchronize vocally, in song, with the vibrations and noise frequencies around me to come up with all the voice parts of a great choral group and/or the various instruments of a large orchestral assembly. There was absolutely no discord in the music I heard. Every part and tone was crystal clear, true, properly amplified, and in unison.'' (279: pp. 43–44)
• Telepathy, clair-voyance.		An incredible power of communication often develops between members of a team—between a quarterback and wide receiver for example—where one can anticipate the moves of the other. See Chapter 3. Skiers tell of sensing a comrade's danger or distress on the slopes. Ocean divers and skydivers have told us the same kind of story.
• Synaesthesia, in which stimulation of one sense causes perception by another.		This crossing of the senses sometimes occurs in golf. (340: pp. 171–172)

Siddhi	Equivalent Psychological Power	Accomplishments in Sport
• Transmission of energy from person to person. Psychological contagion; group inspiration.		Vince Lombardi's inspirational powers were legendary. (122) Other coaches and many athletes have had the power to inspire their fellows in extraordinary ways, and certain teams have been famous for their inspirational momentum.
• The ability to draw nourishment from air.		John Muir and Herman Buhl could live for days in the mountains with little or no food while expending enormous amounts of energy. (70) Ian Jackson describes his twenty-day fasts combined with heavy distance running in *Yoga and the Athlete*. (224)
• Spiritual healing.		Many athletes have helped sports fans recover from illness. Babe Ruth was famous in this regard. (296) Improbable as it might seem to some, healing powers were ascribed to Vince Lombardi by some of his players. (122) There are similar stories about George Best, the soccer star, and other athletes. Many athletes and sport participants have been said to possess extraordinary abilities to heal themselves, and there have been famous recoveries from injuries like Ben Hogan's.
• Control of others, through manipulation of their physiological processes, their thoughts and emotions, and their "bio-energetic fields."		Muhammad Ali, Jim Brown, and other athletes have been legendary for their ability to "psyche out" their opponents. Vince Lombardi and other coaches have been equally famous for their ability to inspire and support their players.

Siddhi	Equivalent Psychological Power	Accomplishments in Sport
• Self-actualizing will.		Nathaniel Hawthorne said that Thoreau could "will a boat in any direction" by merely thinking the direction he wanted. (137) Fight trainer Cus D'Amato claimed he had the power of the "evil eye," by which he could cast a spell over others.
• Power of mass hypnosis.		Certain dancers—Nijinsky and Isadora Duncan for example— have had the ability to cast a spell on the audience, an ability which dozens of authors have tried to analyze with little success. John Brodie and other quarterbacks have talked about breaking the spell cast by an unfriendly crowd. (63) Muhammad Ali has cast many a spell over an opponent and a viewing audience.
• Immunity to harm or danger.		Hockey great Bobby Orr is said to have warded off opponents merely by staring at them. Japanese samurai warriors could train for this ability. Muhammad Ali and other champions have been legendary for their immunity from harm. (See Chapter 4.)
• Harmonizing with the elements while transcending their ordinary effects.		Sailor Adrian Hayter describes his ability to blend with wind and wave during long small-boat voyages. (196) Many skiers possess a similar ability.
• Heaviness and immovability.	Psychic strength and density.	This ability is encouraged in karate and other martial arts. (375: p. 59) Football players and wrestlers have told us about the same kind of power.

Siddhi	Equivalent Psychological Power	Accomplishments in Sport
• Psychokinesis; moving objects at a distance through psychic power.	Mastery of the mind and emotions; will-power in general.	Former quarterback John Brodie wrote, "I would have to say that such things seem to exist—or emerge when your state of mind is right. It has happened to me dozens of times. An intention carries a force, a thought is connected with an energy that can stretch itself out in a pass play or a golf shot or a thirty foot jump shot in basketball. I've seen it happen too many times to deny it." (393) It is a legendary power among certain pool and billiard players, among golfers, and in archery and target shooting.
• Feats of extraordinary strength and endurance as with *lung gom* walkers who, it is claimed, can walk for weeks without stopping through the mountains of Tibet.		Marathon running. Extraordinary moments of strength in weight lifting competition, in wrestling and boxing, and in every other sport. See Chapter 4.
• Perception of internal bodily structures such as organs, cells, and molecules.		Several distance runners have told us that they have caught glimpses of their own insides during a race or hard training. Some have seen capillaries break and heal over; others have reported images of particular tendons and muscles; a few have glimpsed forms that look like "cellular structures." Similar experiences have been reported to us by football players, golfers, and other athletes.

6
. Mind/Body
Training

Given the similarities between sport and religious practice, the question arises whether training programs could deliberately cultivate the spiritual elements in athletics. Could the kinds of experience we have described in the preceding chapters be more fully evoked and nourished? Part of the answer is clear: coaches and athletes all over the world are already using methods from yoga, the martial arts, hypnosis, meditation, and other disciplines to enrich their training programs. For example:

During the 1960s a field of applied psychology called "psychic self regulation" was developed in the Soviet Union. It is based on laboratory studies of our human ability to control various physiological processes, including pulse, muscular relaxation, blood pressure, and breathing. The methods developed in this new discipline are being used in sport now by some Russians and East Europeans. The immensely effective sports training program in East Germany includes meditation, autogenic training, hypnosis, methods of "self-regeneration," dance, and various kinds of group process. (438: p. 32)

The United States Olympic Committee, while not making the effort that Russia and East Germany are in these areas, has recently instituted a few programs in biofeedback training and mental practice at their training centers at Squaw Valley, California, and elsewhere. (130) The Buffalo Bills football team has worked with clinical psychologist Robert Nideffer on methods of mental practice, relaxation, and concentration. (358; 192: p. 4) In baseball, the Detroit Tigers have worked with biofeedback, and the Philadelphia Phillies have used transcendental meditation. Ken Norton has employed hypnosis before several of his fights, including the one in which he beat Muhammad Ali.

Lee Pulos, a Canadian clinical psychologist, has helped the Canadian National Women's Volleyball team and many other world-class athletes by getting them to practice their sports both mentally and physically. Like other sports psychologists Pulos has found that mental practice enhances physical performance, that when the mind and body are simultaneously trained the best results usually follow. His general method is simple. In volleyball, for example, he might have the player imagine a particular shot several hundred times until he or she sees it vividly. Then, when the image is powerfully established, the athlete will begin to practice that shot on the court, bringing his body into alignment with his inner vision. Periods of physical practice alternate with periods of mental practice until the athlete clearly sees what he wants to do—and then does it to his or his coach's satisfaction. Billie Jean King, Olympic 400 meters champion Lee Evans, high jumper Dwight Stones, and bodybuilder Arnold Schwartzenegger have all used mental techniques. The list could go on and on. The point we want to make is clear, however: many coaches and athletes pay attention to the mental aspects of their training. The question is: How far might this be developed? What could be done to bring the spiritual dimensions of games and training out into the open and nurture them more fully?

Elements of a Mind/Body Training Program

What follows is a preliminary answer, a set of suggestions for anyone who wants to explore these possibilities. We are not talking about specific training methods or techniques here, however. This chapter won't improve your golf swing or your tennis serve. The methods we present will focus instead on the psychological and spiritual dimensions which, we think, can apply not only to sports but to the rest of our lives as well.

We will begin by describing approaches that might enhance athletic training programs in general, and then we'll suggest ways to incorporate them into an individual training regimen. Some of these elements—like meditation and biofeedback—are relatively familiar and are used to some extent in training programs now. Others, like "inner seeing" and developing the "energy body," may seem strange, but are promising enough, we believe, to include in this review. There are probably as many ways to combine these approaches as there are coaches and athletes, for their effectiveness depends in large part upon the special situations and makeup of the people involved.

Meditation Practice

As we have seen, sport depends largely upon focusing one's attention, whether on the field in which it happens, on one's teammates and opponents, on the ball, or on the functioning of one's own body. Success depends in large part on the steadiness and clarity of the participant's concentration. We have also seen that ordinary focusing can grow into something more, into something tennis players have called "the zone" and other athletes have labeled the "playing trance." This something more resembles the advanced meditation states we have described—the *dhyana* or *samadhi* of Patanjali's yoga sutras, for example, in which "the true nature of the world shines forth, not distorted by the mind of the perceiver." (377: p. 175)

Sport by its very nature promotes this heightened concentration, but formal meditation practice can help it grow. Several well-known athletes, among them Bill Walton, Joe Namath, rodeo rider Larry Mahan, and Billie Jean King, have testified to the help meditation has given them. The Detroit Tigers, the Philadelphia Phillies, and other teams have encouraged their members to use it. Running coach Mike Spino (467, 469), tennis teacher Tim Gallwey (164, 165), and other instructors describe meditative approaches in their books. The practices these athletes and coaches advocate can improve both performance and enjoyment in sport because they help bring us to a deeper center, a truer and more effective level of personal functioning.

Describing the action of the mind, yogic commentators often employ the image of a lake. If the surface of a lake is lashed into waves, the water becomes muddy and the bottom invisible. In this metaphor the lake represents the ordinary mind with its usual agitations, while the bottom of the lake represents our essential self. After hours of hitting golf shots or watching a fishing fly dance on a stream, you might discover the depths of your own quiet mind just as if you had been meditating. But the formal practice of meditation might quicken the process.

Meditation is profoundly simple in method. Zen sitting, for example, involves simple attention to breath or to the passing contents of your mind. In another Buddhist practice you simply attend to the sensations of walking. (This practice resembles the steady attention required for distance running, swimming, cross-country skiing and other endurance sports.) Many forms of meditation involve the observation of the mind's subtle turns. The Christian "prayer of Quiet" requires a simple focus on the light or form of God, without elaborate imagery. In these and other contemplative methods there is only the barest, most focused activity of mind, a constant indwelling so that a deeper consciousness might emerge, bringing with it a more spontaneous and harmonious action and a growing union with our truest source. The "noise" that intervenes between our truest self and ordinary consciousness is partially or largely eliminated in these practices. Identification with the mind's superficial movements gives way to a sense of something free and eternal.

Meditation practice need not be limited to a quiet retreat. Its popularity among professional rodeo riders (who practice meditation before entering the chutes with Brahma bulls and bucking horses) and among professional football players attests to its power in the midst of the most tumultuous sports. Says basketball star Bill Walton:

> I try to do some form of meditation every day. . . . The nicest thing about meditation is that it puts your body in harmony with your surroundings. And that can be real helpful, because when you're a professional athlete, your surroundings can get pretty unharmonious. (32: p. 84)

Or golf professional Jane Blalock:

> I go into the locker room and find a corner by myself and just sit there. I try to achieve a peaceful state of nothingness that will carry over onto the golf course. If I get that feeling of quiet and obliviousness within myself, I feel I can't lose. (131: p. 174)

There are many ways to set up the practice of meditation. But most important are patience and regularity. In an old religious metaphor the act of meditation is compared to the ringing of a bell, in which the afterglow of the experience is like the dying sound. It is crucial to hit the bell (meditate again) before the ringing (the afterglow) stops. By practicing at regular intervals, the insight and depth of meditation are maintained and amplified. Gradually those qualities became second nature. The specific method you use is less important than faithfulness of practice. Whether you simply attend to your thoughts, count breaths, repeat a prayer, or focus on a point, the important thing is persistence. Two sessions a day—one in the morning and another in the afternoon or evening—will have their effect if you are patient.

Biofeedback

Some athletic programs are already using biofeedback. Recently, for example, it was incorporated into the training of prospective Olympic athletes by the United States Olympic Committee. (130) The method works as follows: An instrument attached to the body gives a continuous record of one or more of the subject's physiological processes so that he or she might alter those processes directly. If someone wants to lower his pulse, for example, a record of it is presented to him as a sound or a squiggle on a moving graph. By watching the record, the subject gradually learns what thoughts, images, feelings, moods, muscular contractions, and other factors are associated with the fluctuations of his pulse. With this growing awareness he can learn to modify his thoughts and feelings so that his pulse drops or rises at will.

Biofeedback is now being used to help people control pulse, blood pressure, electrical activity in the brain, muscular tension, stomach acidity, and several other body processes.

Visualization and Mental Practice

We often picture an activity in our mind before we undertake it. Most of us do this every day, though in a haphazard manner. Reflect for a moment on your own experience. Haven't you seen yourself meeting someone you know or accomplishing a task or trying some impossible feat? Images of future action pass in and out of awareness without our willing them—sometimes showing us performing to perfection, sometimes anticipating defeat. Our imagination can be either helpful or discouraging when it begins to anticipate a course of action. It is a force that can encourage or defeat us.

This anticipatory power of the imagination has been utilized in many sports, and recently a good deal of research has explored its effectiveness for athletes. This research has shown that by picturing the successful completion of moves they want to make, athletes can improve their performance, especially if the mental picture is accompanied by physical practice. (358, 405, 406, 472) Merely imagining a good round of golf or a successful race is ineffective without hitting shots or going through the necessary conditioning. In general, the athletes who do best are those who practice both mental and physical techniques.

Top athletes are good at both mental and physical self control. Think of Ben Hogan, Jack Nicklaus, Bill Russell, or Arnold Schwarzenegger. Some of these champions have described how they picture the moves they want to make. Jack Nicklaus, for example, claims that hitting good shots depends 10 percent on his swing, 40 percent on his setup and stance, and 50 percent on his mental picture. In his book *Golf My Way* he describes how he visualizes a shot before he makes it:

> I never hit a shot, not even in practice, without having a very sharp, in-focus picture of it in my head. It's like a color movie. First I "see" the ball where I want it to finish, nice and white and sitting up high on the bright green grass. Then the scene quickly changes and I "see" the ball going there: its path, trajectory, and shape, even its behavior on landing. Then there is sort of a fade-out, and the next scene shows me making the kind of swing that will turn the previous images into reality. . . .
>
> It may be that handicap golfers also "go to the movies" like this before most of their shots, but I somehow doubt it. Maybe . . . they see only pictures of the swing, rather than of what it's supposed to achieve. If that's true in your case, then I believe a few moments of movie-making might work some small miracles in your game. Just make sure your movies show a perfect shot. We don't want any horror films of shots flying into sand or water or out of bounds. (355: pp. 79-80)

In rodeo riding—a sport very different from golf!—meditation and visualization have become quite popular in recent years. Champion bronco and bull rider Larry Mahan says, "I try to picture a ride in my mind before I get on the bull. Then I try to go by the picture." (299: p. 212)

Francis Tarkenton, who has the leading passing statistics in the history of the National Football League, visualizes an upcoming game as follows:

> On this week, for example, he must think Pittsburgh and nothing else. He must see that Steeler defense in his dreams, every one of them, knowing their names, numbers, bodies, moves. He must be able to tell who is chasing him by the sound of the footsteps, and

which way to turn to evade him, for every man has his weakness. He must see those linebackers eyeing him as they backtrack into pass coverage, know their relative speed and effectiveness, know just how many steps each one will take on specific defensive calls so that he can find the right hole at the right time. "Sometimes I think I'm going into a purple quandary trying to anticipate what's going to happen. By Friday, I'm running whole blocks of plays in my head. . . . I'm trying to visualize every game situation, every defense they're going to throw at me. I tell myself, 'What will I do on their five-yard line and it's third and goal to go, and our short passing game hasn't been going too well and their line looks like a wall and we're six points behind?' I walk around on another planet and I'm not much fun to live with. . . . (17: p. 81)

The testimony of research about visualization's effectiveness combined with these endorsements by sporting champions makes a strong case for this kind of practice in athletic training. The method is simple in principle: just picture the move you want to make until you see it clearly, then imagine how that action would feel. Repeat the procedure until the perfected move comes naturally to you, then take the image and your feeling for it into physical practice.

But a warning here. Though practiced images of desired performance can help us, at times they must give way to even better ones that arise spontaneously. In *Golf and the Kingdom,* the narrator describes such a process:

I saw the path of my ball on the first hole at Burningbush going down the right side of the fairway with a draw, not down the middle as I might have seen it, and so it flew—to the best part of the fairway for an approach to the green. Some invisible radar had superseded my ordinary judgement. This has happened to me many times. Through experience you can learn when to stay with your original image and when to yield to the new one. (340: p. 180)

Sometimes our mind and body unconsciously make adjustments that are superior to the first image we have about a particular move. When we become aware of the readjusted image we have to go with it. Maybe our first image didn't anticipate all the variables in a given situation. Whatever the case, we should surrender to the spontaneous maneuver, as it is the result not only of mental preparation and physical practice but also of on-the-spot intuition.

And sometimes, images arise that might be trying to deliver a message that goes beyond our sports activity.

> Many thoughts that arise as you are playing must be brushed aside. But certain ones that will not be brushed aside must be understood, otherwise they will haunt you until your golf game and your disposition suffer. Some years ago a thought like that began to torment me.
>
> It began entering my mind when I was putting. It said, "You are not lined up straight, line up again." It occurred to me over and over that the angle of my putter face was slightly askew. I would stand back and try to line up at a better angle, but still the thought was there. It kept coming back through the entire round. When I played again, a week or so later, the same voice began again— "You are not lined up straight, line up again," it said, creeping into my mind on every green and eventually as I was addressing the longer shots. I adjusted and readjusted my stance, waggled the club endlessly, the greens and fairways began to look like cubistic drawings as I surveyed them for a better line. Then it slowly dawned upon me that the thought was coming from some deep recess of my mind, that it was one of those thoughts Shivas had said I should listen to. What did it have to say? I let it run through my mind after that second round, let it play itself out, "You are not lined up straight, line up again." Slowly, inexorably, the meaning came clear: indeed I was not lined up straight, in my work, with my friends, during most of the day. I was sleeping in my office then, rising to telephone calls, . . . doing business over every meal. I was as disorganized as I had ever been and my unconscious knew it, and now it was speaking to me clearly on the golf course. I needed to realign my life, it said, not just my putt or my drive. Only during a round of golf did I slow down enough for the word to get through. (340: pp. 173-174)

An athlete can find visualization effective not only in improving performance but also in literally reshaping the body. There are many ways, large and small, gross and subtle, in which a body can change in the course of a training routine. Muscles may be recontoured, fat may disappear, new capillaries (thousands of miles of them) may develop, organelles may be added to cells, tendons may be stretched and made more flexible. This happens naturally, of course, through the physical exercise the athlete does. Each sport or training regimen determines what the athlete's body will be like. But the process can be aided by suggestion, visualization, and other mental techniques.

Bodybuilders use mental imaging to facilitate their physical development. The greatest bodybuilder of the 1970s, Arnold Schwarzenegger (437), and the 1977 Mr. Olympia, Frank Zane, have said that visualizing a particular muscle's contour somehow speeds the process of acquiring it. "A pump when I see the muscle I want," Schwarzenegger told us, "is worth ten with my mind drifting." He talked about sculpting his body in the movie *Pumping Iron:* he would first plan the kind of physique he wanted—aiming for values like symmetry, definition, and elegance—then work to achieve the form he wanted. Like a sculptor, he followed his artistic conception, but worked with his own living flesh. First he saw what he wanted, then he maintained that image during his workouts—indeed during each pump of his muscles. The process began and was maintained by the image of his inner eye. There is evidence from other fields as well that mind can affect body in dramatic ways. We will review some of this evidence in the following chapter.

So visualization can be helpful in various ways. It can give power to performance and help reveal the mind's workings. It can also help remold our physique and catalyze spontaneous powers. Russian and East German coaches have even incorporated it into "rejuvenation" exercises. Not much is known about these exercises in the West, but we have learned that it consists of guided visualization after hard practice and competition in which the athlete imagines his body recovering from the stress it has suffered. At the Esalen Sport Center a few program leaders have worked out similar methods, leading participants through meditations after workouts in which they imagine a healing in their chests, or picture their blood vessels and muscles recuperating, or see various colors entering sore spots to restore vitality. We have encouraged runners to make up their own ways of imagining their bodies healing faster. Generally, such procedures seem to speed recovery from physical stress.

Some athletes use hypnotic and suggestive techniques as an adjunct to visualization and mental practice. There are more methods of hypnosis than we can usefully summarize here, but in general hypnosis is used only to support the kind of mental practice we have already described. The hypnotist-trainer helps athletes make their own images more vivid and certain. Most coaches and sports psychologists say it is better if the athlete can learn to visualize on his or her own. Hypnosis should lead the player toward an independent ability to imagine desired outcomes without the need of external support.

Dreaming

Artists, poets, and scientists have often made discoveries in a dream. The same kind of inspiration happens to athletes. Jack Nicklaus once described a dream that helped him recover from a slump in tournament play:

> I've been trying everything to find out what has been wrong. It was getting to the place where I figured a 76 was a pretty good round. But last Wednesday night I had a dream and it was about my golf swing. I was hitting them pretty good in the dream and all at once I realized I wasn't holding the club the way I've actually been holding it lately. I've been having trouble collapsing my right arm taking the club head away from the ball, but I was doing it perfectly in my sleep. So when I came to the course yesterday morning, I tried it the way I did in my dream and it worked. I shot a 68 yesterday and a 65 today and believe me it's a lot more fun this way. I feel kind of foolish admitting it, but it really happened in a dream. All I had to do was change my grip just a little. (108: p. 101)

As we have seen, dreams can also carry a message about the future. After his devastating premonition of the fight with Jimmy Doyle, Sugar Ray Robinson said he never again disregarded dreams with warnings. Dreams can also have a positive message. Bruce Jenner told Tony Kornheiser that he used to dream of the Olympics constantly—especially of crossing the finish line victoriously in the 1500 meters at the end of the decathlon. (Since winning that event in the

1976 Olympics he has not had the dream again.) (258: p. 6) We suggest that you can learn from your dreams too—new techniques, perhaps, or situations to avoid. They might deliver new perspectives on your sport or on your life in general.

Inner Seeing

A mental ability that goes beyond imagination or visualization as we have described them so far might be called "inner seeing." It involves images that are not deliberately constructed like the kind of mental pictures Nicklaus and Schwarzenegger (437) have recommended. Unlike ordinary visualization this power appears to involve a *direct perception* of structures or processes that are usually invisible to us. To our surprise, we have found that some people appear to catch glimpses of their own insides while involved in sport.

Some distance runners, for example, have told us that they sometimes see organs, muscles, and blood vessels—and even forms that look like cells! Following a hard workout, one runner was flooded with images of breaking capillaries. He had lain down on his back to rest, when in his mind's eye he suddenly saw red cells spurting from broken vessels with startling rapidity. The perception was frightening, but there was a sensation of healing in his chest and a pervasive sense of well-being. A few nights later he had the same kind of vision in a dream, and guessed that through this imagery he was gaining a closer rapport with the process of breakdown and buildup in his training. Stories like his have led me (Murphy) to ask other runners if they have known similar episodes, and I have found that some have. During talks on these subjects I have sometimes asked if anyone in the audience might have had this kind of experience. Generally, about a quarter of those present have said that they have. This consistent finding plus stories of similar phenomena among athletes leads us to believe that many of us possess a latent power through which we can directly perceive our own body structures.

Evidence from other fields of experience supports this belief:

- A woman reported to us that during an acute psychotic episode she hallucinated her internal organs on the outside of her body, as if she "were turned inside out." After her psychosis had passed she was convinced that in some way she had directly perceived her body's insides. We have since discovered that many schizophrenic patients have similar experiences.

- Many people say that they have seen internal body structures during the course of gestalt therapy, encounter groups or in other psychotherapeutic contexts. Such glimpses often come during exercises in which they are imagining what the inside of their bodies looks like.
- As we have seen in Chapter 5, this kind of power has been recognized by yogis and contemplatives for thousands of years.
- The literature on psychedelic and hallucinogenic drugs is filled with similar accounts. (184, 314)

So the phenomenon as it appears in sport finds parallels in yoga, psychotherapy, research with psychedelic drugs, and the accounts of certain schizophrenics. But does this prove that all these people are actually *seeing* their hearts or lungs or capillaries? Aren't such experiences simply the product of these people's imaginations?

At present we have no certain proof that these perceptions are of actual body structures. But we can say this: (1) the experience often carries a sense of conviction with it, (2) it is sometimes accompanied by a sense of healing, which indicates some degree of self-mastery, (3) this kind of power has been described in the yogic and shamanistic traditions for some 3000 years or more, and (4) a few of these perceptions have been verified, as we will see in the next chapter. Taken together, this evidence is certainly suggestive. At the very least, "inner seeing" vivifies one's bodily awareness. And if it is a real power, it could be harnessed to help us achieve increasing rapport with our body's structures and processes. Maybe we possess a rudimentary scanning device—something like a built-in microscope complete with zoom lens and television screen for easy readout—by which we can zero in on whatever ails us or on whatever body part we want to change. In that case, bodybuilders and runners who have glimpsed their own muscles and capillaries might be learning how to use this scanning device. Perhaps they have unknowingly discovered a latent human power.

But how do we incorporate this power into a training program? That's a difficult question, for this ability is much harder to develop than ordinary introspection, imagination, or self-suggestion. It is better not to strain for it, we think. Wait until it happens. Sometimes it appears in meditation, sometimes in the course of visualization exercises. And at times it may come unexpectedly, during a workout perhaps, or in a dream, or while you are absorbed in a game. When it comes let it happen: that is the best advice we know to give at present. See what it wants to say and where it wants to take you.

Sensory and Kinesthetic Awareness

Various methods of sensory and kinesthetic training go under names like *sensory awareness, sensory awakening, body awareness,* and so forth. These disciplines aim to promote a more open, sensitive, untroubled contact with both the internal and external worlds. There are problems in describing them, however, for they depend much more on the nonverbal, artistic, and unique characteristics of their practitioners than they do on automatically repeatable techniques or formulas.

Charles Brooks, who with his wife Charlotte Selver has pioneered this kind of work in the United States, writes:

> Like Zen meditation, sensory awareness is not a teaching but a practice. . . . We have no real theoretical framework, and our experiments are entirely empirical. Our aim is not the acquisition of skills, but the freedom to explore sensitively and to learn from that exploration. We work toward an adult version of the open, curious attitude which healthy children have to the world they are born into. Charlotte Selver has been working for more than forty years with this approach, but she is constantly improvising and coming on approaches that she has not tried before. (64: p. 14)

One experiences a cumulative effect in a workshop led by Selver and Brooks, an atmosphere and caring that are more important than any technique. If you want to explore this kind of approach, you will find that, like meditation, it requires patience and persistence. And like meditation, the various exercises involved are extremely simple. Brooks, for example, describes the way one might learn about standing in a Charlotte Selver workshop:

> We sit down and explore our feet directly. With our own hands we go deeply into them, discovering and enlivening the many joints

and ligaments of which a foot consists. How far and deep must one go to follow the identity of a given toe until it becomes lost in the interior? What can we feel of the architecture of the arch? How does the heel seem to our palm and our fingers, in its aspect as bone and its aspect as padding? . . .

Now come back to standing. . . . Take time to feel where the floor is. How do we relate to it? Many people now feel that they *are* relating to the floor. They no longer stand on their feet but on something which they feel really supports them from below. The feet feel flexible and alive, not stood on but free to explore what they touch, as the hands a moment ago were exploring them.

Now the leader may ask, "Do you allow the connection with the floor upward into you?" And a little later, "Do you allow it through your knees?" Afterward, a number of people may well report that they found their knees were locked. When they gave up this locking, readjustments could be felt taking place in the ankles or the pelvis or higher. . . .

As thighs and calves wake up, slight changes may occur spontaneously. Or we may deliberately tighten our buttocks or our stomach muscles, taking time to notice how this affects our relation to the support under us, and noticing the changes as we gradually give up the constriction to allow more connection through. Reports often follow of an opening, resulting in a sense of contact with the floor throughout the organism. Changes may be felt as far away as in neck, eyes, and lips, together with an increased sense of standing altogether, which is no longer just a gap in living but is now becoming a positive activity. Very often breathing changes, as one release triggers another, or perhaps sets up a constriction somewhere else.

Such deliberate tensing of muscle constellations, when followed by a very gentle and conscious release—quite different from the nerveless "letting go" so often practiced for relaxation—can be very valuable in bringing habitual contractions to consciousness, where they may slowly dissolve as the vital processes which they are inhibiting begin to be felt and permitted. This requires a fresh and new exploration on each occasion, as opposed to the technique or excercise which is repeated always with the same objective in view. For we are working not with ideas, but with consciousness itself.

Still standing, let us bring our hands gently to resting on the top of our heads. Through palms and fingers we can feel, if we are sensitive, not only our hair but also the temperature and perhaps the animation of living tissue underneath. This is as far up as we extend, just as the soles of our feet delimit our extension downward. What is alive in between? Is there some sense of our existing altogether between the meeting of hands and scalp at the top and of soles and floor at the bottom?

Somewhere in this extent air enters, penetrates to a constantly varying distance, and leaves; weight is passed on from bone to bone and muscle to muscle; fluids circulate; metabolic processes generate ever-changing energies. Everywhere sensory nerves are interwoven and there is the possibility of more awakeness. Our standing is an endless readjustment of these happenings to one another, depending on the clear functioning of our proprioceptive nervous system and on the flexibility of our musculature.

In such trips through one's interior there is always a likelihood of getting stalled; so many toll gates and barricades have been set up over the years. Now and then, however, a new path opens: sensation and energy flood through; consciousness expands to regions heretofore out of bounds. One has a new and full recognition: I am alive there too! I exist: and I am standing on something which exists also. (64: pp. 42–46)

We have quoted from Brooks' account at length to convey the spirit of this work as well as its method. As you can see, it requires a good deal of time and patience, but its effectiveness in opening one to the richness of the internal and external worlds is attested to by growing numbers of people in Europe and America.

Many sportspeople find their way naturally to the "open, curious attitude which healthy children have"—but many others do not. Many of us were discouraged by the competitiveness and drudgery of those gym classes we suffered through in grammar school and high school. Who can forget the tough-looking coach bawling us out because we weren't doing our push-ups fast enough?—or the teacher ridiculing the fat girl who was last in the sprints? Physical education courses, all too often, were lessons in how *not* to enjoy the body and its senses. Exploring the various approaches to sensory and kinesthetic awareness, however, can help to right the balance.

The Energy Body

As we saw in Chapter 4, exceptional physical feats are possible when athletes deliberately develop their *ki,* or subtle energy. Certain extraordinary powers are especially apparent in the martial arts: the power to split bricks, the ability to sense an opponent approaching from behind, the power to calm dangerous men or animals. This subtle energy is an aspect of our body that is, in a sense, both separate from and intimately connected with our physical frame.

Recently an approach has been developed in the West that draws on methods of the martial arts to cultivate our awareness and control of these subtle energies. Some of this work has been pioneered by Robert Nadeau and George Leonard, black belt experts in aikido. The main ingredient in their teaching is permission. Once their students find that it's all right to sense forms of energy not generally recognized in the West, they discover openings into a fresh new world of perception and being. Leonard describes this concept of the energy body in *The Ultimate Athlete:*

> Energy Body workshops begin with the assumption that a field of energy exists in and around each human body. . . .
> The individual is viewed as an *energy being,* a center of vibrancy, emanating waves that radiate out through space and time, waves that respond to and interact with myriad other waves. The physical body is seen as one manifestation of the total being, coexisting with the Energy Body. Its reality and importance is in no way denied. It provides us with the most reliable information as to the condition of the total being. The Energy Body, on the other hand, is less reliable and more difficult for us to perceive at this stage in our development. But it is far less limiting than the physical body. It can change shape, size, density, intensity, and other qualities. Each of these changes influences the physical body to some extent. In some mysterious way that we can't yet fully understand, the Energy Body also seems to transcend space and time, connecting each human consciousness to all of existence. (279: pp. 68-71)

Some 20,000 people have attended programs based on these premises that Leonard has conducted at universities and personal growth centers during the past four years. Participants in these programs are frequently able to sense the location of other people in the room with their eyes closed, create an "energy flow" by which they can resist force with considerable ease, transmute pain and shock into positive feelings of being energized, resist being lifted or become effectively lighter at will. Leonard introduces beginners to this kind of experience through exercises in balance and centering, soft eye focus, energy sensing, and energy flow. Here is a description he gave us of one of his exercises:

First have someone try to bend your extended arm at the elbow.

Then stretch and shake your hand with wrist limp. Breathe deeply, allowing the abdomen to swell. Relax. Now stand with your right foot slightly in front of the left, weight evenly distributed on both feet, knees neither locked nor bent. Let your right arm rise to a horizontal position in front of you, hand open, thumb up. Elbows should not be locked.

Now imagine that your arm is part of a beam of pure, smooth, unbendable energy. Your arm is in the center of this beam which extends a few inches all around it. With eyes soft, (that is, not sharply focused on any specific object), imagine the beam of which your arm is a part extending through any object in front of you—the wall or whatever—across the horizon to the ends of the universe. Your arm is part of the beam. The beam is like a laser. It cannot be bent but it takes no effort on your part to keep it from being bent. All you have to do is concentrate on its extension.

Now have the same person try to bend your arm at the elbow, using the same amount of force as he used before. Have him use more force. Note the difference. (279)

Consciously developing a greater awareness of our energy body is one way to enhance our *ki* and increase our overall competence in sport.*

---

* In *The Ultimate Athlete* (279) Leonard outlines ways in which the energy body comes into play during conventional athletics (see Chapter 6, pp. 110–122), and in *The Silent Pulse* (278), he develops a theory that may help account for these phenomena. In *Golf in the Kingdom* (340) I (Murphy) relate some of these phenomena to golf and other sports (see especially "The Pleasures of Practice," pp. 166–180).

By combining the approaches we have reviewed in this chapter with regular physical practice, we believe the athletic enjoyment can be enhanced. This kind of training needn't be limited to championship athletics; it can easily be applied to your own individual program. But just as conventional sports training must fit the physique and temperament of the athlete, so these approaches must be adapted to your readiness and ability. You will have to experiment and try different combinations of them. You may want to find teachers to help you with particular aspects of one approach or another. If you want to read more about any of these training dimensions, we have included books and articles about them in the bibliography.

To show you how these elements might fit into individual training, we have outlined a program for jogging and running, one of the most popular individual sports right now. This model is only meant to get your imagination going. It can easily be adapted for tennis, golf, or any other athletic activity.

A Mind/Body Program for Joggers and Runners

Begin with two 20-minute periods of meditation each day—the first when you arise and the second in the evening. If you have never practiced meditation, begin by observing your thoughts and feelings without judgment or interference, in a quiet room. Maybe a friend or spouse or child can join you.

Your jogging program should begin as prescribed in one of the good books on the subject [Kenneth Cooper's *Aerobics* (91), perhaps, Jim Fixx's *The Complete Runner* (167), or Joan Ullyot's *Women Running* (500)]. Stick with the kind of program these authors describe.

In your jogging sessions try using helpful images like a stream flowing in the direction you are moving, or a giant sail unfurled above you helping to carry you along. Practice holding such images for at least part of your workout until it gets to be an easy thing to do. See how it affects your jogging. Does it add freedom or zest? Does it help you cut through fatigue? If other helpful images come, experiment with them.

When you are jogging, be aware of all the sensations that arise. Don't suppress them. Exercise periods are times to know your body more completely. What do your feet feel like? Your calves and thighs? Your breathing? This flood of sensation is something to learn from and enjoy.

Before and after each run do some stretching exercises: stretch your calves and hamstrings, flex your ankles, limber up your shoulders. While you are doing this, stay aware of the sensations in each part, become your body more fully.

If you have any dreams or reveries that seem to relate to this new regimen, pay attention to them. See if you can learn what they are trying to tell you. See what messages they might be trying to deliver. Because you are engaging new parts of yourself, the unconscious recesses of your organism will start making new connections. Learn what those connections might be.

Such a program would only take forty minutes a day plus the time you spend jogging and stretching. Give this program a couple of months to have its effect.

After you have been jogging for several months, you will be able to increase your speed and distance. Again, there are books that tell you how. [Mike Spino's *Running Home* (469) includes programs for the intermediate runner, with all sorts of ways to incorporate meditation and visualization into your training.]

In general, simply let your abilities stretch out in all the exercises you've been practicing, without forcing them. By now you will have heard about different kinds of workouts from friends and fellow joggers. You may have joined a running group or run in a couple of races. Meditate with companions and share your experiences with them. Experiment with longer periods of meditation and mental practice once a week or so. Try sitting for an hour and see what it's like.

Use your imagination to recombine the elements we have outlined in the preceding pages to make a regimen that suits you. *But stay faithful to practice.* There is a momentum in running and meditation that grows with dedication.

When you are jogging 20 miles a week or more and have spent at least six months in this kind of program, you will be able to try some bolder experiments. Try going two miles farther than you have ever run before. Meditate for two hours without stopping. Then go on a running vacation or retreat in which running, stretching, meditation, and sensory awareness are your only focus.

Set a long-range running goal. By now you should have met people who can join you in your training for a longer run. And set a goal for inner exploration, maybe to try a week-long meditation retreat.

If you are a full-time athlete, work on meditation disciplines while you are building an all-around physical regimen that includes training for cardiopulmonary and muscular endurance, strength, and flexibility. All these amplify the others.

By now you will be getting leads from various quarters, both inside and outside you. Let imagination inform everything you do. Try something new and unique in your training, and aim to surpass at least one personal limit you now think is fixed.

7
Evolutionary
Possibilities

A major question in sport concerns the ultimate limits of performance and record breaking. Is there a limit to how fast the mile or the marathon will eventually be run? How much further can swimming records be lowered? How difficult—or easy—will future ascents in climbing be, or the maneuvers in gymnastics or the turns in skating? Records fall in some event each week, it seems, and sportspeople constantly attempt the impossible.

Our human ability to surpass apparent limits is dramatized in sport in a way that has caught the world's imagination. But as we begin to perceive the spiritual side of this in more of its richness, as we begin to comprehend the range of inward knowing and supernormal power that sport evokes, we can also wonder how far body and mind might develop in the directions these powers suggest.

Is there a significant frontier here? In gathering the material for this book, we have found ourselves frequently asking this question. Could the extraordinary capacities we have explored in this book be more fully developed in the culture at large? Do these aspects of sport point to similar possibilities in all of us, whether we are athletes or not? We believe that they do. Indeed, many programs to explore these possibilities are emerging in Europe, Russia, and the United States. The immense interest in Buddhist, Yogic, Sufi, Christian, and Jewish mysticism; the popularity of experimental psychotherapies; the experimentation with biofeedback and hypnosis; the development of disciplines like suggestology and psychic self-regulation in Russia and Eastern Europe; and the growing fascination with altered states of consciousness demonstrates a readiness in modern culture to explore the kind of experience our sports stories illustrate.

Sports provide a strong and compelling focus for an exploration of mental and physical transformation. But exceptional human capabilities emerge in other fields as well, of course, lending further weight to the proposition that we possess enormous untapped potentials. Let's take a look at some of these fields.

Placebo Research

A placebo is a sugar pill or inert substance that is given to a patient who believes it is a medicine or drug. By accepting the authority of the doctor or experimenter, persons taking the pill often rally their own powers to produce the changes they have been led to expect. Placebos have helped people lower the amount of fat and protein in their blood, change their white cell count, reduce the trembling associated with Parkinson's disease, relieve depression, increase sleepiness, reduce post-operative wound pain, relieve the symptoms of arthritis, eliminate the symptoms of withdrawal from morphine, and produce various specific effects of both stimulant and depressant drugs. Through placebos we are authorized to mobilize our own self-regenerative powers.

The placebo effect often produces astonishing results. Changing our blood cell count is usually considered to be a feat for yogis, yet unsuspecting patients have done it. Placebo research demonstrates how specific and how effective our own powers of self-surpassing can be.

Hypnosis and Suggestion

Hypnosis and suggestion have now been proved effective for a variety of problems from shyness to serious medical illness. Researchers have successfully used hypnotic induction to alleviate congenital ichthyosis, a devastating disease characterized by skin that is black, horny, and covered with scales. It is usually resistant to all forms of treatment, but by using hypnosis and suggestion, at least four researchers have helped victims of this disease achieve from 75 to 90 percent remission. (248, 312, 432, 530)

It has also been shown that women can successfully use suggestive techniques to increase their breast size. In one study (275), L. M. LeCron hypnotized 20 women and suggested that their "inner mind" restart the pubescent process of breast growth. Twelve of the 20 increased their bust line by one to one-and-a-half inches, and five of the remaining eight women increased theirs by two inches. In another study (521), thirteen women who wanted larger breasts were given weekly hypnotic suggestions to reexperience the sensations of puberty. After 12 weeks their average bust measurement increased 2.1 inches as compared with control measurements of the rib cage just below the bust, which showed no change over the same period.

Using hypnosis, James Esdaile, a Scottish surgeon, performed over a thousand operations without anesthesia in India during the mid-nineteenth century. These operations included the amputation of arms, fingers, and toes; the removal of tumors internally and externally; the extraction of teeth; the removal of cataracts. His patients not only felt less pain, but their wounds healed faster than those of patients who were not hypnotized. Esdaile's operations were observed and described by many reliable witnesses, including British government officials. (135, 136)

Results like these have been achieved in many experiments during the past 150 years.* These studies clearly demonstrate that through hypnosis many people can win significant freedom from pain, disease, and allergy, change the structure of their body, and increase certain skills and capacities.

Spiritual or Mind-Assisted Healing

Dr. Carl Simonton and his wife, Stephanie Matthews, maintain a cancer treatment clinic in Fort Worth, Texas, based on the premise that an individual's mental and emotional processes are significant contributors to the creation of cancer in the body. The treatment program consists of regular exercise, psychological counseling, radiation therapy, and mental self-healing. Participants in it visualize a scenario in which their natural immune systems are seen fighting the cancer as a healthy body does. The Simontons' results to date indicate that mental activity of this kind helps rid the body of disease.

One of their patients was a 61-year-old man with extensive throat cancer. By using mental imagery and radiation therapy, he was healed after a year and a half of treatment. In the course of his remission he drew pictures to represent the state of his disease, and Dr. Simonton was amazed to observe his accurate representation of the cancer's size and shape. He seemed to see internally what Dr. Simonton could see with the aid of an instrument. After his cancer was gone, this man used the mental techniques he had learned to eliminate arthritis and sexual impotence. Seven years later, at the time of this writing (1978), he is free of disease or disability. (454)

---

* We recommend F. W. H. Myers' *Human Personality* (344), Ernest R. Hilgard's *Hypnotic Sensibility* (210), and *Hypnosis: Research Developments and Perspectives,* Erika Fromm and Ronald E. Schor, Editors (159), for reviews of hypnosis experiments during the nineteenth and twentieth centuries.

Other researchers are also working along these lines, among them Harold Stone of the Center for the Healing Arts in Los Angeles. Dr. Stone speculates that some of his patients possess a "transformative gift" that may inadvertently contribute to their cancer. In his therapy he helps these people redirect their transformative ability so that it will reverse the growth of the cancer and support a healthy regenerative process in their bodies.

There have always been gifted individuals who appear to possess healing abilities. Drs. Elmer and Alyce Green have studied some of them at the Menninger Foundation in Topeka, Kansas. Healer Jack Schwartz, for example, was able to stop bleeding from puncture wounds in his arms and hands at will in the Greens' laboratory.* The work of the Simontons, Harold Stone, and the Greens is breaking new ground in the scientific study of mind-assisted healing.

Biofeedback

Various mental exercises combined with biofeedback training teach patients how to control heart rate, muscle tension, lymph flow, blood flow, blood pressure, gastrointestinal functions, air flow in bronchial tubes, and electrical characteristics of the skin and brain. These generalized tasks have been effectively applied to the treatment of Raynaud's disease, Parkinson's disease, migraine and tension headaches, hypertension, spastic colon, asthma, neuromuscular problems, epilepsy, and cerebral palsy. (181)

John Basmajian has reported on the voluntary control of single nerve fibers through auditory and visual feedback from electrodes placed in a thumb muscle. Subjects learned such delicate control that they could produce neural rhythms such as "doublets, triplets, gallop rhythms, and drum rolls" at will after 60 to 90 minutes of training. (35, 36) In another study Bernard Engel showed that some people can learn to control individual sections of the heartbeat. (134) Recent pilot studies have demonstrated a person's ability to influence blood sugar levels at will. These various investigations suggest that any aspect of a person's chemistry or physiology that can be brought to awareness,

---

* The Greens have reported the results of their studies in numerous articles and in their book *Beyond Biofeedback* (181), published in 1977.

either directly or through instruments, can become accessible to conscious control.

Russian "Psychic Self-Regulation" (PSR)

PSR is defined by its Russian authors as "a directed, purposeful regulation of the various actions, reactions, and processes of an organism realized by means of its own psychic (mental) activity." The system is a synthesis of yoga, hypnosis, autogenic training, and the martial arts. In it, mastery of muscle relaxation and breathing rhythms, achievement of temperature changes in the arms, chest, abdomen, and head, and control of heart rate are developed in preparation for more selective control of various psychological and physiological functions.

Russian researchers report that they have found a normal distribution curve for this capacity in the general population—though everybody, they say, has it to some degree. But because most people are unaware of this capacity, it is usually used nonconsciously, often contributing to the development of disease. Soviet researchers maintain that mental self-influence occurs through normal physiological pathways, such as the central nervous system, and at the micromolecular level down to the most fundamental structures within living organisms. Published research from the Russian medical and sport communities suggests that PSR techniques can help increase the growth of muscle fiber and affect cellular and subcellular processes. (282, 283, 411, 412)

Psychokinesis and Telepathic Suggestion

The ability to affect physical objects, including one's own body and the bodies of others, without the mediation of any known physical medium has been studied by parapsychologists since the 1880s. If such a power actually exists, it would help explain many of the phenomena we have examined in this book.

There is a class of event in which it is not always clear whether psychokinesis or telepathic suggestion is the mediating factor. F. W. H. Myers, a founder of the (British) Society for Psychical Research and the author of the field's great classic, *Human Personality and Its Survival of Bodily Death,* described several experiments in which a subject was hypnotized telepathically and commanded to perform certain actions. One such experiment was witnessed by Myers and by Pierre Janet, Freud's famous contemporary. Janet and Myers watched while their colleague Dr. Gibert, a physician of Le Havre, induced an unsuspecting patient to leave her home at night and walk across town to his house—a highly unusual excursion. Myers, Janet, and Gibert conducted 25 such experiments between October 1885 and May 1886, of which 19 were deemed successful. (344)

Similar experiments in "suggestion at a distance" have been conducted by many researchers since then. The Russian physiologist L. L. Vasiliev, who established the Soviet Union's first parapsychology laboratory, studied the phenomenon in the 1930s. His experimenters used telepathic suggestion to induce people miles away to sway back and forth. In other experiments, sleep and arousal were telepathically induced in unsuspecting subjects. Vasiliev's experiments have led to current work in Russia along these lines. It is now widely reported that several laboratories in the Soviet Union are trying to develop such powers for military purposes. (74, 505, 520)

Several experiments have been reported in which a person psychokinetically influenced bacteria, plants, or mice. (51, 68, 303, 512) Recent research has developed a teaching mechanism using feedback for the distant influence of another person's physiology. And at the twentieth annual convention of the Parapsychological Association, Dr. William Braud reported on his efforts to influence the galvanic skin response (GSR) of another person while receiving continuous feedback of the target person's GSR acticity. He found a significant correlation between his attempts to increase or decrease the subjects' GSR and the actual GSR fluctuations. (58)

In 1970, Dr. Helmut Schmidt introduced a highly reproducible and consistent approach to the scientific study of psychokinesis. Schmidt designed and built a random-event generator triggered by the radioactive decay of strontium-90 nuclei. The electron emission from such decay is one of nature's most random processes. Since then at least 45 psychokinesis studies using this device or similar equipment have been reported in the scientific literature. In most of these studies, subjects were able to influence this random process mentally, primarily by getting sensory feedback whenever a decrease in the randomness occurred. Interestingly, experienced meditators learn the task more easily than non-meditators. Charles Honorton, in his presidential address to the Parapsychological Association, characterized the process as an ability to bring "order out of disorder, as a function of intention." (214)

In our opinion, these studies confirm the human capacity for intentional psychokinesis. (214, 430, 431) In showing that order can be imposed on randomness by meditation or mere intention, they give us a clue about the mind's role in self-transformation. Increasing harmony within the body and with other people is a fundamental aspect of spiritual growth. This research seems to show that the ability to do so is a relatively accessible capacity.

The extensions of human capacity that we have reviewed in these last few pages come from established fields of research and have been demonstrated in many clinical and experimental settings. There is a growing scientific literature about them. But there are also more exotic phenomena that point to extraordinary powers of self-transformation latent in human nature. Some of these phenomena have not been scrutinized in scientific laboratories like the ones we have just reviewed, but they have been observed by reliable witnesses for centuries and have been attested to in the religious traditions. They include the following.

Religious Stigmata and Tokens of Espousal

Bleeding wounds on hands and feet, apparent lance wounds in the abdomen, bruises on the shoulders, chafing of wrists and ankles, punctures on the forehead simulating the crown of thorns—all these have appeared in the bodies of devotees during contemplation of Christ's crucifixion. They demonstrate how specific and elaborate the mind's effect on the body can be. Apparently, the body will dramatize any image that is passionately embraced by the imagination.

It is generally thought that St. Francis of Assisi was the first to exhibit the stigmata. Thomas de Celano, in the first biography of St. Francis, wrote:

> Marks of nails began to appear in his hands and feet. . . . These marks were rounded on the inner side of the hands and elongated on the outer side, and certain small pieces of flesh were seen like

the ends of nails bent and driven back, projecting from the rest of the flesh. So also the marks of nails were imprinted in his feet, and raised above the rest of the flesh. . . . (492: pp. 45-46)

Since St. Francis, over 300 stigmatics have born the marks of the crucifixion. Certain wounds suggest that the stigmatic's imagination is influenced by his or her surroundings during the wound-forming process. Catherine Emmerich (1774-1824), for example, had a Y-shaped cross on her chest that resembled the unusual Y-shaped cross on top of the church in which she prayed.

Allied to the stigmata is the *token of espousal,* a ring-shaped modification of flesh that forms around a nun's finger as a symbol of her betrothal to Christ. At the beatification of Catherine de Ricci (1522-1589) in 1614, eyewitnesses described "a ring on the index finger of the left hand made entirely of flesh raised up like a ridge." (492: pp. 135-136) A French stigmatic named Marie-Julie Jahenny was studied by Dr. Imbert Gourbeyre, a French physician, who observed the "appearance of a mystical ring, i.e., a hoop of vivid red encircling the ring finger of the left hand." (492: p. 132) Twenty years later Dr. Gourbeyre wrote, "Marie-Julie's ring remains to the present day . . . still a ring made in the fleshy tissues, like a hoop of red coral which had sunk into the skin." (492: pp. 131-133) Like stigmata, this bodily change symbolizes a crucial event in the imaginative life of the devotee—in this case the spiritual marriage to Christ. It is another dramatic example of the specificity with which body structures can be altered through internal processes without external intervention or manipulation.

Incendium Amoris and the Tibetan Tumo

Some contemplatives exhibit an extreme body heat *(incendium amoris)* that they attribute to the warmth of their love for God. Padre Pio of Foggia, Italy (1887-1968), who was stigmatic from 1915 until his death, had a temperature of 112° Fahrenheit at times, reported doctors who studied him. The Dominican nun Suor Maria Villani of Naples (1584-1670) was "continually consumed by an almost unsupportable flame of love." (492: p. 219) When a surgeon opened her body nine hours after her death, smoke issued forth and the heat prevented him from placing his hand in the abdominal cavity. In Tibetan Buddhism the "warmth of spiritual devotion" is called gTum-mo, the "Inner Fire." In certain exercises the devotee contemplates this fire, "which radiates light as well as warmth" and makes it possible to endure the cold of Tibetan snow and ice. (177: p. 165) In the Sufi tradition it is called the "fire of separation":

> Then the saint came to take a meal, and the girl was pouring water on his hands. She noticed that so intense was the fire of separation burning in him that immediately the water would fall on his hands it would pass into vapor. (44, quoted in 425: p. 17)

Bodily Luminosity

Father Francis Suarez, the famous Jesuit theologian, was observed by a laybrother while encompassed in a radiant light. In the words of Jerome da Silva:

> I perceived that a blinding light was coming from the crucifix. . . . This light streamed from the crucifix upon the face and breast of Father Suarez (whose body was lifted in the air five palms above the floor). (492: p. 166)

Thomas à Kempis, in a biography of St. Lydwina of Schiedam, described some of the luminous phenomena seen about her:

> She was discovered . . . surrounded by so great a divine brightness . . . although she always lay in darkness and material light was unbearable to her eyes, nevertheless, the divine light was very agreeable to her. . . . Her cell was often so wondrously flooded by light that to the beholders the cell itself appeared full of material lamps or fires. (492: p. 167)

Similar events were observed in the presence of St. Philip Neri, St. Charles Borromeo, St. Ignatius of Loyola, St. Francis of Sales, and Ramana Maharshi, a modern Indian saint. (492)

Incorruptibility After Death

Some contemplatives have exhibited apparent incorruptibility of their bodies after death. St. Madeline Sophie Barat, founder of the Society of the Sacred Heart, died in 1865. Twenty-eight years later her body was found almost perfectly intact, though the coffin was partly decayed and covered with mildew. St. Bernadette of Lourdes was buried in 1879. Thirty years later her body was exhumed during the beatification process. An eyewitness described the event:

> Not the least trace of corruption nor any bad odour could be perceived in the corpse. . . . Even the habit in which she was buried was intact. The face was somewhat brown, the eyes slightly sunken. (492: p. 235)

The body of Paramahansa Yogananda, founder of the Self-Realization Fellowship, is reputed to have been perfectly preserved 20 days after his death. In a notarized letter, Harry Rowe, mortuary director at Forest Lawn Memorial Park in Los Angeles, wrote:

> No physical disintegration was visible in his body even twenty days after death. . . . No indication of mold was visible on his skin, and no visible desiccation took place in the bodily tissues. . . . The physical appearance of Yogananda on March 27, just before the bronze cover of the casket was put into position, was the same as it had been on March 7 [the date of his death]. (536: p. 000)

The evidence from these various fields shows that the human organism can work wonders of self-transformation. Sometimes it is tricked into assuming this power, as in the placebo effect. Sometimes it is guided, as in the hypnotic removal of allergies, or assisted with instruments, as in biofeedback. Or it can work with self-reliant awareness, as it does in yoga or psychic self-regulation. This power of transformation can be specific enough to alter the blood cell count, powerful enough to help remove cancer, or sufficiently elaborate to cause wounds in the hands and feet that bleed only on Good Friday. It can also touch others in mysterious ways, if we can believe the evidence we have just reviewed.

Many studies are now searching out these untapped powers of mind and body. I (Murphy) am involved in one such project in which my associates and I are exploring the nature of supernormal bodily changes, the ways in which they happen, and the characteristics of the people who have them. We are also beginning to experiment with disciplines that facilitate their development.* To date we have collected several thousand anecdotes involving extraordinary bodily changes like the ones described in this book, have compiled a preliminary inventory of the separate powers they seem to exemplify (such as "inner seeing" and "inner hearing"), and have studied the physical features, personality characteristics and environmental conditions of the people to whom they happen. In the process of collecting this material, we have discovered that many people possess exotic capacities like "inner seeing." These exceptional powers, which are generally unknown to modern psychology and physical science, are often involved in the dramatic bodily changes we are investigating—and sometimes seem to mediate them. We have mentioned the distance runner, for example, who saw images of his capillaries breaking while healing sensations passed through his chest, and the bodybuilders who have vivid pictures of the muscles they are training.

Another such power is a subtle internal hearing that accompanies moments of change or surpassing performance. The sounds heard in this way may be loud or faint, harsh or musical, human or unearthly. One champion bodybuilder, for example, says that he heard his muscles growing in his sleep when he was training heavily. They sounded like "cornflakes being poured into a bowl." (163: p. 72) Bobby Jones claimed he often heard a melody as he approached a round of golf and that if he swung the club to its rhythm he would play his best game. Barbra Streisand described a similar though more painful kind of internal hearing in a *Playboy* interview:

> I had clicks in my ears. I told my mother and she said, "Well, sleep on a hot-water bottle." She never asked me about it again.

---

* James L. Hickman is my principal associate in this project. We are being helped by Dulce Murphy, Mary Payne, Rhea White, Keith Thompson, and others. For a fictional account of the possibilities we are looking at, see *Jacob Atabet,* by Michael Murphy (341).

From that day, I led a whole secret life. . . . Two years later, I developed a high-pitched noise that I have heard all my life. I never hear the silence. When I used to have my ears examined, it turned out I had supersonic hearing. I hear high-range, high-pitch noises off the machine. . . .

When I was a kid, I used to go around with scarves to try to cut out the noise, which only made it worse, because it drives it more inside your head. I had this secret, I never told anybody. I didn't want to be different. I felt totally abnormal.

Playboy: How do you connect that with your musical talent?

Streisand: Strange connection. It made me listen very carefully to life. I would listen like nobody listened. But it's not good, it's not fun. I'm like inside my body, I hear my body. I'm very aware of my body's functions. It's very frightening. I see many colors.

Playboy: In your head?

Streisand: In my eyes. When I look at a wall, I don't just see a white wall. I see other things.

Playboy: Textures or colors?

Streisand: Textures *and* colors. It's like overemphasizing the processes of being alive.

Playboy: Is it like being stoned?

Streisand: I don't know. That's what people talk about. Maybe I'm stoned all the time. (382)

Subtle hearing and seeing, clairvoyant sensing or "touching," and the ability to affect one's environment by a power like psychokinesis might look like symptoms of disease if they come uninvited. (Indeed, many psychotics claim they possess them.) Disembodied voices or glimpses of your own insides can be profoundly disturbing. But the very fact that such powers arise spontaneously in many people suggests that they are a fundamental part of human nature. The fact that they burst in upon so many of us might indicate that we are designed to use them. Perhaps these strange abilities are part of a larger awareness and capacity that is pressing to be born.

Indeed, this is the belief of many spiritual traditions. In some schools of yoga, Buddhism, and Taoism, the aspirant is taught the meaning of subtle sounds and sights that lead to larger realms of consciousness and beauty. Such leadings were honored by shamans thousands of years ago. The same can be said for almost all the capacities we have looked at in this book: nearly all of them were cultivated somewhere, at some period in the human past. And nearly all of them arise spontaneously even in people who do not expect or do not welcome them. Apparently they cannot be suppressed completely, even in a culture that is generally blind to their existence. Taken as a whole, they shadow forth a vast unexplored realm. Cultivated wisely, they may lead us to a new evolutionary adventure.

The exploration of the mind's further reaches has already been joined on several fronts. Research in biofeedback, hypnosis, and meditation; the psychic self-regulation developed in Russia and Eastern Europe; the dissemination of Eastern religions in the West; the growing interest in altered states of consciousness—all are openings onto a great frontier. We suspect that still bolder explorations will follow. Like all advances in human knowledge, these developments will have practical by-products, we think—ways to make education more effective, perhaps, to help cure disease, or to lengthen life.

If a large-scale enterprise were mounted to explore these immense potentials of human nature, who knows what discoveries we might make? Couldn't we support highly trained researchers who would investigate the openings we have looked at in these pages? It would bring a new zest of adventure to us all, we believe, just to know that such attempts were being made. It is even conceivable that through such explorations we might win radical new insights not only into the structure of the mind but also into the most fundamental processes of the physical universe.

The extraordinary capabilities in sport that we have presented in this book are probably only a glimmer of what human beings can achieve. We simply do not know the limits of long-term research into these phenomena. But if the pattern we have seen so often in human history holds, every new plateau of knowledge and mastery will reveal further vistas to engage those of us who want to explore the limits of the human spirit.

Recommended Readings

Butt, Dorcas S., *The Psychology of Sport* (New York: Van Nostrand Reinhold, 1976).

Chow, David, and Richard Spangler, *Kung Fu: Philosophy and Technique* (Garden City, N.Y.: Doubleday, 1977).

Gallwey, Timothy, *The Inner Game of Tennis* (New York: Random House, 1974).

Gerber, Ellen W. (ed.), *Sport and the Body* (Philadelphia: Lea and Febiger, 1972).

Herrigel, Eugen, *Zen in the Art of Archery* (New York: Pantheon, 1953).

Hickman, James, "You Are What You Think," *Runner's World* **12**, 5 (May 1977).

Huizinga, John, *Homo Ludens* (Boston: Beacon Press, 1950).

Keen, Sam, and Michael Murphy, "Our Bodies, Our Souls: A New Age Interview," *New Age* **3**, 8 (January 1978).

Leonard, George, *The Ultimate Athlete* (New York: Viking, 1975).

Lowe, Benjamin, *The Beauty of Sport* (Englewood Cliffs, N.J.: Prentice-Hall, 1977).

Murphy, Michael, *Golf in the Kingdom* (New York: Viking, 1972).

———, *Jacob Atabet* (Millbrae, Calif.: Celestial Arts, 1977).

Nideffer, Robert M., *The Inner Athlete* (New York: Crowell, 1976).

Sheehan, George, *Running and Being* (New York: Simon and Schuster, 1978).

Slusher, Howard, *Man, Sport and Existence* (Philadelphia: Lea and Febiger, 1967).

Spino, Mike, "Going Beyond Jogging," *Runner's World* **12**, 8 (August 1977).

Spino, Mike, and James Hickman, "Beyond the Physical Limits," *Runner's World* **12**, 3 (March 1977).

Spino, Mike, and James Warren, *Running and the Mind* (New York: Bantam Books, in press).

Weiss, Paul, *Sport: A Philosophic Inquiry* (Carbondale: Southern Illinois University Press, 1969).

Westbrook, Adde, and Oscar Ratti, *Aikido and the Dynamic Sphere* (Rutland, Vt.: Charles E. Tuttle, 1970).

Bibliography

This bibliography includes both the references cited in the text and additional books and articles which we recommend for further reading on aspects of the extraordinary sports experience. Sometimes these recommended titles are not about sport per se, but are listed because they provide background on the unusual states and capacities we have discussed in this book. A boldface letter following a citation refers to one of the ten subject categories listed below. These categories are not exclusive. Although only one subject category has been assigned to an entry, many titles fit two or more categories. The letters for each category are as follows:

A Altered states of consciousness.

B Biographies and autobiographies containing unusual sports experiences.

C Creativity in athletics.

E "Extraphysical" energies and out-of-body experiences.

G General works on the extraordinary sports experience.

I Works on individual sports containing material on the extraordinary sports experience.

M Martial arts.

O The ordeal in sport.

P Psychology and sports.

Y Sport as yoga.

1. Alderman, R. B., *Psychological Behavior in Sport* (Philadelphia: Saunders, 1974). **P**

2. Alderman, R. B., "A Sociopsychological Assessment of Attitude toward Physical Activity in Champion Athletes," *Research Quarterly,* vol. 41 (Mar. 1970), pp. 1-9. **P**

3. Algonzin, Keith, "Man and Sport," *Philosophy Today,* vol. 20 (Fall 1976), pp. 190-195. **G**

4. Ali, Muhammad, with Richard Durham, *The Greatest* (New York: Random House, 1975). **B**

5. Allen, Jim, *Locked In: Surfing for Life* (New York: Barnes and Noble, 1970). **I**

6. Allen, Woody, "A Fan's Notes on Earl Monroe," *Sport,* vol. 65, no. 5 (Nov. 1977), pp. 20-21 + . **I**

7. Anderson, Dave, "Ali's Radar Waves," *New York Times* (Jan. 11, 1976).

8. Andretti, Mario, *What's It Like Out There?* (Chicago: Regnery, 1970). **B**

9. Andrews, Peter, "Sooner or Later, the Altitude Gets You," *Signature,* vol. 11, no. 3 (Mar. 1976), pp. 34-37 + . **A**

10. Andrews, Valerie, "The Joy of Jogging," *New York,* vol. 10, no. 1 (Dec. 27, 1976/Jan. 3, 1977), pp. 60-63. **I**

11. Angell, Roger, "The Sporting Scene: Down the Drain," *New Yorker,* vol. 51, no. 18 (June 23, 1975), pp. 42-59. **A**

12. Angell, Roger, "Still Getting the Ink," *New York Times Book Review* (Oct. 13, 1974), pp. 6-8.

13. Aran, Gideon, "Parachuting," *American Journal of Sociology,* vol. 80, no. 1 (July 1974), pp. 124-152. **I**

14. Arens, William, "Great American Football Ritual," *Natural History,* vol. 84, no. 8 (Oct. 1975), pp. 72-81. **Y**

15. Ashe, Arthur, "Catching Connors in the Stretch," *Sports Illustrated,* vol. 45, no. 6 (Aug. 9, 1976), pp. 20-21. **A**

16. Ashe, Arthur, with Frank DeFord, *Arthur Ashe: Portrait in Motion* (Boston: Houghton Mifflin, 1975). **B**

17. Asinof, Eliot, *Seven Days to Sunday* (New York: Simon and Schuster, 1968). **I**

18. Assagioli, Roberto, *Psychosynthesis* (New York: Hobbs Dorman, 1965). **Y**

19. Aultman, Dick, "Gain More Leverage—Start Down Slow," *Golf Digest,* vol. 24, no. 9 (Sept. 1973), pp. 28-33.

20. Aurobindo, Sri, *The Collected Works of Sri Aurobindo,* vol. 22 (Pondicherry, India: Sri Aurobindo Ashram Trust, 1970).

21. Aurobindo, Sri, *The Collected Works of Sri Aurobindo,* vol. 23 (Pondicherry, India: Sri Aurobindo Ashram Trust, 1970). **E**

22. Aurobindo, Sri, *The Life Divine* (New York: Dutton, 1951).

23. Avalon, Arthur (Sir John Woodruffe), *The Serpent Power* (New York: Dover, 1974). **E**

24. Axthelm, Pete, *The City Game: Basketball in New York* (New York: Harper's Magazine Press, 1970). **B**

25. Axthelm, Pete, "O.J.—The Juice Really Flows," *Newsweek,* vol. 82 (Nov. 26, 1973), pp. 67–70.

26. Axthelm, Pete, "Sky King," *Newsweek,* vol. 87, no. 21 (May 24, 1976), p. 55. **C**

27. Axthelm, Pete, "The Year of the Runner," *Newsweek,* vol. 80, no. 23 (Dec. 4, 1972), pp. 76–84. **O**

28. Bach, Richard, *Stranger to the Ground* (New York: Avon Books, 1972). **I**

29. Banner, Bob, "Physical Exercises: An Overview," *Preparation,* vol. 1, no. 1 (June 1977), pp. 14–21. **Y**

30. Bannister, Roger, *The Four-Minute Mile* (New York: Dodd, Mead, 1955). **B**

31. Bannister, Roger, "The Meaning of Athletic Performance," in John Talamini and Charles H. Page (eds.), *Sport and Society* (Boston: Little, Brown, 1973), pp. 325–335. **G**

32. Barbieri, Ralph, "A Visit with Bill Walton . . . and from FBI," *Sport,* vol. 61, no. 2 (Aug. 1975), pp. 74–76+.

33. Barclay, Glen, *Mind over Matter* (Indianapolis: Bobbs-Merrill, 1973). **M**

34. "Baryshnikov: Gotta Dance," *Time,* vol. 105, no. 21 (May 19, 1975), pp. 44–50.

35. Basmajian, John V., "Control and Training of Individual Motor Units," *Science,* vol. 41 (Aug. 21, 1963), pp. 440–441. **Y**

36. Basmajian, John V., *Muscles Alive: Their Functions Revealed by Electromyography* (Baltimore: Williams and Wilkins, 1962). **Y**

37. Baumbach, Jonathan, "Aesthetics of Basketball," *Esquire,* vol. 73 (Jan. 1970), pp. 140–146. **I**

38. Beard, Frank, and Dick Schaap, *Pro: Frank Beard on the Golf Tour* (Cleveland: World, 1970). **B**

39. Beisser, Arnold, *The Madness in Sport* (New York: Appleton-Century-Crofts, 1967). **P**

40. Bell, Marty, "Hypnosis in Sports," *Sport,* vol. 57, no. 3 (Mar. 1974), pp. 92–95+. **A**

41. Bell, Marty, *The Legend of Dr. J.* (New York: Coward-McCann, 1975). **B**

42. Belmonte, Juan, "The Making of a Bullfighter," *Atlantic,* vol. 159 (Feb. 1937), pp. 129–148. **B**

43. Bennet, Glin, "Medical and Psychological Problems in the 1972 Single-handed Transatlantic Yacht Race," *Lancet,* vol. 2 (Oct. 6, 1973), pp. 747–754. **O**

44. Bhavan, B., *Sufis, Mystics and Yogis of India* (Bombay: Bankey Behari, 1971).

45. Block, Alex Ben, *The Legend of Bruce Lee* (New York: Dell, 1974). **B**

46. Blofeld, John, *The Secret and Sublime* (London: Allen and Unwin, 1973).

47. Blount, Roy, Jr., *About Three Bricks Shy of a Load* (Boston: Little, Brown, 1974). **I**

48. Bodo, Peter, and David Hirshey, *Pele's New World* (New York: Norton, 1977). **B**

49. Bolt, Tommy, *The Hole Truth* (Philadelphia: Lippincott, 1971).

50. Bonatti, Walter, *On the Heights* (London: Rupert Hart-Davis, 1964 [©1961]). **B**

51. Bond, Donald, *The Love and Fear of Flying* (New York: International Universities Press, 1952). **P**

52. Bongartz, Roy, "The $100,000 Bowling Machine," *Sports Illustrated,* vol. 46, no. 11 (Mar. 7, 1977), pp. 66–76. **I**

53. Bonington, Chris, *Annapurna South Face* (New York: McGraw-Hill, 1971).

54. Bonington, Chris, *Everest the Hard Way* (New York: Random House, 1976).

55. Borden, Charles A., *Sea Quest: Global Blue-Water Adventuring in Small Craft.* (Philadelphia: Macrae Smith, 1967). **I**

56. Bradley, Bill, *Life on the Run* (New York: Quadrangle/New York Times Book Co., 1976). **B**

57. Bradshaw, Terry, and C. Conn, *No Easy Game* (Old Tappan, N.Y.: H. Fleming Revell, 1973). **B**

58. Braud, William, "Allobiofeedback: Immediate Feedback for a Psychokinetic Influence Upon Another Person's Psychology," *Research in Parapsychology 1977* (Metuchen, N.J.: Scarecrow, 1978), in press.

59. Breslin, Jimmy, "A Day with the Doctor," *Sport,* vol. 60, no. 3 (Mar. 1975), pp. 28–32.

60. Brier, Bob. Personal communication.

61. Brier, Robert M., "PK on a Bio-electrical System," *Journal of Parapsychology,* vol. 33 (Sept. 1969), pp. 187–205.

62. Brock, Lou, and Franz Schulze, *Stealing Is My Game* (Englewood Cliffs, N.J.: Prentice-Hall, 1976). **B**

63. Brodie, John, and James D. Houston, *Open Field* (New York: Bantam, 1974). **B**

64. Brooks, Charles V. W., *Sensory Awareness: The Rediscovery of Experiences* (New York: Viking, 1974). **Y**

65. Brown, Barbara B., *Stress and the Art of Biofeedback* (New York: Harper and Row, 1977). **A**

66. Brown, George I., and Donald Gaynor, "Athletic Action as Creativity," *Journal of Creative Behavior,* vol. 1, no. 2 (1967), pp. 155–162. **C**

67. Brown, John Porter, *The Darvishes; or Oriental Spiritualism,* 2d ed. (London: Frank Cass, 1968 [© 1927]).

68. Buckle, Richard, *Nijinsky 1909* (New York: Simon and Schuster, 1971).

69. Budge, E. A. Wallis (ed.), *The Egyptian Book of the Dead* (New York: Dover, 1967). **E**

70. Buhl, Hermann, *Lonely Challenge* (New York: Dutton, 1956). **O**

71. Butt, Dorcas Susan, *The Psychology of Sport* (New York: Van Nostrand Reinhold, 1976). **P**

72. Byrd, Richard E., *Alone* (New York: Putnam's, 1938).

73. Cahill, Tim, "A Man for Off Season," *Rolling Stone,* Issue 247 (Sept. 8, 1977), pp. 24–30.

74. Caldwell, Carol, "Beyond ESP," *New Times,* vol. 10, no. 7 (Apr. 3, 1978), pp. 42–50.

75. Campbell, Gail, *Marathon: The World of Long-Distance Athletes* (New York: Sterling, 1977). **O**

76. Capra, Fritjof, *The Tao of Physics: An Exploration of the Parallels*

Between Modern Physics and Eastern Mysticism (Berkeley, Calif.: Shambhala, 1975).

77. Castaneda, Carlos, *Tales of Power* (New York: Simon and Schuster, 1974).

78. Cath, S. H., A. Kahn, and N. Cobb, *Love and Hate on the Tennis Court* (New York: Scribner's, 1977). **I**

79. Chouminard, Yvan, "Chouminard on Ice," *Outside,* vol. 1 (Dec. 1977), pp. 30–33. **I**

80. Chow, David, and Richard Spangler, *Kung Fu: Philosophy and Technique* (Garden City, N.Y.: Doubleday, 1977). **M**

81. Cleary, William, *Surfing: All the Young Wave Hunters* (New York: New American Library, 1967). **I**

82. Cochran, Jacqueline, with Floyd Odlum, *The Stars at Noon* (Boston: Little, Brown, 1954).

83. Cohen, Marvin, "Baseball and Religion," *Dial,* vol. 67 (July 26, 1919), pp. 57–59. **G**

84. Cohen, Marvin, *Baseball the Beautiful* (New York: Link Books, 1974). **I**

85. Colbert, Jim, "Fine-tuning Your Concentration," *Golf Magazine,* vol. 17, no. 6 (June 1975), pp. 54–58. **Y**

86. Coleman, Kate, "Because It's There . . . Outward Bound: Not for the Social Climber," *WomenSports,* Vol. 2, no. 9 (Sept, 1955), pp. 30–33 + .

87. Colletto, Jerry, with Hack L. Sloan, *Yoga Conditioning and Football* (Millbrae, Calif.: Celestial Arts, 1975). **Y**

88. Collins, Larry, and Downe Lapiere, *Or I'll Dress You in Mourning* (New York: Simon and Schuster, 1968).

89. Columbo, Franco, and George Fels, *Winning Bodybuilding* (Chicago: Regnery, 1977).

90. Connolly, Olga, *Rings of Destiny* (New York: David McKay, 1968). **B**

91. Cooper, Kenneth, *Aerobics* (New York: M. Evans, 1968). **Y**

92. Cooper, Kenneth, *The Aerobics Way* (New York: M. Evans, 1977). **Y**

93. Cooper, Linn F., and Milton H. Erickson, *Time Distortion in Hypnosis* (Baltimore: Williams and Wilkins, 1954).

94. Cousteau, Jacques Y., with Frederic Dumas, *The Silent World* (New York: Harper and Row, 1953).

95. Cousy, Bob, as told to Al Hirshberg, *Basketball Is My Life* (Englewood Cliffs, N.J.: Prentice-Hall, 1958). **B**

96. Cousy, Robert, *The Last Loud Roar* (Englewood Cliffs, N.J.: Prentice-Hall, 1964). **B**

97. Cratty, Bernard J., *Psychology in Contemporary Sport* (Englewood Cliffs, N.J.: Prentice-Hall, 1973). **P**

98. Crompton, Paul H., *Kung Fu: Theory and Practice* (Toronto: Pagurian Press, 1975). **M**

99. Crookall, Robert, *Casebook of Astral Projection* (Secaucus, N.J.: University Books, 1972). **E**

100. Crookall, Robert, *The Study and Practice of Astral Projection* (Secaucus, N.J.: University Books, 1966 [©1960]). **E**

101. Crookall, Robert, *The Techniques of Astral Projection* (New York: Samuel Weiser, 1964). **E**

102. Csikzentmihalyi, Mihalyi, *Beyond Boredom and Anxiety* (San Francisco: Jossey-Bass, 1976). **A**

103. Csikzentmihalyi, Mihalyi, "Play and Intrinsic Rewards," *Journal of Humanistic Psychology,* vol. 15, no. 3 (Summer 1975), pp. 41–63. **A**

104. Csonka, Larry, and Jim Kiick, *Always on the Run* (New York: Random House, 1973). **B**

105. David-Neel, Alexandra, *Magic and Mystery in Tibet* (Secaucus, N.J.: University Books, 1965 [©1956]).

106. Davidson, Art, *Minus 148: The Winter Ascent of Mt. McKinley* (New York: Norton, 1969). **O**

107. Delatire, Edwin J., "Some Reflections on Success and Failure in Competitive Athletics," *Journal of the Philosophy of Sport,* vol. 2 (Sept. 1975), pp. 133–139.

108. Dement, William C., *Some Must Watch While Some Must Sleep* (San Francisco: W. H. Freeman, 1974).

109. Demaret, Jimmy, *My Partner, Ben Hogan* (New York: McGraw-Hill, 1954). **B**

110. DeMille, Richard, *Castaneda's Journey* (Santa Barbara, Calif.: Capra Press, 1976).

111. DeMott, Benjamin, "An Unprofessional Eye . . . Suspended Youth," *American Scholar,* vol. 32 (Winter 1962–1963), pp. 107–112.

112. Dennis, Larry, "Weiskopf Walking Slower and Swinging Smoother," *Golf Digest,* vol. 24, no. 11 (Nov. 1973), pp. 80–81.

113. Devaney, John, *Bob Cousy* (New York: G. P. Putnam's, 1965). **B**

114. Devaney, John, *The Bobby Orr Story* (New York: Random House, 1973). **B**

115. Diaz-Canabate, Antonio, *The Magic World of the Bullfighter* (London: Burke, 1956). **I**

116. Dickinson, Mary Lindsay. Personal communication.

117. Dingwall, E. J., "D. D. Home: Sorcerer of Kings," in E. J. Dingwall, *Some Human Oddities* (Secaucus, N.J.: University Books, 1962), ch. 5.

118. Dingwall, E. J., "Eusapia Palladino: Queen of the Cabinet," in E. J. Dingwall, *Very Peculiar People* (Secaucus, N.J.: University Books, 1962), ch. 5.

119. Dobereiner, Peter, "The Day Joe Ezar Called his Shots for a Remarkable 64," *Golf Digest,* vol. 27, no. 11 (Nov. 1976), pp. 66–67.

120. Doust, Dudley, "Opening the Mystical Door of Perception in Sport," *The Sunday Times* (Nov. 4, 1973).

121. Doust, Dudley, "Tony Jacklin, Mystical Perception in Sport," *Intellectual Digest,* vol. 4 (Apr. 1974), pp. 32–33. **A**

122. Dowling, Tom, *Coach! A Season with Lombardi* (New York: Norton, 1970). **B**

123. Draeger, Donn F., and Robert W. Smith, *Asian Fighting Arts* (New York: Berkley, 1974 [©1969]). **M**

124. Duncan, Isadora. *The Art of the Dance* (New York: Theatre Arts, 1928). **B**

125. Duncan, Isadora, *My Life* (New York: Boni and Liveright, 1927). **B**

126. Durckheim, Karlfried, *Hara* (New York: Weiser, 1975). **M**

127. Ebon, Martin (ed.), *The Amazing Uri Geller* (New York: New American Library, 1975).

128. Eccles, Sir John, "The Human Person in its Two-Way Relationship to the Brain," *Research in Parapsychology 1976* (Metuchen, N.J.: Scarecrow Press, 1977), pp. 251–262.

129. Eckhart, Meister, *Meister Eckhart; a Modern Translation,* trans. Raymond Bernard Blakney (New York: Harper and Row, 1941).

130. Editorial, *Olympian,* vol. 1, no. 10 (July–Aug. 1977), pp. 13–15.

131. Edmiston, Susan, "Winners and How They Win," *Woman's Day,* vol. 33 (Sept. 1976), p. 174+ .

132. Ellen, Arthur, with Dean Jennings, *The Intimate Casebook of a Hypnotist* (New York: New American Library, 1968). **A**

133. Elliot, Herb, *The Herb Elliot Story* (New York: Thomas Nelson, 1961). **B**

134. Engel, Bernard T., "Visceral Control: Some Implications for Psychiatry." Paper presented at the American Psychiatric Association Conference, Anaheim, California, 1975.

135. Esdaile, James, *Mesmerism in India* (New York: Arno Press, 1976 [©1846]).

136. Esdaile, James, *Natural and Mesmeric Clairvoyance* (New York: Arno Press, 1975 [©1852]).

137. Evans, Jay, and Robert R. Anderson, *Kayaking: The New White Water Sport for Everybody* (Brattleboro, Vt.: Stephen Greene Press, 1975).

138. Evans, Lee. Personal communication.

139. Fairfax, John, *Britannia: Rowing Alone Across the Atlantic* (New York: Simon and Schuster, 1971).

140. Falls, Joe, *The Boston Marathon* (New York: Macmillan, 1977).

141. Farrelly, Midget, as told to Craig McGregor, *The Surfing Life* (New York: Arco, 1967). **I**

142. Ferguson, Marilyn, *The Brain Revolution* (New York: Taplinger, 1973).

143. Fessier, Michael, Jr., "Transcendental Running," *Human Behavior,* vol. 5, no. 7 (July 1976), pp. 17-20. **I**

144. Fimrite, Ron, "Bringer of the Big Hit," *Sports Illustrated,* vol. 42, no. 24 (June 16, 1975), p. 33 + .

145. Fincher, Jack, "If Russ Francis Can't Beat You, His 'Kahuna' Can," *Sport,* vol. 65, no. 4 (Oct. 1977), p. 76 + .

146. Fischler, Stan, *Bobby Orr and the Big, Bad Bruins* (New York: Dodd, Mead, 1969). **B**

147. Fixx, James, *The Complete Book of Running* (New York: Random House, 1977). **I**

148. Floyd, Keith, "Of Time and the Mind," *Fields Within Fields Within Fields*, no. 10 (Win. 1973-1974), pp. 47-57. **P**

149. Fluegelman, Andrew, *The New Games Book* (Garden City, N.Y.: Doubleday, 1976). **A**

150. Flying Magazine Editors, *Sport Flying* (New York: Scribner's, 1976). **I**

151. Fodor, Nandor, "The Riddle of Nijinsky," in his *Between Two Worlds* (West Nyack, N.Y.: Parker, 1964), pp. 24–29.

152. Ford, Whitey, Mickey Mantle, and Joseph Durso, *Whitey and Mickey* (New York: Viking, 1977).

153. Fox, Matthew, *Whee! We, Wee All the Way Home* (Gaithersburg, Md.: Consortium Books, 1976).

154. Fox, Oliver, *Astral Projection* (Secaucus, N.J.: University Books, 1963). **E**

155. Frady, Marshall, "The Little Man Is a Big Man on the N.C. State Campus," *Sport,* vol. 60, no. 2 (Feb. 1975), p. 30+.

156. Frager, Robert, "Psychology of the Samurai," *Psychology Today,* vol. 2 (Jan. 1969), pp. 48–53+. **M**

157. Frazier, Walt, *Rockin' Steady* (Englewood Cliffs, N.J.: Prentice-Hall, 1974). **B**

158. Frazier, Walt, and Joe Jares, *Clyde* (New York: Holt, Rinehart and Winston, 1970).

159. Fromm, Erika, and Ronald E. Shor (eds.), *Hypnosis: Research Developments and Perspectives* (Chicago: Aldine, 1972).

160. Furlong, William B., "Danger as a Way of Joy," *Sports Illustrated,* vol. 30 (Jan. 27, 1969), pp. 52–53. **A**

161. Furlong, William Barry, "The Fun in Fun," *Psychology Today,* vol. 10, no. 1 (June 1976), p. 35+.

162. Furst, Peter, *Flesh of the Gods* (New York: Praeger, 1972).

163. Gaines, Charles, and George Butler, *Pumping Iron* (New York: Simon and Schuster, 1974). **I**

164. Gallwey, Timothy, *The Inner Game of Tennis* (New York: Random House, 1974). **I**

165. Gallwey, Timothy, *Inner Tennis* (New York: Random House, 1976). **I**

166. Gallwey, Timothy, and Bob Kriegel, *Inner Skiing* (New York: Random House, 1977). **I**

167. Gaskins, G., and D. W. Masterson, "The Work of Art in Sport," *Journal of the Philosophy of Sport,* vol. 1 (Sept. 1974), pp. 36–66. **C**

168. Genasci, James E., and Vasillis Klissouras, "The Delphic Spirit in Sports," *Journal of Health, Physical Education, and Recreation,* vol. 37, no. 2 (Feb. 1966), pp. 43–45. **G**

169. Gerber, Dan, "The Way It Feels: Sailfishing off Key West," *Outside,* vol. 1 (May 1978), pp. 53-54. **Y**

170. Gerber, Ellen W. (ed.), *Sport and the Body* (Philadelphia: Lea and Febiger, 1972). **G**

171. Ghiselin, Brewster (ed.), *The Creative Process: A Symposium* (New York: New American Library, 1955 [© 1952]).

172. Gilbey, John, *Secret Fighting Arts of the World* (Rutland: Tuttle, 1963). **M**

173. Glasser, William, *Positive Addiction* (New York: Harper and Row, 1976). **P**

174. Gluck, Jay, *Zen Combat* (New York: Ballantine Books, 1962). **M**

175. Golf Digest's Professional Teaching Panel, "How Your Game Can Brighten Under Pressure," *Golf Digest,* vol. 26, no. 11 (Nov. 1973), pp. 85-88.

176. Gott, Jim, with Norman Lewis Smith, *Amphibian* (Chicago: Playboy Press, 1976).

177. Govinda, Lama Anagarika, *Foundations of Tibetan Mysticism* (New York: Samuel Weiser, 1969). **E**

178. Grange, Red, as told to Ira Morton, *The Red Grange Story* (New York: Putnam's, 1953).

179. Greeley, Andrew, and William C. McCready, "Are We a Nation of Mystics?" *New York Times Magazine* (Jan. 26, 1975), pp. 12-13 + .

180. Green, Celia, *Out-of-the-Body Experiences* (Oxford: Institute of Psychophysical Research, 1968).

181. Green, Elmer, and Alyce Green, *Beyond Biofeedback* (New York: Dial Press, 1977). **Y**

182. Greenhouse, Herbert, *The Astral Journey* (Garden City, N.Y.: Doubleday, 1974). **E**

183. Gregg, Jearald, "A Philosophical Analysis of the Sports Experience" (Ph.D. diss., University of Southern California, 1971). **G**

184. Grof, Stanislav, *The Realms of the Human Unconscious* (New York: Viking, 1975). **A**

185. Grossinger, Richard, *The Unfinished Business of Doctor Hermes* (Plainfield, Vt: North Atlantic Books, 1976).

186. Gutkind, Lee, *Bike Fever* (Chicago: Follett, 1973). **I**

187. Hagen, Walter, as told to Margaret S. Heck, *The Walter Hagen Story* (New York: Simon and Schuster, 1956).

188. Hano, Arnold, "John F. Kennedy: His Legacy to Sports," in Al Silverman (ed.), *The Best of Sport* (New York: Viking, 1971).

189. Harper, William, "Man Alone," *Quest,* Monograph XII (May 1969), pp. 57–60. **G**

190. Harris, Dorothy V., *Involvement in Sport* (Philadelphia: Lea and Febiger, 1973). **P**

191. Harris, Dorothy V., "Sports Science: The Happy Addict," *WomenSports,* vol. 5, no. 1 (Jan. 1978), p. 53.

192. Harris, T. George, "Why Pros Meditate," *Psychology Today,* vol. 9, no. 5 (Oct. 1975), p. 4.

193. Harrison, E. J., *The Fighting Spirit of Japan* (New York: Foulsham, 1955). **A**

194. Haskins, James, *Doctor J* (Garden City, N.Y.: Doubleday, 1975).

195. Haston, Dougal, *In High Places* (New York: Macmillan, 1972).

196. Hayter, Adrian, *The Long Voyage* (New York: Harper and Row, 1959).

197. Heinz, William C., "The Ghost of the Gridiron," in Red Smith (ed.)., *Press Box* (New York: Norton, 1976), pp. 45–59.

198. Heller, Peter, *"In this Corner"* (New York: Simon and Schuster, 1973). **I**

199. Hellison, Donald, *Humanistic Physical Education* (Englewood Cliffs, N.J.: Prentice-Hall, 1973). **C**

200. Hemery, David, *Another Hurdle* (New York: Taplinger, 1976). **B**

201. Hemingway, Ernest, *Death in the Afternoon* (New York: Scribner's, 1932). **I**

202. Hemingway, Patricia Drake, *Transcendental Meditation Primer* (New York: David McKay, 1975). **Y**

203. Herrigel, Eugen, *Zen in the Art of Archery* (New York: Pantheon, 1953). **Y**

204. Herrington, Nancy, "Body Work: A Guide to the New Physical Therapies," *New Age,* vol. 3, no. 8 (Jan. 1978), pp. 48–53 + . **Y**

205. Herzog, Maurice, *Annapurna* (New York: Dutton, 1952).

206. Hickman, James C., Michael Murphy, and Michael Spino, "Psychophysical Transformations Through Meditation and Sport," *Simulational Games,* vol. 8, no. 1 (Mar. 1977), pp. 49–60. **Y**

207. Hicks, Gail F., "Creativity and Body Awareness" (Ph.D. diss., Washington State University, 1974). **C**

208. Higdon, Hal, "Can Running Cure Mental Illness?" [Part 1] *Runner's World,* vol. 13, no. 1 (Jan. 1978), pp. 36–43. **P**

209. Higdon, Hal, "Can Running Put Mental Patients on Their Feet?" [Part 2] *Runner's World,* vol. 13, no. 2 (Feb. 1978), pp. 36–43. **P**

210. Hilgard, Ernest R. *Hypnotic Susceptibility* (New York: Harcourt, Brace and World, 1965).

211. Hoffman, S. J., "Athletae Dei: Missing the Meaning of Sport," *Journal of the Philosophy of Sport,* vol. 3 (Sept. 1976), pp. 42–51. **G**

212. Hogan, Ben, "This Is My Secret," *Life,* vol. 39, no. 6 (Aug. 8, 1955), pp. 60–63. **I**

213. Honig, Donald, *Baseball Between the Lines* (New York: Coward, McCann and Geoghegan, 1976).

214. Honorton, Charles R., "Has Science Developed the Competence to Confront Claims of the Paranormal?" *Research in Parapsychology 1975* (Metuchen, N.J.: Scarecrow Press, 1976), pp. 199–223.

215. Hornbein, Thomas F., *Everest—The West Ridge* (San Francisco: Sierra Club, 1965). **O**

216. Horwitz, Tom, and Susan Kimmelman, with H. H. Lui, *Tai Chi Ch'uan: The Technique of Power* (Chicago: Chicago Review Press, 1976). **M**

217. Houston, Charles S., "The Last Blue Mountain," in Samuel S. Klausner (ed.), *Why Men Take Chances* (Garden City, N.Y.: Doubleday/Anchor, 1968), pp. 48–58. **G**

218. Houts, Jo Ann, "Feeling and Perception in the Sport Experience," *Journal of Health, Physical Education, and Recreation,* vol. 111, no. 8 (Oct. 1972), pp. 71–72. **A**

219. Huizinga, Johan, *Homo Ludens* (Boston: Beacon Press, 1950). **G**

220. Hunter, Catfish, as told to George Vass, "The Game I'll Never Forget," *Baseball Digest,* vol. 32, no. 6 (June 1973), pp. 35–37.

221. Huxley, Aldous, *The Perennial Philosophy* (New York: Harper and Row, 1945).

222. Ismail, A. H., and L. E. Trachtman, "Jogging the Imagination," *Psychology Today,* vol. 6, no. 10 (Mar. 1973), pp. 78–82 + . **P**

223. Jacklin, Tony, *Jacklin* (New York: Simon and Schuster, 1970). **B**

224. Jackson, Ian, *Yoga and the Athlete* (Mountain View, Calif: World Publications, 1975). **Y**

225. Jackson, Marni, "Wheeling for Distance," *Outside,* vol. 1, no. 7 (Mar. 1978), pp. 49–54. **I**

226. James, William, *The Energies of Men* (New York: Moffat, Yard, 1908). **A**

227. James, William, *The Varieties of Religious Experience* (New York: Modern Library, 1902).

228. Jenner, Bruce, "It Was Too Easy," *Sport,* vol. 63, no. 5 (Nov. 1976), pp. 67–78.

229. Jenner, Bruce, and Philip Finch, *Decathlon Challenge* (Englewood Cliffs, N.J.: Prentice-Hall, 1977). **B**

230. Jennings, Melchior, *Instinct Shooting* (New York: Dodd, Mead, 1965). **I**

231. Jerome, John, "Frank Shorter: The Man Who Invented Running," *Outside,* vol. 1, no. 8 (April 1978), pp. 33–37. **B**

232. Johansson, Ingemar, "New Challenger Scouts a Fight," *Life,* vol. 46, no. 19 (May 11, 1959), p. 40+.

233. Johnston, Richard W., "Dangerous Delusion," *Sports Illustrated,* vol. 45 (Oct. 18, 1976), pp. 88–92+.

234. Jolivet, Regis, "Work, Meditation, Play, Contemplation," *Philosophy Today,* vol. 5 (Summer 1961), pp. 114–120. **Y**

235. Jones, Robert F., "The World's First Peace Pentathlon," *Sports Illustrated,* vol. 32 (May 11, 1970), pp. 50–58+.

236. Jones, Robert F., "You Learn the Art of Invisibility," *Sports Illustrated,* vol. 33 (Nov. 16, 1970), pp. 23–25.

237. Jones, Robert Tyre, Jr., *Bobby Jones on Golf* (Garden City, N.Y.: Doubleday, 1966). **I**

238. Jones, Robert Tyre, Jr., *Golf Is My Game* (Garden City, N.Y.: Doubleday, 1960). **I**

239. Jordan, Pat, *Broken Patterns* (New York: Dodd, Mead, 1977). **G**

240. Kaelin, E. F., "The Well-Played Game: Notes Toward an Aesthetics of Sport," *Quest,* Monograph X (May 1968), pp. 16–28. **C**

241. Kahn, Roger, *The Boys of Summer* (New York: Harper and Row, 1971).

242. Kahn, Roger, "Stan Musial: Pride of the St. Louis Cardinals," in Ed Fitzgerald (ed.), *Heroes of Sport* (New York: Bartholomew House, 1960), pp. 5–22.

243. Keen, Sam, and Michael Murphy, "Our Bodies, Our Souls: A New Age Interview," *New Age,* vol. 3, no. 8 (Jan. 1978), pp. 34–37+. **G**

244. Kellogg, Curtiss, "Running Loose," *Runner's World,* vol. 12, no. 8 (Aug. 1977), p. 64. **Y**

245. Kenn, C. W., *Firewalking from the Inside* (Los Angeles: Franklin Thomas, 1949).

246. Kenyon, Gerald S., "A Conceptual Model for Characterizing Physical Activity," *Research Quarterly,* vol. 39, no. 1 (Mar. 1968), pp. 96–105. **G**

247. Kerley, M. R., "Kitty O'Neil; a Deaf Stunt Woman Races the Speed of Sound," *WomenSports,* vol. 4, no. 4 (April 1977), pp. 17–19.

248. Kidd, C., "Congenital Ichthyosiform Erythroermia Treated by Hypnosis," *British Journal of Dermatology,* vol. 78, 1966, pp. 101–105.

249. Kiernan, Thomas, *The Miracle at Coogan's Bluff* (New York: Crowell, 1975).

250. Kilner, Walter J., *The Human Aura* (Secaucus, N.J.: University Books, 1965). **E**

251. King, Billie Jean, with Kim Chapin, *Billie Jean* (New York: Harper and Row, 1974). **B**

252. Kirkpatrick, Harvey, "Wayne Estes' Final Game," *Sport,* vol. 60, no. 2 (Feb. 1975), pp. 25–26.

253. Kirshenbaum, Jerry, "They're All Out to Launch," *Sports Illustrated,* vol. 31 (July 21, 1969), pp. 38–41.

254. Kleinfield, Sonny, *A Month at the Brickyard* (New York: Holt, Rinehart and Winston, 1977). **I**

255. Kleinman, Seymour, "The Nature of a Self and its Relation to an Other in Sport," *Journal of the Philosophy of Sport,* vol. 2 (Sept. 1975), pp. 45–50. **A**

256. Klobucher, Jim, and Fran Tarkenton, *Tarkenton* (New York: Harper and Row, 1976). **B**

257. Koestler, Arthur, *The Act of Creation* (New York: Macmillan, 1964).

258. Kornheiser, Tony, "Bruce Jenner: Apple Pie Hero," *New York Times* (Mar. 13, 1977).

259. Kostrubala, Thaddeus, *The Joy of Running* (Philadelphia: Lippincott, 1976). **P**

260. Koufax, Sandy, with Ed Linn, *Koufax* (New York: Viking, 1966). **B**

261. Kram, Mark, "All the Best," [George Best] *Sports Illustrated,* vol. 36, no. 13 (Mar. 27, 1972), pp. 60–69. **B**

262. Kram, Mark, "The Face of Pain," *Sports Illustrated,* vol. 44, no. 10 (Mar. 8, 1976), pp. 58–66. **O**

263. Kram, Mark, "The Not-So Melancholy Dane," [Torben Ulrich] *Sports Illustrated,* vol. 30 (Apr. 7, 1969), pp. 78–86. **B**

264. Krikler, Bernice, "A Preliminary Psychological Assessment of the Skills of Motor Racing Drivers," *British Journal of Psychiatry,* vol. III (Feb. 1965), pp. 192–194.

265. Krippner, Stanley, and Daniel Rubin (eds.), *The Energies of Consciousness* (New York: Gordon and Breach, 1975). **E**

266. Krippner, Stanley, and Daniel Rubin (eds.), *The Kirlian Aura* (Garden City, N.Y.: Doubleday, 1974). **E**

267. Krumdick, Victor F., and Norman C. Lumian, "The Psychology of Athletic Success," *Athletic Journal,* vol. 44, no. 1 (Sept. 1963), p. 52 + . **P**

268. Kupfer, Joseph, "Purpose and Beauty in Sport," *Journal of the Philosophy of Sport,* vol. 2 (Sept. 1975), pp. 83–90. **G**

269. Lampe, David, "Yesterday," *Sports Illustrated,* vol. 47 (Dec. 19–26, 1977), pp. E6 + . **O**

270. Lance, Kathryn, *Running for Health and Beauty* (Indianapolis: Bobbs-Merrill, 1977). **A**

271. Lang, Andrew, "The Fire Walk," *Proceedings of the Society for Psychical Research,* vol. 15, Part 36 (Feb. 1900), pp. 2–15.

272. Larned, Dorothy, "Fantasies and Fatigue: Diana Nyad Floats Alone," *WomenSports,* vol. 3, no. 3 (Mar. 1976), pp. 36–39. **O**

273. Laski, Marghanita, *Ecstasy* (Bloomington: University of Indiana Press, 1961). **A**

274. Lauck, Dan, "Has the King's Crown Slipped?" *Newsday* (Aug. 21, 1977), pp. 10–11.

275. LeCron, L. "Breast Development Through Hypnotic Suggestion," *Journal of the American Society of Psychosomatic Dentistry and Medicine,* vol. 6, 1969, pp. 58–61.

276. Leonard, George B., "Aikido and the Mind of the West," *Intellectual Digest,* vol. 4 (June 1973), pp. 17–20.

277. Leonard, George, "Running for Life: How the Masters are Redefining Human Potential," *New West,* vol. 1 (Aug. 16, 1976), pp. 34–45. **I**

278. Leonard, George, *The Silent Pulse* (New York: Dutton, in press).

279. Leonard, George, *The Ultimate Athlete* (New York: Viking, 1975). **G**

280. LeShan, Lawrence, *The Medium, the Mystic, and the Physicist* (New York: Viking, 1974).

281. Leuchs, Arne, and Patricia Skulka, *Ski with Yoga* (Matteson, Ill.: Greatlakes Living Press, 1976). **Y**

282. Lewis, A. J., "Influence of Self-Suggestion on the Human Organism" (Los Angeles: Garrett AiResearch Corp., 1976).

283. Lewis, A. J., "Psychic Self-Regulation," paper presented at the Fourth Annual Western Regional Association for Humanistic Psychology Conference, San Diego, California, 1977.

284. Lewis, Jesse Francis, "Ecstatic Experience: A Classification" (Ph.D diss., University of Arizona, 1974). **A**

285. Libby, Bill, *Bud Harrelson* (New York: Putnam's, 1975).

286. Libby, Bill, *Foyt* (New York: Hawthorn Books, 1974). **B**

287. Libby, Bill, "Jack Is Nimble, Jack Is Quick," *Sport,* vol. 49, no. 1 (Jan. 1970), pp. 48–49 + .

288. Libby, Bill, *O. J.* (New York: Putnam's, 1974). **B**

289. Libby, Bill, *Parnelli* (New York: Dutton, 1969).

290. Libby, Bill, with Richard Petty, *King Richard* (Garden City, N.Y.: Doubleday, 1977). **B**

291. Lindbergh, Charles, *Autobiography of Values* (New York: Harcourt Brace Jovanovich, 1977).

292. Lindbergh, Charles, "Man's Potential," in Charles Muses (ed.), *Consciousness and Reality* (New York: Outerbridge and Lazard, 1969), pp. 304–312. **C**

293. Lindbergh, Charles, *The Spirit of St. Louis* (New York: Scribner's, 1953). **B**

294. Linn, Ed, "Warm Breeze from the Past," *Sport,* vol. 52, no. 3 (Sept. 1971), pp. 50–52 + . **G**

295. Lipsyte, Robert, *Sportsworld* (New York: Quadrangle/New York Times Book Co., 1975).

296. Lloyd, F. R., "The Home Run King," *Journal of Popular Culture,* vol. 9, no. 4 (Spring 1976), pp. 983–995.

297. Loader, W. R., *Sprinter* (New York: Macmillan, 1961). **I**

298. Lowe, Benjamin, *The Beauty of Sport* (Englewood Cliffs, N.J.: Prentice-Hall, 1977). **G**

299. Ludwig, Jack, *Games of Fear and Winning* (Garden City, N.Y.: Doubleday, 1976).

300. Lunn, Sir Arnold, *A Century of Mountaineering, 1857–1967* (London: Allen and Unwin, 1957). **O**

301. McClintock, Jack, *The Book of Darts* (New York: Random House, 1977). **I**

302. McCluggage, Denise, *The Centered Skier* (Vermont Crossroads: Vermont Crossroads Press, 1977). **Y**

303. MacDonald, R. G., J. L. Hickman, and H. S. Dakin, "Preliminary Physical Measurements of Psychophysical Effects Associated with Three Alleged Psychic Healers," Mimeograph (San Francisco: 3101 Washington St., 1976).

304. McKinney, Steve, "How I Broke the World's Speed Ski Record," *Ski Magazine,* vol. 39, no. 7 (Spring 1975), pp. 36–39+.

305. McPhee, John, *A Sense of Where You Are* (New York: Farrar, Straus, 1965). **B**

306. Maheu, Rene, "Sport and Culture," *Journal of Health, Physical Education and Recreation,* vol. 34, no. 8 (Oct. 1963), pp. 30–32+. **G**

307. Manry, Robert, *Tinkerbelle* (New York: Harper and Row, 1966).

308. Manso, Peter, *Vroom! Conversations with Grand Prix Champions* (New York: Funk and Wagnalls, 1969). **I**

309. Maravich, Pete, with Curry Kirkpatrick, "I Want to Put on a Show," *Sports Illustrated,* vol. 31 (Dec. 1, 1969), p. 39+. **I**

310. Marcus, Joe, *The World of Pele* (New York: Mason/Charter, 1976).

311. Maslow, Abraham, *Motivation and Human Personality* (New York: Harper and Row, 1954).

312. Mason, A., "A Case of Congenital Ichthyosiform Erythrodermia of Brocq Treated by Hypnosis," *British Medical Journal,* vol. 2 (1952), pp. 422–423.

313. Masters, Robert, "Psychophysical Education: Recovering the Body," *Saturday Review,* vol. 2, no. 11 (Feb. 22, 1975), pp. 30–31. **Y**

314. Masters, Robert E. L., and Jean Houston, *The Varieties of Psychedelic Experience* (New York: Holt, Rinehart and Winston, 1966). **A**

315. Maule, Tex, "Masterpiece in Milwaukee," *Sports Illustrated,* vol. 14 (May 8, 1961), pp. 24–27.

316. Mead, George R., *The Doctrine of the Subtle Body in Western Tradition,* 2d ed. (Wheaton, Ill.: Theosophical Publishing House, 1967). **S**

317. Meggyesey, David. Personal communication.

318. Merrien, Jean, *Lonely Voyagers* (New York: Putnam, 1954). **O**

319. Meryman, R., "The Flake and the Old Man," *Life,* vol. 68, no. 8 (Mar. 6, 1970), pp. 54–56+. **I**

320. Messner, Reinhold, *The Seventh Grade* (New York: Oxford University Press, 1974). **I**

321. Metheny, Eleanor, *Movement and Meaning* (New York: McGraw-Hill, 1968). **G**

322. Michener, James A., *Sports in America* (New York: Random House, 1976).

323. Middlecoff, Cary, "The Winning Feeling," *Esquire,* vol. 45, no. 4 (Apr. 1956), p. 67 + . **A**

324. Miller, David L., *Gods and Games* (Cleveland: World, 1970).

325. Miller, Johnny, with Dean Shanklin, *Pure Golf* (Garden City, N.Y.: Doubleday, 1976).

326. Minick, Michael, *The Wisdom of Kung Fu* (New York: Morrow, 1974). **M**

327. Mishima, Yukio, *Sun and Steel* (Palo Alto, Calif.: Kodansha International, 1970). **B**

328. Mishra, Rammurti S. *Yoga Sutras* (Garden City, N.Y.: Doubleday, 1973). **E**

329. Monkerud, Donald, "Aikido, Art of the Velvet Fist," *New Realities,* vol. 1, no. 6, pp. 26–31. **M**

330. Monroe, Robert, *Journeys Out of the Body* (Garden City, N.Y.: Doubleday, 1971). **E**

331. Moody, Raymond A., Jr., *Life after Life* (Atlanta: Mockingbird Books, 1975).

332. Moore, Kenny, "The Kenya Connection," *Sports Illustrated,* vol. 48 (June 5, 1978), pp. 40–42 + .

333. Moore, Kenny, "A Night for Stars, Both Born and Reborn," *Sports Illustrated,* vol. 46 (May 23, 1977), pp. 32–34.

334. Morgan, William P., "The Mind of the Marathoner," *Psychology Today,* vol. 11, no. 11 (Apr. 1978), pp. 38–49. **P**

335. Morgan, William P., "Selected Psychological Considerations in Sport," *Research Quarterly,* vol. 45 (Dec. 1974), pp. 374–390. **P**

336. Morley, David C., *The Missing Links: Golf and the Mind* (New York: Atheneum/SMI, 1976). **P**

337. Moses, Sam, "Suddenly Mario Is the Magician Again," *Sports Illustrated,* vol. 46 (May 30, 1977).

338. Moss, Stirling, with Ken Purdy, *All But My Life* (New York: Dutton, 1963). **B**

339. Muldoon, Sylvan, and Hereward Carrington, *The Projection of the Astral Body* (London: Rider, 1956). **E**

340. Murphy, Michael, *Golf in the Kingdom* (New York: Viking, 1972).

341. Murphy, Michael, *Jacob Atabet: A Speculative Fiction* (Millbrae, Calif.: Celestial Arts, 1977).

342. Murphy, Michael, "Sport as Yoga," *Journal of Humanistic Psychology,* vol. 17, no. 4 (Fall 1977), pp. 21–33. **Y**

343. Murphy, Michael, and John Brodie, "I Experience a Kind of Clarity," *Intellectual Digest,* vol. 3, no. 5 (Jan. 1973), pp. 19–22. **A**

344. Myers, Frederic W. H., *Human Personality and its Survival of Bodily Death* (New York: Longmans, Green, 1954, 2 vols.). **E**

345. "Mystery of Firewalking," *Human Behavior,* vol. 7, no. 3 (Mar. 1978), p. 51 + .

346. Namath, Joe, with Bob Oates, Jr., *A Matter of Style* (Boston: Little, Brown, 1973). **I**

347. Namath, Joe, with Dick Schaap, *I Can't Wait Until Tomorrow— 'Cause I Get Better-Looking Every Day* (New York: Random House, 1969).

348. Naruse, Gosaku, "The Hypnotic Treatment of Stage Fright in Champion Athletes," *International Journal of Clinical and Experimental Hypnosis,* vol. 13 (Jan. 1965), pp. 63–70. **A**

349. National Football League. Properties, Inc. The Creative Staff, *The First Fifty Years* (New York: Ridge Press/Benjamin Co., 1969). **B**

350. Neal, Patsy, *Sport and Identity* (Philadelphia: Dorrance, 1972). **G**

351. Neale, Robert E., "Play and the Sacred," in Ralph Slovenko and James A. Knight (eds.), *Motivation in Play, Games and Sport* (Springfield, Ill.: Charles C Thomas, 1967), pp. 148–157. **G**

352. Netto, Aranjo, and Claudio Melloe Souza, *"King of the Booters,"* *Reader's Digest,* vol. 43 (Oct. 1964), pp. 203–209.

353. Neumann, Randy, "Randy Neumann," *Sport,* vol. 58 (July 1974), pp. 85–89 + .

354. Newman, Roscoe Lee. Personal communication. In George Leonard, *The Ultimate Athlete* (New York: Viking, 1975).

355. Nicklaus, Jack, *Golf My Way* (New York: Simon and Schuster, 1974). **I**

356. Nicklaus, Jack, "Nicklaus Psychoanalyzes the Superstars," *Golf Digest,* vol. 28, no. 3 (March 1977), pp. 38–41. **P**

357. Nicol, J. Fraser, "Historical Background," in Benjamin B. Wolman (ed.), *Handbook of Parapsychology* (New York: Van Nostrand Reinhold, 1977), pp. 305–323.

358. Nideffer, Robert M., *The Inner Athlete* (New York: Crowell, 1976).

359. Nieporte, Tom, and Don Sauers, *Mind over Golf* (Garden City, N.Y.: Doubleday, 1968). **I**

360. Nishiyama, Hidetaka, and Richard C. Brown, *Karate: The Art of "Empty Hand" Fighting* (Rutland, Vt.: Tuttle, 1960 [© 1959]).

361. Nitschke, Ray, as told to Robert W. Wells, *Mean on Sunday* (Garden City, N.Y.: Doubleday, 1953).

362. Novak, Michael, *The Joy of Sports* (New York: Basic Books, 1976). **G**

363. Noyce, Wilfred, *The Springs of Adventure* (Cleveland: World, 1958). **G**

364. Nyad, Diana, "Mind over Water," *Esquire,* vol. 84, no. 4 (Oct. 1975), pp. 132–139. **O**

365. Oglanby, Elva, *Toller* (New York: Vanguard, 1976). **B**

366. Otto, Rudolf, *The Idea of the Holy,* 2d ed. (London: Oxford University Press, 1950).

367. "Our Olympic Hopes," *Soviet Life,* vol. 8, no. 239 (Aug. 1976), pp. 60–65.

368. Owen, A. R. G., "Stigmata," in Richard Cavendish (ed.), *Man, Myth & Magic,* vol. 20 (New York: Marshall Cavendish, 1970), pp. 2647–2703.

369. Oxendine, Joseph B., *The Psychology of Motor Learning* (New York: Appleton-Century-Crofts, 1968). **P**

370. Oyama, Masutatsu, *This Is Karate* (Rutland, Vt.: Japan Publications, 1965). **M**

371. Palmer, Arnold, *Go for Broke* (New York: Simon and Schuster, 1973). **I**

372. Panati, Charles (ed.), *The Geller Papers* (Boston: Houghton Mifflin, 1976).

373. Papanek, John, "Strutting Their Stuffs," *Sports Illustrated,* vol. 44 (Feb. 9, 1976), pp. 50–52.

374. Park, Roberta, "Raising the Consciousness of Sport," *Quest,* Monograph XIX (Win. 1973), pp. 78–82. **A**

375. Parker, Edmund K., *Secrets of Chinese Karate* (Englewood Cliffs, N.J.: Prentice-Hall, 1963).

376. Parr, Jeanne, *The Superwives* (New York: Coward, McCann and Geoghegan, 1976).

377. Patanjali, *How to Know God; the Yoga Aphorisms of Patanjali,* trans. and with a new commentary by Swami Prabhavananda and Christopher Isherwood (New York: Harper and Row, 1953).

378. Pele, with Robert L. Fish, *My Life and the Beautiful Game* (Garden City, N.Y.: Doubleday, 1977). **B**

379. Peterson, Robert, *Only the Ball Was White* (Englewood Cliffs, N.J.: Prentice-Hall, 1970).

380. Pettit, Bob, with Bob Wolff, *Bob Pettit* (Englewood Cliffs, N.J.: Prentice-Hall, 1966). **B**

381. Pirie, Gordon, *Running Wild* (London: W. H. Allen, 1961). **B**

382. "Playboy Interview: Barbra Streisand," *Playboy,* vol. 24 (Oct. 1977), p. 79 +.

383. Player, Gary, *Positive Golf* (New York: McGraw-Hill, 1967). **I**

384. Plimpton, George, *The Bogeyman* (New York: Harper and Row, 1968).

385. Plimpton, George, "In the Mind's Eye," *Sports Illustrated,* vol. 35 (July 5, 1971), pp. 50–52 +. **P**

386. Plimpton, George, "Watching the Man in the Mirror," *Sports Illustrated,* vol. 33 (Nov. 23, 1970), pp. 80–83 +.

387. Plimpton, George, and Bill Curry, *One More July* (New York: Harper and Row, 1977). **B**

388. Ponsonby, David, "Soccer in the Kingdom," Part 1, *Soccer America,* vol. 4, no. 22 (May 29, 1973), p. 12 +. **I**

389. Ponsonby, David, "Soccer in the Kingdom," Part 2, *Soccer America,* vol. 4, no. 23 (June 5, 1973), p. 17. **I**

390. Powell, Arthur E. *The Astral Body* (Wheaton, Ill.: Theosophical Publishing House, 1973). **E**

391. Powell, Arthur E., *The Etheric Double* (Wheaton, Ill.: Theosophical Publishing House, 1969). **E**

392. Proxmire, William, *You Can Do It* (New York: Simon and Schuster, 1973).

393. Pye, David, *George Leish Mallory: A Memoir* (London: Oxford University Press, 1927). **B**

394. Ratti, Oscar, and Adde Westbrook, *Secrets of the Samurai* (Rutland, Vt.: Tuttle, 1973). **M**

395. Ravizza, Kenneth, "Peak Experiences in Sport," *Journal of Humanistic Psychology,* vol. 17, no. 4 (Fall 1977), pp. 35–40. **A**

396. Ravizza, Kenneth, "A Study of the Peak-Experiences in Sport" (Ph.D. diss., University of Southern California, 1973). **A**

397. Rebuffat, Gaston, *Starlight and Storm* (New York: Oxford University Press, 1968 [©1957]). **B**

398. Reich, Leonard, "Try Not to Think About It," *Runner's World,* vol. 9 (Feb. 1974), p. 17. **Y**

399. Reid, Ron, "Handy Pair of Brainy Bengals," *Sports Illustrated,* vol. 37 (Oct. 16, 1972), pp. 46–51.

400. Rhine, Louisa E., "Frequency of Types of Experience in Spontaneous Precognition," *Journal of Parapsychology,* vol. 18 (June 1954), pp. 93–123.

401. Rhine, Louisa E., "Subjective Forms of Spontaneous Psi Experiences," *Journal of Parapsychology,* vol. 17 (June 1953), pp. 77–114.

402. Rice, Grantland, *The Tumult and the Shouting* (New York: A. S. Barnes, 1954).

403. Richard, Colette, *Climbing Blind* (New York: Dutton, 1967). **B**

404. Richards, Bob, *Heart of a Champion* (Old Tappan, N.Y.: Fleming H. Revell, 1973). **B**

405. Richardson, Alan, "Mental Practice: A Review and Discussion, Part I," *Research Quarterly,* vol. 38 (Mar. 1967), pp. 95–107. **P**

406. Richardson, Alan, "Mental Practice: A Review and Discussion, Part II," *Research Quarterly,* vol. 38 (May 1967), pp. 263–273. **P**

407. Rickard, Rodger S., "An Explication of the Role of Aesthetic Value in American Physical Education" (Ed. D. diss., Stanford University, 1970). **G**

408. Robinson, Doug, "The Climber as Visionary," *Ascent,* vol. 9, 1969, pp. 4–10. **I**

409. Robinson, Doug, "Ice Nine," *Outside,* vol. 1 (Dec. 1977), pp. 26–29. **B**

410. Robinson, Sugar Ray, with Dave Anderson, *Sugar Ray* (New York: Viking, 1970). **B**

411. Romen, A. S., *et al.* (eds.), *Psychical Self-Regulation,* vols. I and II (Alma-Alta, U.S.S.R., 1974).

412. Romen, A. S., *et al. Psychical Self-Regulation* (Alma-Alta, U.S.S.R., 1974).

413. Ronberg, Gary, "Tea Party for Bobby's Bruins," *Sports Illustrated,* vol. 32 (May 4, 1970), pp. 18–21.

414. Rosenthal, Saul R., "Risk Exercise and the Physically Handicapped," *Rehabilitation Literature,* vol. 36, no. 5 (May 1975), pp. 144–149.

415. Rush, Joseph, *New Directions in Parapsychological Research* (New York: Parapsychology Foundation, 1964).

416. Rush, Joseph H., "Problems and Methods in Psychokinesis Research," in Stanley Krippner (ed.), *Advances in Parapsychological Research,* vol. 1 (New York: Plenum, 1977), pp. 15–78.

417. Russell, W. Scott, *Karate; The Energy Connection* (New York: Delacorte Press/Eleanor Friede, 1976). **M**

418. Ruth, Babe, as told to Bob Considine, *The Babe Ruth Story* (New York: Dutton, 1948).

419. Ryback, Eric, *The High Adventure of Eric Ryback* (San Francisco: Chronicle Books, 1971).

420. Saal, Herbert, "The Great Leap," *Newsweek,* vol. 84, no. 7 (Aug. 12, 1974), p. 84.

421. Sadler, William A., "Creative Existence: Play as a Pathway to Personal Freedom and Community," *Review of Existential Psychology and Psychiatry,* vol. 6, no. 3 (Fall 1966), pp. 237–245. **C**

422. Sage, George H., "Humanistic Theory, the Counter-Culture, and Sport," in his *Sport and American Society,* 2d ed. (Reading, Mass.: Addison-Wesley, 1974), pp. 415–429. **G**

423. Sanderson, Derek, with Stan Fischler, *I've Got to Be Me* (New York: Dodd, Mead, 1970).

424. Sanford, Bob, *Riding the Dirt* (Newport Beach, Calif.: Bond/Parkhurst Books, 1972). **I**

425. Sannella, Lee, *Kundalini: Psychosis or Transcendence?* (San Francisco: H. S. Dakin Co., 1976). **E**

426. Sawyer, Benjamin, and Sandy Dorbin, "Athletics as Art," *Synergy,* no. 41 (Summer 1973), pp. 19–30. **C**

427. Schaap, Dick, *The Perfect Jump* (New York: New American Library, 1976). **B**

428. Schaap, Dick, "The Second Coming of St. Francis," *Sport,* vol. 54 (Dec. 1972), pp. 84–94.

429. Schmeidler, Gertrude R., "Research Findings in Psychokinesis," in Stanley Krippner (ed.), *Advances in Parapsychological Research,* vol. 1 (New York: Plenum, 1977), pp. 79–132.

430. Schmidt, Helmut, "A PK Test with Electronic Equipment," *Journal of Parapsychology,* vol. 34 (Sept. 1970), pp. 175–181.

431. Schmidt, Helmut, "Quantum-Mechanical Random Number Generator," *Journal of Applied Physics,* vol. 41 (Feb. 1970), pp. 462–468.

432. Schneck, Jerome, "Hypnotherapy of Ichthyosis," *Psychosomatics,* vol. 7, 1966, pp. 233–235.

433. Schofield, Len J., and Stephanie Abbuhl, "The Stimulation of Insight and Self-Awareness Through Body-Movement," *Journal of Clinical Psychology,* vol. 31, no. 4 (Oct. 1975), pp. 745–746. **C**

434. Schollander, Don, *Deep Water* (New York: Crown, 1971). **B**

435. Schultheis, Rob, "Skiing Out of Bounds," *Outside,* vol. 1 (Nov. 1977), pp. 38–41. **I**

436. Schutz, William C., *Here Comes Everybody* (New York: Harper and Row, 1971).

437. Schwarzenegger, Arnold, and Douglas Kent Hall, *Arnold: The Education of a Bodybuilder* (New York: Simon and Schuster, 1977). **I**

438. "Scorecard: The Sporting Look," *Sports Illustrated,* vol. 31 (Nov. 24, 1969). p. 14.

439. Scott, Jack, *The Athletic Revolution* (New York: Free Press, 1971). **G**

440. Seaver, Tom, with Dick Schapp, *The Perfect Game* (New York: Dutton, 1970).

441. Seitz, Nick, "Is This the Man to Succeed Palmer?" in Irving T. Marsh and Edward Ehre (eds.), *Thirty Years of Best Sports Stories* (New York: Dutton, 1975), pp. 252–259.

442. Seitz, Nick, "What Makes a Golfer Unique in Pro Sports? The Onlyness," *Golf Digest,* vol. 27, no. 1 (Jan. 1976), pp. 52–55. **B**

443. Seligman, Martin E. P., "Submissive Death: Giving up on Life," *Psychology Today,* vol. 7, no. 12 (May 1974), pp. 80–85 + .

444. Sevier, Vernon A., "Physical Fitness and the Integrated Personality," *Journal of Physical Education,* vol. 71 (May 1974), p. 145 + . **C**

445. Shackleton, Ernest H., *South* (New York: Macmillan, 1947 [©1920]).

446. Sharman, Bill, *Sharman on Basketball Shooting* (Englewood Cliffs, N.J.: Prentice-Hall, 1965). **I**

447. Shaw, Gary, *Meat on the Hoof* (New York: St. Martin's, 1972).

448. Sheehan, George, "Basics of Jogging," *Runner's World,* vol. 12 (Aug. 1977), pp. 34–37.

449. Sheehan, George, *Dr. Sheehan on Running* (Mt. View, Calif: World Publications, 1975). **G**

450. Sheehan, George, "I Found It in Running," *New Times,* vol. 10, no. 7 (Apr. 3, 1978), pp. R22–R23. **C**

451. Sheehan, George, *Running and Being: The Total Experience* (New York: Simon and Schuster, 1978). **G**

452. Shoemaker, Willie, *The Shoe* (Chicago: Rand McNally, 1976).

453. Silverman, Al (ed.), *The Best of Sport 1946–71* (New York: Viking, 1971).

454. Simonton, Carl, and Stephanie Simonton, *Getting Well Again* (Los Angeles: J. P. Tarcher; distributed by St. Martin's, 1978).

455. Singer, Robert R., *Myths and Truths in Sport Psychology* (New York: Harper and Row, 1975). **P**

456. Slocum, Joshua, *Sailing Alone Around the World* (New York: Sheridan House, 1963 [©1900]). **B**

457. Slovenko, Ralph, and James Knight (eds.), *Motivation in Play, Games and Sports* (Springfield, Ill.: Charles C Thomas, 1967). **G**

458. Slusher, Howard, *Man, Sport and Existence* (Philadelphia: Lea and Febiger, 1967). **G**

459. Smith, Adam, "Sport is a Western Yoga," *Psychology Today,* vol. 9 (Oct. 1975), pp. 48–51+. **Y**

460. Smith, Adam, "Trying the Dance of Shiva," *Sports Illustrated,* vol. 39, no. 7 (Aug. 13, 1973), pp. 36–38+. **Y**

461. Smith, Marshall, "Wary Old Devil" [Juan Fangio] *Life,* vol. 43, no. 6 (Aug. 5, 1951), pp. 82–90. **B**

462. Smith, Robert W., *Hsing-I* (Tokyo and New York: Kodansha International, 1974). **M**

463. Smythe, Frank, *The Adventures of a Mountaineer* (London: J. M. Dent, 1940). **B**

464. Smythe, Frank, *The Mountain Vision* (London: Hodder and Stoughton, 1949). **I**

465. Sollier, Andre, and Zsolt Gyorbiro, *Japanese Archery: Zen in Action* (New York: Walker/Weatherhill, 1969).

466. Solomon, Ted J., " 'Para' Normal Powers Actually Normal," *Gateway,* vol. 9, no. 2 (Feb. 1964), pp. 21–23.

467. Spino, Mike, *Beyond Jogging: The Innerspaces of Running* (Millbrae, Calif.: Celestial Arts, 1976).

468. Spino, Mike, "Running as a Spiritual Experience," Appendix B in Jack Scott, *The Athletic Revolution* (New York: Free Press, 1971), pp. 222-225. **A**

469. Spino, Mike, *Running Home* (Millbrae, Calif.: Celestial Arts, 1977). **Y**

470. Spino, Mike, and James Hickman, "Beyond the Physical Limits," *Runner's World*, vol. 12, no. 3 (Mar. 1977), pp. 52-53. **Y**

471. Stanford, Rex G., "Experimental Psychokinesis," in Benjamin B. Wolman (ed.), *Handbook of Parapsychology* (New York: Van Nostrand Reinhold, 1977), pp. 324-381.

472. Start, Kenneth B., and Alan Richardson, "Imagery and Mental Practice," *British Journal of Educational Psychology*, vol. 34, no. 3 (1964), pp. 280-284. **P**

473. Stebbins, R. J., "A Comparison of Effects of Physical and Mental Practice in Learning a Motor Skill," *Research Quarterly*, vol. 39 (Oct. 1938), pp. 714-720. **P**

474. Stewart, Jackie, and Peter Manso, *Faster: A Racer's Diary* (New York: Farrar, Straus, 1972). **I**

475. Stone, Roselyn E., "Meanings Found in the Acts of Surfing and Skiing" (Ph.D. diss. University of Southern California, 1970). **G**

476. Suinn, Richard M., "Body Thinking: Psychology for Olympic Champs," *Psychology Today*, vol. 10, no. 2 (July 1976), pp. 38-41 + . **P**

477. Summers, Montague, *The Physical Phenomena of Mysticism* (New York: Barnes and Noble, 1950).

478. Sutton, Don, "Hypnosis Snapped My Slump," *Sport*, vol. 60, no. 2 (Feb. 1975), pp. 62-65. **A**

479. Suzuki, Daisetz T., *Zen and Japanese Culture* (New York: Pantheon, 1959).

480. Swedenborg, Emmanuel, *The Heavenly Arcana* (New York: American Swedenborg Publishing Society, 1873). **E**

481. Tansley, David, V., *Subtle Body* (London: Thames and Hudson, 1977). **E**

482. Tarshis, Barry, *Tennis and the Mind* (New York: Atheneum, 1977). **I**

483. Tart, Charles T., *States of Consciousness* (New York: Dutton, 1975). **A**

484. "Tech Talk: East German Secrets?" *Track and Field News,* vol. 29, no. 10 (Nov. 1976), p. 32.

485. Tekeyan, Charles, "The Athlete and Death: Immortality Wrestles with Reality," *New York Times* (Dec. 28, 1975).

486. Telander, Rick, *Joe Namath and the Other Guys* (New York: Holt, Rinehart and Winston, 1976). **I**

487. Terray, Lionel, *The Borders of the Impossible* (Garden City, N.Y.: Doubleday, 1964). **B**

488. Thomas, Caroline, "The Perfect Moment" (Ph.D. diss., Ohio State University, 1972). **G**

489. Thomas, Caroline, "Toward an Experimental Sport Aesthetic," *Journal of the Philosophy of Sport,* vol. 1 (Sept. 1974), pp. 67–91. **G**

490. Thomas, Vaughn, *Science and Sport* (Boston: Little, Brown, 1970). **P**

491. Thouless, R. H., and B. P. Wiesner, "The Psi Processes in Normal and 'Paranormal' Psychology," *Journal of Parapsychology,* vol. 12, no. 3 (Sept. 1948). pp. 192–212.

492. Thurston, Herbert, *The Physical Phenomena of Mysticism* (London: Burns, Oates and Washbourne, 1952).

493. Tiller, William A., *Kirlian Photography: Its Scientific Foundations and Future Potentials* (Stanford, Calif.: Stanford University Press, 1975). **E**

494. Tohei, Koichi, *Aikido in Daily Life* (Tokyo; Rikugei Publishing House, 1966).

495. Torres, Jose, *Sting like a Bee* (New York: Abelard-Schuman, 1970).

496. Trias, Robert A., *The Hand Is My Sword: A Karate Handbook* (Rutland, Vt.: Charles E. Tuttle, 1973). **M**

497. Trippett, Frank, "The Ordeal of Fun," *Look,* vol. 33, no. 15 (July 29, 1969), pp. 24–34. **A**

498. Twining, Wilbur E., "Mental Practice and Physical Practice in Learning a Motor Skill," *Research Quarterly,* vol. 20 (Dec. 1949), pp. 432–435. **P**

499. Ullman, James Ramsay, *Kingdom of Adventure: Everest* (New York: William Sloane, 1947). **O**

500. Ullyot, Joan, *Women's Running* (Mt. View, Calif.: World Publications, 1976).

501. Uyeshiba, Kisshomara, *Aikido* (Tokyo: Hozansha Publishing Co., 1974). **M**

502. Vandell, Roland A., Robert A. Davis, and Herbert A. Clugston, "The Function of Mental Practice in the Acquisition of Motor Skills," *Journal of General Psychology,* vol. 29 (Oct. 1943), pp. 243–250. **P**

503. Vanderzwang, H. J., *Toward a Philosophy of Sport* (Reading, Mass.: Addison-Wesley, 1972). **G**

504. Vanek, M., and B. Cratty, *Psychology and the Superior Athlete* (New York: Macmillan, 1970). **P**

505. Vasiliev, Leonid L., *Experiments in Mental Suggestion* (Church Crookham, Hampshire, England: Institute for the Study of Mental Images, 1963).

506. Wallace, William N., "Psychic Phenomena on the Ball Field," *New York Times* (Aug. 25, 1973).

507. Ward, Robert, "The Mutilation of a Work of Art," *Sport,* vol. 64, no. 5 (May 1977), pp. 96–104 + .

508. Watanabe, Jiichi, and Lindy Avakian, *The Secrets of Judo* (Rutland, Vt.: Charles E. Tuttle, 1960). **M**

509. Watts, Barrie, "World's Fastest Miler Says: 'My Psychic Powers Help Me to Win,' " *The Star* (Aug. 31, 1976).

510. Webb, James, *The Occult Underground* (LaSalle, Ill.: Open Court, 1974).

511. Weiss, Paul, *Sport: A Philosophic Inquiry* (Carbondale: Southern Illinois University Press, 1969). **G**

512. Wells, Roger, and Judith Klein, "A Replication of a 'Psychic Healing' Paradigm," *Journal of Parapsychology,* vol. 36 (June 1972), pp. 144–149.

513. Wentz, Walter Yeeling Evans (ed.), *The Tibetan Book of the Dead* (London: Oxford University Press, 1960). **E**

514. Wepukhulu, Hezekiah, "Seriff, Soccer Soothsayer," *Africa Report,* vol. 18 (Nov-Dec. 1973), pp. 22–23.

515. West, Jerry, with Bill Libby, *Mr. Clutch* (Englewood Cliffs, N.J.: Prentice-Hall, 1969). **B**

516. Westbrook, Adde, and Oscar Ratti, *Aikido and the Dynamic Sphere* (Rutland, Vt.: Charles E. Tuttle, 1970). **M**

517. White, David A., "Great Moments in Sport: The One and the

Many," *Journal of the Philosophy of Sport,* vol. 2 (Sept. 1975), pp. 124–132. **A**

518. White, Rhea A. (ed.), *Surveys in Parapsychology* (Metuchen, N.J.: Scarecrow Press, 1976).

519. White, Rhea A., and Laura A. Dale, *Parapsychology: Sources of Information* (Metuchen, N.J.: Scarecrow Press, 1973).

520. Wilhelm, John L., "Psychic Spying?" *Washington Post,* Aug. 7, 1977.

521. Williams, J., "Stimulation of Breast Growth by Hypnosis?" *Journal of Sex Research,* vol. 10, 1974, pp. 316–326.

522. Williams, Ted, with John Underwood, *My Turn at Bat* (New York: Simon and Schuster, 1969). **B**

523. Williamson, C. J., "The Everest 'Message,' " *Journal of the Society for Psychical Research,* vol. 48, no. 769 (Sept. 1976), pp. 318–320.

524. Willis, William, *The Gods Were Kind* (New York: Dutton, 1955). **B**

525. Willis, William, *Whom the Sea Has Taken* (New York: Meredith, 1967). **B**

526. Wills, Maury, and Don Freeman, *How to Steal a Pennant* (New York: Putnam's, 1976). **B**

527. Wind, Herbert Warren (ed.), *The Gilded Age of Sport* (New York: Simon and Schuster, 1961). **G**

528. Wind, Herbert Warren (ed.), *The Realm of Sport* (New York: Simon and Schuster, 1966). **G**

529. Winderbaum, Larry, *The Martial Arts Encyclopedia* (Washington, D.C.: Inscape Publishers, 1977). **M**

530. Wink, C., "Congenital Ichthyosiform Erthrodermia Treated by Hypnosis: Report of Two Cases," *British Medical Journal,* vol. 2, 1961, pp. 741–743.

531. Wolf, David, *Foul! The Connie Hawkins Story* (New York: Holt, Rinehart and Winston, 1972). **B**

532. Wolman, Benjamin B. (ed.), *Handbook of Parapsychology* (New York: Van Nostrand Reinhold, 1977).

533. Wolters, Richard A., *The Art and Technique of Soaring* (New York: McGraw-Hill, 1971). **I**

534. Worsley, F. A., *Shackkton's Boat Journey* (New York: Norton, 1977).

535. "Wraparound: High: What's Up There?" *Harper's,* vol. 247 (Oct. 1973), pp. 3-10.

536. Yogananda, Paramahansa, *The Autobiography of a Yogi,* 10th ed. (Los Angeles: Self-Realization Fellowship, 1969).

537. Zimmer, Heinrich, *Myths and Symbols in Indian Art and Civilization* (New York: Pantheon, 1946).

538. Zimmerman, Paul, *A Thinking Man's Guide to Pro Football* (New York: Dutton, 1970). **I**

Index

Index